Habitations

by Robert J. Leeney

"The lunatic, the lover, and the poet

Are of imagination all compact...

...And as imagination bodies forth

The forms of things unknown, the poet's pen

Turns them to shapes, and gives to airy nothing

A local habitation and a name."

Theseus, Duke of Athens
A Midsummer Night's Dream, Act V

Selected Comments from
30 Years of the Saturday New Haven Register

Cover design for "Habitations" by John R. Cummings.

Photos from the New Haven Colony Historical Society used with permission.

Cover Photo: Arcade of Elms on New Haven Green, about 1870. The two young men, foreground, are on Chapel St. sidewalk. Photographer unknown.

Printed in the United States of America.

Published by Robert J. Leeney
Bethany, CT

ISBN 0-9773028-0-6
HABITATIONS
By
Robert J. Leeney

Acknowledgements

I extend my thanks, also to the innumerable, and always special, news gatherers, photographers, and other newspaper colleagues who aided me down the decades and are exemplified today by Editor Jack Kramer and Editorial Page Editor Charles Kochakian at the New Haven Register.

I am also grateful for the counsel and support I have had from Peter Thomas LaMothe and Amy Trout of the New Haven Colony Historical Society, Fred Guida, Virginia Marangell, Elrond Wojtkiewicz, John R. Cummings, and those family stalwarts David, Anne, and son-in-law Kevin Panagrossi.

Habitations

by Robert J. Leeney

Foreward

I joined the news staff of the New Haven Register as a reporter at aged 24 in the summer of 1940. Ever since I have had the great privilege of writing regularly, and often almost daily, about events and issues in my home place.

In the best tradition of the American newspaper, at its zenith as a public institution communicating through the written word, I covered news on city streets, edited the book page, took a place on the editorial page, became the principal drama reviewer in the Shubert Theater's Broadway-linked heyday, and was for 20 years the editor of the Register and the Journal Courier before I retired in 1981. In three years of World War II, 1943-1945, I sent my editors letters from the Pacific that were intermittently published in the Sunday paper.

This book is a selection of Saturday columns that I started as an Editor's Note in 1974 and have continued every week, without interruption, since then. A full life, a cherished wife, a loving and supportive family, good friends have all been background to my locally-focused observation of events and opinions that made news in New Haven and in the Register.

This is not a solid definition of our era but a shared rumination, in a given day or week, about the way we moved through the 20th and into the 21st Centuries. Thank you for reviewing with me some neighborly reporting endeavors that William Shakespeare saw as "giving to airy nothing a local habitation and a name."

The art shows habitations, old and new, for the idea discussed.

R.J.L.

Saturday, January 19, 1985
Editor's note

Reprising an old sweet song

Down the arches of time the tune I hear this week is a Thirties melody, "Sophisticated Lady." It vibrates in the ribs and vaultings of the Hotel Taft's once-busy Colonnade Room in the photograph taken last week for the Register by Kirby Kennedy. Owner Joel Schiavone says he's seeking 1985 uses, probably retail, for the space two stories beneath the comer of Chapel and College. Back in 1934 I whiled away the Yale football season in that gracious cavern as the Taft's owners tried to find a profitable response to the repeal of Prohibition and the return of civilized drinking.

The hotel was in its heyday, nearly 20 years old and a key New Haven institution. There were no superhighways then, only a railroad. A few "cabins" on the edge of town and a "commercial" hotel or two were the alternate hostelries. From its busy circular lobby a three-piece string ensemble in the formal dining room could be heard at any proper hour, enmeshed in the restrained raptures of "dinner music" or some politely sweetened Gypsy dance.

Mr. Bob Richardson held forth, amiably Irish and dapper, behind the registration desk. Mr. Louis Horvath, continental in accent and disciplined in demeanor, striped trousers in the morning and black tie after dark, directed the staff. Mr. Edson Fiske was the controller - in the only office I had then seen with a fireplace. On a more Olympian level, Mr. Craig Lavin ran the Taft and was host to everybody of importance passing through New Haven.

A year out of high school and without work in the Great Depression, I was brought by a relative to see Mr. Fiske, questioned about my arithmetic and my sense of duty, acquainted with a cash box and some columnar bookkeeping sheets, and then sent to the Colonnade Room. My job involved totaling the waiters' table checks, providing them with the right change for whatever payment they received, documenting each transaction in the account sheets, and keeping everything in balance. There was no cash register, and nothing like a credit card machine.

Those were the routine perimeters of the job. Beyond them was adventure. I set up shop at 4 each afternoon in the glamour of the deserted dining room, its pillar lamps softly lit, waiters moving to arrange tables, musicians hob-nobbing by the piano. I was entitled between 5 and 6 to order dinner from the menu and have it served in a flourish of silver and white linen, complete with a closing finger bowl and advice from a friendly waiter on which was the day's best dessert. After dinner the crowds were rarely pressing, though on football weekends every table was often filled.

At some point a boy and a girl began to show up regularly for dinner and dancing, probably a Yale student and his heartthrob. She made my heart throb as well.

Dressed always in a basic black frock or cocktail dress, elegant at dinner, easy to laugh, a splendid dancer, she illuminated the shadowy room. Once, as I gazed, I realized they were dancing romantically to the slow fox-trot tempo of a Duke Ellington piece called "Sophisticated Lady" - and the song has ever since borne her imprint.

I wondered if she was a rich girl, from Prospect Street or Westville. I wondered if she was what my mother called a "college" girl (which was not the same as being Betty Co-ed) - a girl like Cole Porter's Miss Antoinette Birby who "lived way out in Derby" and found that "as a fountain of knowledge, believe me, some college is Yale, Yale, Yale." Whatever I wondered, her grace and glow were ideal.

Her escort made less impression. He was tall. He wore prep style tweeds and was probably, in today's parlance, a "hunk." But we shared something - for he, too, was smitten. From my place behind the cash drawer I could see him, absorbed in each word, each move, each bubble of silver laughter from his girl. One night, for reasons unperceived, he came in a tuxedo. She was, as always, smart in her black dress. His birthday? Hers? A proposal? At any rate they gratified the orchestra, which didn't have a lot of dancers, with their languorous grace, their affectionate exchanges and their style.

Those regular trysts showed no sign of ending. But the deep-down grillroom was not a downtown hit. In hard times, despite the availability of drink after a decade of drought, New Haveners were neither high steppers nor big spenders. And after the Harvard game that year the Colonnade Room was closed. I turned in my neat cash drawer. I was again a fellow looking for a job. "Sophisticated Lady" moved down the list of top songs. The boy and the girl disappeared, to become wraiths in a fading memory.

I wonder if somewhere they still swirl and dip - in Sun City, San Diego or St. Petersburg - as an aging combo plays the chorus and the trumpeter lightly mutes his song. The picture is still a pretty one in my mind.

So, Mr. Schiavone, if in renovating the Taft you find something new to sell beneath all those arches, and if you have a dedication "do" to celebrate such change, let the band again play "Sophisticated Lady" for me - and for them. Just once.

Saturday, March 4, 1978
Editor's Note

Can We Save The Shubert

Can the Shubert be saved? A rising volume of personal mail, as well as letters to the editor, raises this question about the show house which for 60 years was synonymous with New Haven in American theater circles.

I lean toward a negative answer-but I certainly think it worthwhile to try to save the Shubert. What must be overcome, however, is a compound of negative circumstances that .will not easily yield to good will and good works.

The commercial theater everywhere in this country is in a slump - creatively as well as economically. The logistics of theater production and of "try out" performances are no longer what the Shubert knew in its heyday. Television in the homes of suburbia and urban street crime statistics have changed our perceptions of night life. The theater building itself is in increasing disrepair. The Taft Hotel - to which the theater is linked structurally and in reciprocal vitality - is a darkened ghost. The immediate neighborhood is slipping toward honky-tonk.

All of these things, plus a myriad of other needs and problems which have been given a higher priority on the local scene, make me fear that the Shubert is beyond revival.

That is why The Register has proposed that at least the remembered magic of those six wonderful and significant decades of Shubert history - and American stagecraft - be kept alive by a timely salvage of the lobby panels which established the Shubert's claim to be "the birthplace of the nation's hits." The panels list, for year after golden year, the plays that opened for premier viewing here in New Haven.

They, at least, should be saved. The idea is one we still support.

But other more hopeful voices say, in effect, that saving the panels is good but saving the Shubert would be better. Rita Bailey Gwin, daughter of Maurice Bailey who was the guiding genius of Shubert operations in its most successful years, has started to tap out letters with an S-O-S theme. Save Our Shubert! "Let's band together and try to keep the theater, open on a new level."

Even more eloquently, Walter F. Mulconry of this city has urged that New-Haven be awakened to the loss it has thus far accepted so quietly. He provided me with an overwhelming list of 450 names, a "partial list of performers who played the Shubert Theatre." The first 15 names on the list are:

Betty Grable, Fred Astaire, Jimmy Durante, Bob Hope, Sophie Tucker, Mary Martin, Ethel Merman, Gene Kelly, Bert Lahr, Betty Hutton, Liza Minnelli, Al Jolson, Pearl Bailey, Ginger Rogers and Danny Kaye. Among the last 15 names are those of John Carradine, Pat Hingle, Kim Hunter, Gene Wilder, Barbara Baxley, Ed Begley, Chester Morris, Michael Rennie, MacDonald Carey, and Faye Emerson. In between is a plum pudding of celebrity from which you may pluck all kinds of pleasure and nostalgia: Eddie Cantor, Alfred Drake, Carol Channing, Beverly Sills, William Gaxton and Victor Moore, Hermione Gingold, Ethel Barrymore, Dame May Whitty, Eva LeGallienne, Sidney Poitier, Jean Stapleton - and hundreds more.

The claim, in this context, is that the performers and their performances can best be enshrined by keeping the Shubert a living theater.

"The memories which are documented in programs, newspaper archives, countless theater annals, and in the hearts and minds of so many," says Walter F. Mu1conry, "are best enshrined within "those walls which held their birth. More great and famous performers have graced the boards of the Shubert stage than any other theater stage in the United States and, perhaps, the world.

"The most important producers, playwrights, composers, lyricists, directors, choreographers, scenic, costume, and lighting designers of the last 60 years have created many of their most important and innovative theatrical productions at the Shubert Theatre.

"America's unique contribution to the theater arts - 'the musical theater' - evolved to its most sophisticated form through a long line of musicals, which came to life in Shubert opening nights. Shubert Theatre patrons over the years watched the development of musical theater as Cole Porter, Rodgers and Hart; Irving Berlin, Rodgers and Hammerstein, and, Lerner and Loewe contributed to its artistic growth.

"This 'house', so rich in theater history, must not be lost!

"The Shubert Theatre is a historical treasure, a national cultural resource, and an important link in any effort to revitalize the central city. The City of New Haven has a strong obligation to acquire the Adams-Shubert Theatre building and to restore and renovate the theater into a desirable theater property..."

Mr. Mulconry points out that the Shubert did more than handle legitimate plays and musicals. He cites the many dance and opera companies which performed there. Present day performance halls like the Lyman Auditorium and Hillhouse High 'School are, in his opinion, less suited than the Shubert to effective presentation of the performing arts. So a restored Shubert could become a new focal point for dance and music forms which have enlarging popular audiences.

His long and careful letter continues:

"When the Hartford Civic Center roof collapsed in January, representatives of the state and federal governments assured the City of Hartford of financial aid to quickly rebuild the Civic Center Coliseum, citing the negative effect upon the economy by the loss of the auditorium. The same observations about the Hartford Civic Center Coliseum bringing people into the center of the city are no less valid for the Shubert Theatre.

"The Shubert Theatre once contributed significantly to downtown life. Audiences came from a wide geographic area - from as far as Bridgeport, Waterbury, and New London. Restaurants and bars, parking lots and garages did considerable business. Shubert crowds often· came early for dinner and stayed late for after-theater drinks.

"Across the country many theaters with less illustrious histories are being restored through grants from private and corporate donors, federal and state agencies and cultural foundations. Among the more recent: Burts Theatre, Toledo, Ohio; Shea's Buffalo Theatre (New York) which received a $600,000 Federal redevelopment grant; Tivoli Theatre, Frederick, Maryland, restored and opened as the Weinberg Center for the arts; Opera House, Newberry, S.C. – aided by 50-50 National Preservation grants-in-aid co-financing.

"There are outside sources which might be tapped for help in obtaining funds to preserve and restore the Shubert Theatre - the National Endowment for the Arts, the Connecticut Commission on the Arts; the Ford Foundation; the Mellon Foundation; the Shubert Foundation; New Haven Foundation; the Rockefeller Foundation; The Preservation Trust; The National Historic Trust.

"One of the first steps, I believe, would be to have the theater added to the National Register of Historic 11 Places. This might be accomplished with the help of Connecticut's senators and congressmen and the New Haven Preservation Trust. . ."

The case for the Shubert is impressive.

Twenty-five years ago this week Tennessee Williams' nearly allegorical "Camino Real" completed a six-day run at the Shubert. It was not the best of Williams – and in some ways it signaled the onset of his long dramatic decline. It was a complex play, unheralded by a lot of advance analysis here, and it was difficult to review.

But as a reminder this morning of a play once reviewed it exemplified the glitter of the Shubert and what it once brought to New Haven: a play by Tennessee Williams, produced by Cheryl Crawford and Ethel Reiner, with Eli Wallach, Jo Van Fleet, Hurd Hatfield, Barbara Baxley, Frank Silvera, and Joseph Anthony. Elia Kazan was the director. Lemuel Ayers designed the entire production, Anna Sokolow assisted Kazan. All gilded names. And down deep in the playbill were names that have since emerged: Nehemiah Persoff, Martin Balsam, and Mike Gazzo.

In this single quarter-century retrospect is a glimpse of what the Shubert meant week after week to the theater ~ in this community and in the country at large.

Can we save the Shubert? I'm not sure that we can.

But it's surely worth a try.

Saturday, January 3, 1981
Editor's Note

A Case for the Shubert

The case for the Shubert - its preservation and its renovation as a theater - is a matter that worries New Haven. Yet it seems to me that we will be throwing away something unique, an asset of special value and special potential for this community, if the Shubert is squeezed out of the municipal budget in the months ahead.

On this third day in the second year of the second- last decade of the 20th Century in New Haven our city government faces difficult problems. Jobs here are declining as industries move out. Neighborhood deterioration and housing decay mean that traditional sources of revenue are faltering. At the same time the prospect of state or federal transfusions of cash grow dimmer. Nothing we need to do as a community looks easy of accomplishment.

So why are we kicking around the idea of putting six million taxpayer dollars into the Shubert?

I'd say because we are not dealing with an idle dream but with a hard reality which may bring us much good if we embrace it -- and leave us forever regretful if we permit it to slip away.

The Shubert exists. It is something that stands there on College Street, that is tangible, that does not have to be created. There are four walls and a roof, a great stage and a fly-loft capable of handling tons of scenery, two balconies and seats for 1,500 people. It is something that cannot be found in Hartford, or Bridgeport, or Springfield. It is New Haven's own.

It has identity - a name, a function, a recognizable purpose and a pleasurable image. Refurbishing is in order. But some 60 years of success make it familiar in aim and accomplishment for theater professionals and theater enthusiasts not just in Connecticut, or on Broadway, but across the United States.

For New Haven it also offers bread and butter opportunities to refresh our downtown redevelopment hopes as perhaps nothing else can.

For a long time the Shubert has been a key element in the idea of a back-of-Chapel-Street shopping arcade and walkway that could run all the way from the Sheraton-Park Plaza on Temple Street through the Joel Schiavone properties on College Street to the Mellon Art Gallery and beyond. The Shubert, in this concept, permits us to attempt something involving human energy, pleasure, and social dynamics that - if it works – will do for downtown far more than we can do by tinkering with new parking spaces or brighter lighting.

The Shubert is a natural component of the cityscape where it stands. The designers' and builders of the Hotel Taft made the hotel and the theater a unified building project back in 1913. Their vision has changed with time, as has the hotel. But the interplay between the Taft, as a residence for today and tomorrow, and the Shubert as a performance center, can create parallel benefits. The Taft will better preserve its present high potential if there is a flow of theater-goers and related street activities nearby. At the other end of the block, the Crown Street garage was designed and built, basically, to serve Shubert parking needs. Both, facilities would continue to support each other.

And what is the alternative to a living Shubert on College Street? It could be nothing more than a row of cinderblock-rear and plastic-front stores just to fill the space. In time it might be another business building or a downtown apartment. But whatever might eventually occupy the spot, the opportunity that exists .today will be gone forever if the Shubert project is neglected or abandoned.

There is risk, of course, in the undertaking. The city is subsidizing the Memorial Coliseum on an annual basis. New Haven taxpayers can't afford unlimited burdens of this type.

The estimated annual operating deficit of the Shubert in its initial period of new operations is about $350,000. The debt service on $7 million in bonds (figured before the prime rate hit 20 percent) is another $350,000 as presented by city development administrator John Sawyer to the Board of Aldermen last August. The theater's total expected subsidy would be about $700,000 per year - a substantial challenge.

Yet conservatively angled studies indicate that a full Shubert season will bring 250,000 people to downtown New Haven each year. And on the basis of experience in other places, the studies project that the "multiplier effect of the Shubert Theater on downtown New Haven would amount to $7.5 million of new spending each year."

Such a tenfold return on the theater's annual subsidy would seem to be worth a measure of risk.

The theater's renewal has got to be weighed in purely arithmetical terms since no other terms will make it workable. But if the arithmetic can be done in ways that make sense, there are other advantages to be pursued in terms of the "quality of life" as it is enriched by access to drama, music and dance in a good theater building.

New Haven is blessed in the cultural depth and diversity it generates. Its music, museums, dance and drama are unmatched in a city its size. In the early 70s when the Shubert went into eclipse as a "commercial" theater center for all Connecticut, we had the strongly rooted Long Wharf company and the Yale Repertory group to prevent a void through their own creative and impressively successful dramatic productions. Neither of these ventures is in the least fazed by the prospect of a reopened Shubert, so far as I can see, and ardent supporters of both have done much to keep the Shubert hopes alive.

Over the not-so-long haul toward the 21st Century New Haven's chief' challenge is to reshape itself as a community. The Olin Company's withdrawal from the key job-creating project we have known as the Olin Scientific Park, the continued frustration over uses for the former U.S. Steel site on the Quinnipiac River, the coming occupancy of the handsome Gant Shirtmakers building by our Jackson Newspapers are all symbolic of factory-job decay in New Haven. Our future, we are told, lies with a service-job economy. This means extensive recruiting of enterprises that might locate here. In attracting the needed new business and new jobs the "quality of life" is an obvious talking point - and a going Shubert, will have strong elements of recognizability, appeal, and even self-identification for business people exploring our local assets.

Is there blindness in this pitch? I don't think so.

After 25 years of reviewing almost every new show at the Shubert, my wife and I have developed a special anatomical feeling for seats 2 and 4, Row D, Left Orchestra at the theater. We saw there everyone and everything from Katharine Hepburn, Ezio Pinza, Sir Laurence Olivier, the Ballet Russe de Monte Carlo with Fokine and Danilova, Margaret Sullivan, Boris Carnovsky, and Barbara Bel Geddes (who now, graces "Dallas" as Miz Elly) to Diana Barrymore drunk and Liza Minelli pudgy. Our understanding of our lives and our time has been illuminated by those 500-or-so nights at the Shubert.

I am an officer of the Friends of the Shubert. I sat for a while on Mayor Frank Logue's first committee to explore the Shubert's continuing potential. I've just worked with the group which recommended to Mayor Ben DiLieto most of the names he will consider for appointment to a Shubert management board. So I have opinions on the issue. - none of which is stronger than the conviction that the theater is a people-serving, non-elitist experience which can send its human insights into the most troubled neighborhoods of our community at the same time it is helping to keep prosperous a city core around which the neighborhoods can cluster.

The old "birthplace of the nation's hits" is not coming back to College Street in a world where cable television's "home box office" is a drama shaper. A new Shubert will hardly be able to offer more than 10 or 12 Broadway-type shows yearly. It will have to develop and encourage other kinds of performance by touring drama, dance or music groups as well as by local organizations like the Connecticut Ballet if it is to fulfill the 260 "event days" per year that the studies consider possible. But other civic theaters meet and surmount such tests regularly.

Whether the Shubert needs all the high-cost polish that the architects have built into their redesign - a three-story glass lobby, a 200-seat small performance hall - remains to be argued, mostly in mortgage terms. Whether the ideal operation - by private managers at private risk - can be attained is also dubious, though it should be a goal. Minimal political involvement in "show biz" should clearly be another prime goal - at the theater and among our aldermen well.

There's much still to be decided. There's something still to be risked. But there's much, much more to be gained for New Haven - and what makes the case for the Shubert, in the end, is the building that's standing, the record, and the reputation it supports, and the future reward it can offer as a place, a name, and a people-pleasing purpose at the heart of the city.

Saturday, February 23, 1985
Editor's note

New Deal at the Shubert

The Shubert Performing Arts Center is not going to dry up and blow away like tumbleweed. It shouldn't be wasted. It is a beautifully renovated, effectively modernized playhouse - the kind of civic asset we would be eager to create if it did not exist on College Street.

The Shubert, on the other hand, is clearly not going to soar phoenix-like from the ashes of its decline and shutdown in the mid-'70s. Why? Because Broadway as a source of sellout shows is no healthier now than it was then. And theater production today is a high-risk, high-cost venture for technical investment makers.

So the Shubert is troubled - which was predictable. It has been saddled with a false start - which was probably unnecessary. But it continues to have the magnet potential for downtown New Haven that it was designed to have - and that it has begun to demonstrate in measurable terms.

What the Shubert needs now is to be worked at, to be tinkered with. It needs tender loving care and an infusion of new confidence from people who believe in and enjoy the special pleasures and insights that the stage can offer. It needs community support at the box office when there's entertainment afoot - plus a dash of vintage civic pride when it comes to sharing jokes or barbed judgments at happy hours around town. And it needs what it admittedly hasn't had to date but seems about to get - hardnosed management that has a feeling for show biz, for municipal responsibility, and for the bottom line.

How did we get where we are? These are some of the elements of the problem - not necessarily in order of importance - which I perceive as a current board member, as one of Mayor Frank Logue's original Shubert committee members, and as a member of Friends of the Shubert before that:

1. The pre-Broadway, post-Broadway "product" flow of Shubert memory no longer exists. The New York dilemma is demonstrated in three facts: (a) One of the hottest tickets in town is Yul Brynner's "King and I," which started here more than 25 years ago. (b) There's an uptown revue that parodies the top shows. Its uproarious "tribute" to last year's Broadway musical hits is several seconds of complete silence. (c) The Goodspeed Opera's carefully polished musical, "Harrigan and Hart," got so-so reviews, nothing pulverizing but no raves either. It opened on a Thursday and closed on Sunday because the producers couldn't spend $50,000 to $75,000 per week to build an audience over time - a common practice when costs were less. Each of these examples illustrates reasons for the slow going at the Shubert.

2. The Shubert has been burned twice in a year by unsuccessful managers, men whose performance did not match their reputations or their professional recommendations. They used large 20- person staffs plus outside consultants. They went wrong by applying the standards of endowed cultural centers in places such as Washington or Los Angeles or New York to the totally different circumstances at the Shubert, where penny pinching and shrewd planning are indigenous necessities. At the Shubert's peak Maurice Bailey managed with five full-time staffers and fewer part-timers.

3. The Shubert's board of directors has been involved from the beginning in a fairly frantic game of catch-up. The essential direction and thrust that any board expects from a knowledgeable management were never forthcoming. Shows that were booked and canceled, advertised and sold and then unsold, by staff professionals were dumped onto the board and its executive committee for solutions. Poor contracts and amateurishly handled finances moved board members from crisis to crisis without much chance for perspective. The fact that many of these work-willing board members are from the suburbs doesn't lessen their concern for costs that affect New Haven's budget and tax rate.

But the Shubert can't be run by a board alone. A theater's funding and its audience-building policies are proper board considerations. The plays that are booked, the deals that are made to bring them in and entertainment successes, however, all depend on professionally skilled managers.

4. The Palace. In a limited market the Shubert's original financing and scheduling projections all assumed a single new theater downtown. Then, suddenly, there were two - in the same block. Enuf sed.

5. The question of the basic contractual arrangements that made a revived Shubert possible is probably central to any formal review, aldermanic or other, at this juncture. There is a case for the logic of the public-private funding as it developed. Thoughtful and ingenious adjustments were made to bring the performing arts center to reality. But the joint venture developers - The Fusco Corp. and Schiavone Realty - are now guaranteed, whether the house is open or shut, roughly $7,000 a week in "rent" for the Shubert. Is there a way to lighten that burden as the Shubert reorganizes?

For today and tomorrow the stress is on austerity along College Street. Much has been made of the fact that the Shubert will "go dark" from late spring through summer. But this a natural way to organize a theater season of many weeks, and many shows, for autumn sale and subscription.

Mayor DiLieto has involved City Hall directly in the supervision of finances and in the shaping of new accountability inside the theater. A better next year is possible.

The emergency is regrettable. The deficit must be faced as a long-term burden that can only be chipped at patiently. But even the Shubert's most recent experience has shown strong "ups" along with the "downs." Making the "ups" predominate is the challenge.

There are responsible people who would now shrug and drop the curtain permanently. To me, this would be a lost opportunity. We can take a civic asset, embrace the obvious negatives, and write the Shubert off. Or we can take that civic asset, with a history and a name recognized worldwide, deal affirmatively with its problems and its potential, impose sensible safeguards on its finances, and try (using George S. Kauffman's play title) to "Light Up The Sky." Let's try!

Saturday July 1, 1978
Editor's Note

Bicentennial Plus Two

Independence Day celebrations on Bicentennial Plus Two will have a quiet focus. Two years after the excitement of the nation's 200th year the fervor has died down. But the search for freedom goes on. And the need to defend it keeps recurring. "Eternal vigilance is the price of liberty."

It's no waste of a pleasant Saturday to ponder briefly the current pressures on "life, liberty, and the pursuit of happiness" which arrive out of efforts to improve or interpret our institutions. This column dedicates itself frequently to explaining the journalistic view. But very often what affects the press and news gatherers in general also has substantial implications for the individual citizen.

Are wire taps on the way out? It's easy to assume so. But hear this.

In this week when New Haven finally saw its first limited release of the names of wire tap victims, there was a rising flap in Washington over proposed legislation labeled the Foreign Intelligence Surveillance Act of 1978.

Pride and frustration in nearly equal parts have been the lot of The Journal-Courier in its exposure of illegal wire tapping here in New Haven. Reporter Andrew Houlding and the paper's editors reported, and proved, that there had been frequent police wire taps without court orders in the Sixties and early Seventies. The full facts of the abuse of personal rights by public agencies continue, however, to be muted and concealed by officials resisting full disclosure.

And the hope that exposure here may have, somehow, threatened wire tapping everywhere, begins to shrivel in the word of Washington's new approach.

The legislation we first discussed as an antidote for warrantless wire tapping. In the House it has been introduced by Judiciary Committee chairman Peter Rodino. In the Senate much the same bill bears the sponsorship of Edward Kennedy and Birch Bayh. These are impeccable liberal credentials. And to anyone familiar with the New Haven illegalities, some firming up of wire tap laws seems essential.

But Pulitzer Prize columnist William Safire sounded an alarm in The New York Times this week. An "exception" in the Rodino bill authorizes the President and the Attorney General to tap telephones without a court order provided the Executive Branch reports its action to House and Senate Intelligence committees. "Thus," says Satire, "the check on abuse is not judicial, but congressional." And the politically sensitive Congress as a watchdog of personal rights is not a very reassuring concept.

The bill authorizes "officers, employees, or agents of the United States" to test equipment and to train wiretappers - in the field - without court warrant.

And finally, in an echo of one of the most haunting aspects of our New Haven wiretap experience, the proposed new legislation unabashedly involves the telephone company. Says Safire:

"Currently, the telephone company provides the government only with 'line access information' - that is, it will point out which wires in the central terminal are on the target phone, and will rent the government a private line from that point to the lawmen's recording equipment. Nothing else.

"But under the proposed law, the phone company and the target's landlord must provide 'any and all information, facilities, or technical assistance necessary to accomplish the electronic surveillance in such a manner as will protect its secrecy.'"

None of this is yet law.

Looking at it from the New Haven perspective, on the weekend before Independence Day, let's hope the proposal is substantially improved before it does become law.

Questions previously raised here about the Supreme Court's decision on warrantless newsroom searches have pretty much stuck to the journalist's view. But here's a wider reading on how the push for evidence may involve many other citizens. The Los Angeles Times has editorialized in part:

"...The U.S. Supreme Court, in a 5-3 decision, said the police may conduct surprise raids on the offices of news organizations in hunting for evidence relevant to a criminal investigation.

But the decision extends far beyond that.

"It renders every home and every place of business vulnerable to a surprise search by police.

"It threatens the confidential relationship between priest and penitent, between doctor and patient, between lawyer and client.

"It sabotages the Fourth Amendment, the historic barrier between the massive power of the state and the individual citizen.

"It mocks the First Amendment in taunting language.

"It eviscerates the due-process clause of the 14th Amendment.

"It comes close to reinstating the evils of the general search warrant in England, and the writs of assistance in the American colonies, that the Fourth Amendment was intended to abolish.

"It opens up the homes of persons innocent of any crime to a sudden knock on the door and the invasion by police in a search for mere evidence of a crime ... "

It is not, therefore, simply a threat to newspapers and news gatherers which is being criticized. It is a potential threat to every citizen.

Colleague Bill Ryan did a column recently on a collector of antique newspapers. He brought to me a copy of the New-Haven Gazette (predecessor of The Journal-Courier) for July 13, 1786. It reported on the toasts, salutes, and sentiments of the first significant anniversary of Independence Day - 10 years after the Declaration's signing. There were 13 toasts, as there were 13 original states. The newspaper reported them in this way:

"On Tuesday, the Fourth, the Tenth Anniversary of the glorious Independence of America, was celebrated at the coffee house in this city, by the mayor, aldermen, common-council-men, sheriffs, and a large number of respectable inhabitants; where an excellent dinner was provided, after which the following toasts were drank under the discharge of thirteen cannon, viz.

"1. The United States of America.

"2. The President and Congress of the United States.

"3. His most Christian Majesty.

"4 The governor of the State of Connecticut.

"5. His Excellency General Washington.

"6. The European powers in Alliance.

"7 The Officers and Soldiers of the late Federal Army.

"8. May we commemorate the virtues of those brave men who have fallen in defense of freedom.

"9. The commissioners who negotiated the late glorious peace.

"10. Success to the measures adopted by Congress for speedy payment of the national Debt, and may all obstacles to
that success be annihilated.

"11. May the trade of the United States be under such regulations as to render it extensive, profitable, and permanent.

"12. May the Happiness of Mankind be as diffusive as their existence, as perfect as their nature is capable of, and as
Eternal as the flux of time.

"13. May the laurels of this day's acquisition be preserved to the latest posterity."

What about that toast No. 3 – an interesting gesture of détente – to his "Christian Majesty", that George III, who 10 years before was charged with having "plundered our seas, ravaged our coasts, burned our towns, and destroyed the lives of our people."

Some honest money man spoke to item 10. A sturdy business type probably put in that prophetic word against too much government regulation in 11. And perhaps a glowing minister, mixing grog with the milk of human kindness, held forth for Number 12.

At any rate, a happy day in 1786 for the Declaration of Independence.

From remembered fireworks to a remembrance of roses. On

this pre-holiday Saturday 37 years ago in 1941, I waited warm in the sunny vestry of St. Joseph's Church on Edwards Street for the organ to blare out. It did – and a smiling girl in veil and bridal gown came down the aisle to put her hand into my hand. They have never come unclasped. And two hands, like two heads, are always better than one.

A declaration of inter-dependence.

Pardee-Morris House, *Lighthouse Rd. New Haven's oldest habitation. Built about 1690, burned by the British in 1779, restored in 19th Century and still later bequeathed to New Haven Citizens, administered by the Colony Historical Society.* *Engraving by Don Forrer.*

Saturday, February 17, 1979
Editor's Note

Words and Musings

"I understand a fury in your words," says Desdemona to Othello, "but not the words."

And that's what local admirers of Robert Brustein may feel about the closing quote from a recent Brustein interview in The Boston Globe. Yale's retiring Drama dean, readying his move to Harvard, was quoted thusly at the end of a long Boston interview:

" ... New Haven is not a pleasurable place in which to live. The environment really is repellent. It's been bearable for us because we're workaholics. Since there is no city, since there's nothing much to do, we've been able to lose ourselves in theater. New Haven is just like what Gertrude Stein said of the West Coast. 'There is no there there.' There is no there here. But there is a there in Boston and in Cambridge. And we're, going to start living for the first time in 13 years ..."

The dean misremembers.

New Haven is secure in its sense of the "there" that's here. And the Brusteins have added to it in their 13 years along York Street.

There was there-ness here, under Brustein auspices, that still-remembered night when the Living Theatre company burst naked from the Yale Theatre in the late Sixties, their old stomach wounds and repaired herniations and painted toenails livid under the street lamps as they pursued Melpomene, the muse of tragedy, down the gutters while cops and Yalies gazed agog.

There was there-ness here when Brustein's fierce insistence on a physical center for his Repertory Company transformed the old Calvary Baptist Church into a stern but modishly effective theater.

There was there-ness here back in 1970 when Brustein, unlike so many groveling colleagues, greeted with open disdain the cultural and political banditry that expressed itself in the May Day riots on the Green and on the Campus.

And then there was the dramatic event itself, how many-score Brustein-imprinted play openings here - some awful, many uplifting, all challenging.

Cambridge as a civic entity can't hold a candle to New Haven for thereness or hereness. We stand, or fall, in this town as a total community. Cambridge has never, even slightly, risen above being an academic appendage to Boston. And while the Hub at times does glow with urbane disorder and dowdy charm, its virtues - and its flaws - are simply those of New Haven multiplied six-fold.

It's my guess that Robert and Norma Brustein, workaholics self-defined, will continue to lose themselves in the theater more than in the there they're abandoning here and looking for elsewhere.

All of which is, I suppose, a way of saying that Dean Brustein has been a neighbor worth having in New Haven - and one who will actually be missed a little more than HIS own words concede.

Saturday, August 20, 1977
Editor's Note

An Ice Cream Sandwich

TOP WAFER: THE CULT OF PERSONALITY.

The gossip revival is one of the trends in newspaper journalism today. And it is reflected, in a way, in the personal response of so many ordinary people to the death this week of Elvis Presley. Without generally realizing it - because most Americans were a little too old, or a little too young themselves - Presley is a deeply personal symbol of the Nineteen Fifties for people who were young when he first erupted on the television and rock record scene.

In his death Elvis Presley, who seemed to be moving toward almost certain eclipse in career terms, has now become a pop-culture immortal.

The devotion and recognition given him this week is a reminder of the close ties that the public develops with those who, for whatever reasons, become its heroes. And it provides an explanation, at least in part, of the continuing universal preoccupation with those columns and commentaries which provide some insights and some "inside" information about people who are big in the news - and, in varying ways, big in our lives and times.

The humanization of heroes and headline makers is a psychological interest, perhaps a need, we all apparently share. And the newspaper gossip column, while its weaknesses are apparent, is a source most readers rarely reject.

SANDWICH FILLING: TODAY'S ICE CREAM.

The Journal-Courier has published a lengthy story about the

substitution of a chemical formulate called caseinate for powdered milk in our cones and sundaes.

I can't believe that "nonfat dry milk" is the key to ice cream's current pleasures and virtues. Yet great agencies of government and commerce are arguing legalistically over how much protein can be manufactured and masqueraded as true nonfat dry milk in the chemical concoctions which today are sanctioned as ice cream.

It wasn't always so.

As an ice cream consumer I go back 50 years to steamy August nights in Fair Haven when, on the edge of darkness, a boy in sneakers - without socks for the cooling effect - would be dispatched a city block-and-a-half to the drug store for a pint of hand-packed vanilla and strawberry. It was an errand to be done running.

Mr. Sullivan, the druggist, spruce in a linen jacket that was unblemished after a long day's work, would emerge from the mysterious back room where he mixed medicines using brass scales and a mortar. He would take the order gravely, and standing beneath the paddles of his two slow-turning ceiling fans, he would pull out a nickel-plated device, half spoon and half small spade, to dig into the ice cream containers buried behind his marble soda fountain.

If the druggist seemed particularly permissive and the boy felt particularly daring he might sidle up to the cigar case and, standing on tiptoe, press a sudden jet of blue and gold flame out of the ever-burning cigar lighter. Mr. Sullivan might turn or blink to signal the recklessness of such conduct, but unless his mood was very bad he said nothing.

Meanwhile, he packed and pressed and pushed hard at vanilla and strawberry, and sometimes chocolate, until the plain unprinted pint measure in manila cardboard could hold no smidgeon more of the frozen delight.

The 35 cents paid in exact change, the green and scarlet glass of the pharmaceutical urns passed in the window like race pylons, the boy sped home - a messenger from Marathon. There the pint container would be opened with anticipations that in themselves created ceremony, the dishes lined up on the kitchen table, spoons at the ready on the dining room buffet.

And in those happy times, when nobody was truly sugar-sated as we all are today, a pint of firm-packed ice cream went a long way; it could provide a week's "treat" for three adults, two children, and perhaps a lucky passing neighbor. And the eating provided, it seems in memory, at least an hour of homey conversation and reminiscence.

Today I am, like so many middle aged males I know, compulsive about ice cream as the universal dessert-of-choice and the snack above all other snacks. At banquets, ice cream makes a lip-smacking climax to one more evening on the rubber chicken circuit. Abroad and eager for new experiences, I still must teeter past the pastries du pays or the whimsical foreign puddings to reach, guiltily, for the ices, the spumoni, and the creams.

I have refused to harbor the notion that Mr. Sullivan's ice cream in its unlabeled 1927 container is different from the ice cream I now hurry by the half gallon from the supermarket to the kitchen freezer. I make this refusal in the face of the obviously plastic residuals which stick in the cardboard ice cream box even after you've rinsed it in a boiling stream of tap water or left it exposed overnight on the counter. I resist the notion even as I observe worriedly that this new ice cream hardly melts in a hot wind on a sun-baked terrace. (Mr. Sullivan's would run down your hand after 60 seconds in the summer air.)

The statisticians indicate that we currently eat about 805 million gallons of ice cream annually in this country. But the moguls of the Food and Drug Administration have long forgotten - or never knew about Mr. Sullivan and his drug store.

They have been busy all this summer consulting "frozen dessert" experts who cheerfully demonstrate that it doesn't take cream to make ice cream, that it doesn't even take "nonfat dry milk" anymore. They insist that we can get the same amounts of protein out of "safe and suitable substitutes", and that - in the process, the ice cream makers will have a chance to make and sell their products at lower prices.

So, okay. Mr. Sullivan himself banished the hand-turned cream freezer. But he bought his ice cream from a dairy. And the dairy had cows that ate buttercups and left slippery spots in the meadows before they surrendered their warm milk to a farmer's pail. And despite this memory I'll probably eat everything the new dessert makers concoct because I was so long ago hooked by Mr. Sullivan on milk and cream from certified cows, and sugar, and ice, and pure flavorings pressed from fruits and roots and berries.

Today's marketers, afloat in a sea of wordy regulations about vegetable shortening, salt, artificial and natural colorings, lecithin, flour, and sugar don't even want to make or sell the old fangled ice cream.

I know I'm in no position to resist them come dessert time. And maybe they will triumphantly substitute caseinate for nonfat dry milk in the cost-cutting formula they pursue with such determination. They may thus replace the product of a somewhat artificial and industrialized cow with something more unassailably synthetic, something unchurned by bovine udder and distilled by the hand of man alone.

Suffering but still salivating I must take such success with my eyes open, my mind closed, and my taste buds couchant.

Despite the ingredients, what I savor is probably beyond taste and texture. Firm, cold, delicious on spoon and tongue and palate it is the memory of Mr. Sullivan's hand-packed pint of cream - home's simple ambrosia in the sweet family sharing of those Augusts past.

Saturday, November 29, 1975
Editor's Note

Remembering A Reporter

The pre-game activity (at the Yale Bowl) was immense. There was so much going on that it seemed for a while the start of the game itself might be overlooked ... Outside of Portal 15 hundreds of women stood in a rambling, confused line. Above their heads a sign said, inscrutably: Women ... The stands were a moving mass of humanity, howling and cheering everything in sight ... Spelling 'ELI' unerringly the (Yale) band marched grandly down, and then off, the field ..."

These are jottings from one of the last news stories - a "color" piece on the Yale-Princeton football game of 1956 - written for The Register by reporter Phil Casey.

In this season 19 years ago, Casey bade a jaunty farewell to New Haven and the newspaper. It was a graceful, quip-filled going – because Phil Casey handled everything in life as if he had a light heart, and because he was taking a job at The Washington Post where the pay was good and high professionalism was the recognized standard. It was a little sad, too, because Phil was a blithe companion to lose after seven years here, and because a marriage on the rocks had much to do with his leaving.

At any rate, we had a post- Thanksgiving party for him. In the tradition of news crews everywhere, Casey and his editors and companions traded jibes that seemed close to insults and jokes full of disrespect and affection. On December 1, 1956, he closed up the battered green desk in the Register's second floor newsroom. He took the train to Washington (Phil never drove a car). And at The Post he became - gradually - a resident character, the personification of a reporting ideal, a man who turned his back on all the big stories in the city of unending big stories so that he and the readers of The Post could examine realities that he considered important - and funny.

Phil Casey died a couple of weeks ago of cancer. And what they remember him for in Washington are the stories he wrote about people of no importance in the streets behind those marble avenues, the stories he wrote again and again about the inward-looking, splendid, lonely animals he observed among crowds in the zoo at Rock Creek Park, the annual story he wrote when the circus came to town.

Over the years Phil kept a lively interest in New Haven, visiting rarely but hanging on every word or rumor about the people he knew. When Dick Lee went down as mayor to hook another Federal grant or loan there were always reunions. And in recent years I saw him at least every spring during conventions of the American Society of Newspaper Editors. He was not impressed by editors. He obviously considered them as exotic as some of his subjects in the park or the circus, people and friends self-caged in management zoos when they could have been out on the scent of a feature story.

One drink with Casey matched a full convention in the perspectives it offered. And the laughter, self-directed, self-illuminating, is what remains.

When we saw him in April, my wife and I didn't know he was going to die. In retrospect, it's clear that he did. At the end his body went first to the doctors as he sought once again, answers to the straight reporter's questions he was asking, and as he tried, once again, to immerse himself meaningfully in the stream of human fellowship. It's unfair to impose upon New Haven readers mere, shimmering recollections of a personality now beyond reach. As tribute to a reporter, though, the editorial they wrote at The Washington Post says a lot about what lingers of Phil Casey in New Haven and Washington and wherever else his whimsical reporting is remembered.

The editorial was headed simply:

"Phil Casey, The Washington Post reporter who died Tuesday, once covered the story of some mynah birds at the zoo, one of which was said to have uttered certain Anglo Saxon horrors in the presence of some elderly ladies. Both birds were thereupon incarcerated. The thing we like to recall of that incident is that

Mr. Casey, while not insensible to such reportorial joys as the allegation that an Israeli sailor had taught the bird bad words in a drunken stupor, also said something that not every reporter would have thought of:

"-Perhaps, he speculated, the bird only uttered the obscenity to persons it disliked. Surely that makes a difference?

"-Perhaps there was a First Amendment issue here, especially since two birds were banished, though only one had cursed.

"-Perhaps the birds did not so much say the scandalous phrase as the visitors thought they heard it.

"Justice, Mr. Casey strongly implied, is not always automatically served merely by doing the 'right' and conventional and proper thing: it can be more complex than that, and in the rush of getting through the world we allow many 'mynah tragedies' to occur, as he somewhat outrageously said at the time.

"We hardly presume to praise Phil Casey in this space because, first of all, we are not sure that we are up to it, and second, it was his honor to do as workmanlike a job of recording the world for us all as he could manage, and that is praise enough.

"Besides, innumerable readers already knew him through his more than 1,600 bylined pieces about almost everything, in which he attracted their affection with his special gift for provoking compassionate mirth. In life as in print, he poked fun at the absurdities he saw in people and institutions, but always made a sympathy and gentleness that made the subtle distinctions between amusement at the human condition and meanness.

"In our midst, where both the work and the man could be appreciated to the fullest, there will always be the Casey stories, by and about one of the most talented. selfless and skilled general practitioners of the newspaper trade we've ever known - and loved."

And so, the bylines end.

Saturday, August 26, 1978
Editor's Note

In Milford And In Memory

Amid the pleasantries, the white and rose wines and the shop talk I stumbled on an old family friend now working at the Milford Redevelopment office and I chatted briefly with a sociable guest whose label said "The Sunshine Factory." Both personify the change that has come to Milford over the decades since 1939 when I got my first summer reporting job covering the beaches. Federal cash and public reconstruction were no part of Milford's prudent Yankee image then. And the town's only sunshine factory was not a whimsically titled giftshop but the blue sky over Milford's far-reaching farms and its nearly-unpolluted beaches.

Population then was under 15,000. Now the figures are reversed and the 51,000 last counted continue to increase. The Milford Turnpike in those days was a billboarded link between towns, a place where you might go to buy gasoline or bait or to carouse occasionally at a "roadhouse" like the Seven Gables Inn. There wasn't a single shopping center between New Haven Green and Milford Green; but there was a portent of things to come in the new Wayside Furniture Shop about halfway between.

"Covering the beaches" was a good beginning reporter's job. It meant providing long columns of personals for the Sunday Register, detailed lists by name of the cousins from Trenton or Topeka who had arrived at Bide-A-Wee cottage in Silver Beach to spend a week with George and Priscilla Spelvin, careful accounts of the Youth Fellowship picnic which had been held at the Pond Point home of Ramona Frost and her parents.

For a fellow who wanted to write and hated to ask questions it was often sun-scalded frustration. But it forced a door to door confrontation with people who said they had no news and then had to be educated to see that there was news in a birthday party on the sand - or even in the arrival of somebody's mother-in-law. The "beat" ran all the way from Oyster River and Woodmont past Sylvester Poli's beflowered Villa Rosa, to Merwin's Beach, and Morningside, past Point Beach, Pond Point, Bayview, Welch's Point and the Milford Gulf.

There were kindly housewives who might offer you lemonade when you knocked (in shirt and tie to properly "represent" the newspaper) at their door. And there were ice cream stands.

Milford itself punctuated the long route. Up Gulf Street you passed the house of Register reporter Jimmy Rose - and in lieu of a bureau or office I might meet with him once in a while on his front porch to pick up a pointer about summer politics or the way to cover the sailing races at the Milford Yacht Club.

Then it was through town, past the Green, down to the Yacht Club and Fort Trumbull, around to Silver Beach, Myrtle Beach and Wildemere, and on to Laurel Beach where the houses were big, the shaded streets were quiet, and the "casino" was the center of everybody's day, and night.

A girl in a two-piece bathing suit was still nearly a sensation in those quiet days. Even the macho males (unheard of adjective) wore suit-tops, too. But the suits were wool knit and clinging. And there were berry-brown nymphs, and naiads, and nymphets who smiled along the way and who linger in the memory of four decades, coy beneath their beach umbrellas or behind screen doors, golden images, still, in a season that might have been comfortably misspent if only there were not always mothers nearby on the porch or a copy-hungry editor back at the office.

My father helped me finance a used Model A Ford to cover the territory. I still mount that first car registration number on my bumper. And on Sunday I'd drive down for extra coverage of the sailing races, beside the girl with whom I still spend all my Sundays.

There was a Catholic retreat house then on Charles Island. If you parked near the long sand-bar at Silver Beach on a Sunday evening you could hear across the water a faint, reflective bell. Pealing vespers? Ringing dinner? Or tolling for an oldtime Milford on the edge of change?

The season ended - as did the reporting job suddenly at Labor Day. The previous summer of '38 had been followed in September by the great New England hurricane. The beaches suffered but endured. This summer of 1939 we all lived, nearly unperturbed, beneath the rising thunderheads of World War II. In that September there was no hurricane - but Hitler's armies rolled into Poland to start the carnage that ended six years later with the explosion of the A-bomb.

By then I could write features. The shore apprenticeship was done.

Milford's sun-tanned mermaids, the old town, and I - and my own girl and our generation the world over - had come to a cutoff more abrupt and lasting than Labor Day. The memories still glow. But change took hold and altered things - as it does again today, on the video screen of our "news machine" in the thriving heart of Milford.

Saturday March 17, 1979
Editor's Note

The Wearing Of The Green

Top 0' the morning is the greeting of the moment.

But the fact that it comes six days after New Haven's St. Patrick's Day parade has marched out of the headlines and into history says something about the contradictions we now embrace as we mix convenience, commercialism, and ethnicity.

Back in Fair Haven when I was a boy everybody was Irish - almost - but there was no St. Paddy's Day parade. The Irish were close to their roots, consumed by their jobs, and so immersed in family pursuits, which were often religious pursuits, that public manifestations like local parades were out of the picture.

St. Patrick's Day might provide a brief respite from the mortifications of Lent - but it wouldn't be much more than a cake with green frosting on the table, a sentimental serving of Irish soda bread (which was not normally held in the highest regard), or, for the man of the house, a bottle of the homemade beer which was brewed in most kitchens during the Prohibition era.

For children St. Patrick's Day meant a green tie, green ribbons, or a green silk shamrock or harp pinned near the shoulder before the trip to school. And in the afternoon in St. Francis classrooms the nuns would let the seventh or eighth grade boy with the sweetest singing voice - Francis Kenefick in my time - sing "Danny Boy," or "That Tumble Down Shack In Athlone," or "A Little Bit Of Heaven (Fell From Out The Sky One Day)." But that came only after the full stint of lessons and learning and occasional head rapping had been observed.

On the evening of the 17th the Holy Name Society would have its annual Irish Night of amateur songs and amateur dances, starting in the church basement at 7:30 p.m. and over by 10. It was an uncomplicated one-day celebration - and while everybody participated it all came mutually, naturally, and without great intensity or emphasis.

The simplicity, I see now, came from the certitude of it all. Everybody was Irish, so there was no need - or at best a very small need - to proclaim Irishness. Ethnic pride and ethnic conviction had not yet become competitive.

The surprise part of such recollection, for me more than for you, is the knowledge that this memory of childhood goes back 50 years. The arithmetic is not depressing - it's merely unbelievable.

Also unbelievable – from the vantage point of today's consciously "pluralistic" society - is the homogenousness of the neighborhood that ran block after block from Grand to Middletown Avenues, from about Clay or Monroe streets down to the Quinnipiac River.

Looking up or down the street from a summer front porch you could put Irish face to Irish name almost endlessly:

Burns, McDonald, Conway, Riley, Brandon, Sullivan, Geenty, Hussey, Keogh, Carroll, O'Dea, Kelliher, Carey, Watson, Dinneen, Enright, Daley, Nolan, Falsey, Brady, Murphy, Cafferty, Deeley, Fleming, Geary, Cleary, McManus, Looney, Cooney, Dillon, Killeen, Lenihan, Flannery, Heffernan, Harkins, McGinnis, McGuire, Foley, Quinn, Mulligan, Mcloughlin, Coyle, Deskin, Griffin, Grady ... and many more.

And if you look back at the jobs, house by house, the same insistent uniformity comes through:

Railroad engineer, railway mail clerk, Folding Box machinist, post office man, iron worker, Candee rubber worker, railroad clerk, gas company man, engineer, railroad fireman, streetcar motorman, railroad engineer, brakeman, trolley conductor, policeman, another policeman, railroad engineer, butcher, city fireman, plumber, clerk at the Yellow Building (railroad headquarters), brakeman, railroad engineer, city fireman, railroad fireman, policeman, railyard worker, policeman, trolley motorman, druggist, grocer ...

In so close-knit a community, personality and idiosyncracy clearly came in for intense scrutiny. We were all so much alike that differences had value and Irishness had a thousand facets.

There was a satisfactory hint of the variety we now call "pluralism". A Swedish tailor, a Jewish tailor, an Italian barber, a German barber, a Belgian carpenter whose son became a monsignor, a German printer, a railroad engineer born to the Yankee reticence of Martha's Vineyard. One day when we lived in a three family house a taxi arrived at the front door - as exotic a conveyance in Fair Haven as a rickshaw. Out of it stepped a strange lady (in recollection I see she was a frightened girl). She was the destined bride of the brother of the Armenian man who lived with his family above us. There was nobody at home up there. Everybody was at work. So the baggage from Asia Minor was piled in the hallway. And my mother and the dark eyed girl who had no word of English spent a strained afternoon over tea in the front room.

Later, on her wedding day, she sang, still in an alien tongue - and I got sick on too much orange soda.

Other nationalities, however, were only grace notes in the Hibernian harmony of Fair Haven. The nuns at St. Francis School had saintly names: Immaculata, Alphonsus, Rosita (?), Basilia, Denise. Yet there was often a touch of brogue in their speech, and you knew they were holier than you but Irish. So, too, the priests: Smith, and Fitzmaurice, Casey, Doran, and Quinn.

Times were hard, and housewives were frugal, but few felt poor. Irish militancy, so far as I can recall, had no great following. But one friend's parlor was dominated by a large, fiercely colored print of the Battle of the Boyne. Those brave, agonized Irish patriots whose blood stained the rushing river were my introduction to Ireland's history, and I see the same oppression - and self-torture in the headlines out of Belfast now.

The green ties and the emerald ribbons we flourished on the 17th of March were bright adornments - but they signified a harsh memory:

"They're hanging men and women there, for the wearing of the green."

My father had been a country schoolmate of Eamon DeValera. And late in life they exchanged a couple of reminiscent letters when the old Irish eagle was living in Eire's presidential house at Dublin's Phoenix Park. But that link had no inflammatory effect upon our lives.

The old country was then far away. The one- way ocean voyage to which so many of these Fair Haveners pledged themselves had been difficult, and expensive, and emotion-ridden. There was little thought of turning back, despite the sentimental songs and prayers and the letters from home.

As for parading, the standard 50-hour week kept fathers and husbands busy until 1 p.m. on Saturday. Fair Haven was an Irish community intent on being American. If Fair Haven's Irish marched for St. Patrick's Day, who'd be there from the outside to watch? So we didn't march.

But I've marched the old neighborhood in review today because the time is ripe in memory - and because last Sunday's official parade came so early on the calendar.

Top O' the morning to you!

Saturday, July 15, 1978
Editor's note

Some Future And Some Past

In quiet news times journalists always look to the future, or to the past, for immediate inspiration.

The July-August "Bulletin" of the American Society of Newspaper Editors, which arrived on my desk in mid-week, has a speculative piece about the step that lies beyond today's revolution in printing methods.

The daily newspaper, it comfortingly concludes, is in no danger of becoming obsolete.

But because newspapers gather together such large quantities of information - and discard much of it for lack of space or paper - some forward-thinkers are saying that it may not be too long before newspapers begin to provide alternative delivery of special categories of news.

In England the British Post Office, BBC, and an enterprise called ITV are all experimenting with systems for providing print news services on home television screens. Some viewers subscribe to a service which gives sports results, news flashes, market prices, weather and travel reports, gardening tips, and other special data. Other viewers, or readers, can order specific categories of information at the push of a button. The Post Office's Viewdata system has a current capacity of 70,000 pages of information which may be called up in a private home on an ordinary television set.

One editor, describing this approach, says:

"Delivering print information is our business. We have the information, but don't always use it, and sometimes we're appealing to a limited audience at high cost. For example, suppose newspapers could supply their readers with stock listings, electronically, presumably within their normal subscription rates.

"Think of the newsprint savings, plus in many instances, more timeliness. Add to this weather reports, restaurant ratings, movie timetables, sports results and box scores, recipes, community events, dispositions of criminal cases, texts of major speeches, research services, and television listings. You've just saved a lot of space in your newspaper and people who want that information are getting it from you."

It's still pie-in-the-sky on a daily basis. But it offers a modernization and convenience-packaging of our standard news content which may some day supplement the paper you hold in your hand. But don't be in a hurry.

The obituary page is a basic newspaper feature, something important to our sense of community. But it resists change.

A conscientious reader has written:

"I know it is a sign of old age, but please put the death notices back where they belong, (on the) last inside page of the front section."

We appreciate the interest and the request. It is a sign, not of old age, but of healthily ingrained habit. After 14 months in its "new" location we think today's Register obituary page is not too hard to find.

We have tried to support new habit and make the obituary page just as easy to locate as before by "anchoring" it in its new location. We run it every day on the first inside page of the second section of the newspaper.

You used to take the first section of the Register and open to the inside of its last page to find the obituaries. Now you simply go past that whole first section. Take the first page of the second section. Open it - and inside is the obituary page with its death notices. This seems to us to be quite as convenient as the old page. And it permitted us to link the editorial page and the Forum page in a solid presentation of issue information and opinion across two pages of your afternoon paper.

In the more concise Journal-Courier the death notices are still published each morning, as they have been for years, on the last inside page of the first section, opposite the editorial page. So while some things do change, everything doesn't.

And remember - in either paper you need only to look at the Page One index to get the number of any special page you want.

Summer's fullness ripens bean and pea along with every known weed, turns rabbits ravenous, gives beetles buzz-saw power. The kitchen garden is schizophrenic, fruiting prolifically in the sun, wilting in the heat. What better time to ponder a list of old time seeds from the Connecticut Journal of 1794 - a hint of what New Haven ancestors were cultivating after reading the ads in the ancestor of The Journal-Courier 184 years ago.

It was a busy enough year for news in New Haven.

The Chamber of Commerce had just been formed. There was yellow fever here at epidemic level; 164 people were stricken and 64 died. The French Revolution was slipping toward the Reign of Terror, and the Connecticut Journal - in the same edition with our seed sale - printed a letter by Robespierre and his colleagues on the Committee of Public Safety about the battle for Toulon. Robespierre himself would die bloodily at the end of July, before New Haven's seeds had produced their sweeter harvest.

Though the list is utilitarian, and unadorned by the color photography that lures us through today's catalogues, it still sounds, as does every offering of seeds, like a litany of health and hope and digestive pleasure.

"Garden Seeds," says the advertisement, "To be sold by Daniel Punderson, in York Street." And then the mouth-watering menu:

"Early dwarf peas, Golden hotspur peas, Early Carlton peas, Dwarf marrowfat peas, Large marrowfat peas, Dwarf sugar peas, Large sugar peas, Large sugar redblows, Green imperial peas, Green nonperial peas, Spanish merotto peas, White rouncival peas, Dwarf bush peas;

"Early York cabbage, Sugar loaf cabbage, Red Dutch cabbage, Drum head cabbage, Green Savoy cabbage;

"Early curl'd lettuce, White head lettuce, Brown head lettuce, Green head lettuce, Asparagus, Red onion, Lemon carrot, Orange carrot, Purple carrot, Red beet, Blood beet, Early Dutch turnip, Salmon radish, Short top radish, Turnip radish;

"Curled endive, curled parsley, Spinage, White mustard, Pepper-grass, Summer savory, Sage, Early cucumber, Long green cucumber, Bush squash, Summer crook neck squash, Muskmelon, Watermelon, and a general assortment of garden Beans."

A Yankee horn of plenty! And though the produce comes from a time long ago and far away in our perspective, many of the gardens here in old New Haven Colony had been tilled for 150 years by the time that ad was run.

Less specific a list, but at least as exotic a promise is offered in the same edition by Asahel Benham of Wallingford. His advertisement says:

"To be sold by the Subscriber, Garden Seeds, of all kinds:

"From that celebrated Garden belonging to the Shaking Quakers of New Lebanon. Those people not only take pains to have the earliest and best seeds, but they import them once in two or three years fresh from their friends in London.

"N.B. Some of the seed called Scarcity. (is also available). "

The seed called Scarcity has a mystery element in its name, but if Chastity, Prudence, Virtue, Faith and Patience found a Puritan application as personal names, why not Scarcity for a fecund seed? At any rate, who'd risk sowing it for fear the harvest would live up to the name?

The promise of everything else was bounteous.

As advertised.

News of that week in the same Connecticut Journal demonstrated remarkable brevity, by today's standards, in dealings between the White House and Congress. The newspaper says:

"A message in writing from the President of the United States, by Mr. Dandridge, his Secretary, as follows:

"United States, 18th March 1794

"Gentlemen of the Senate, and of the House of Representatives,

"The Minister Plenipotentiary of the French Republic, having requested an advance of money, I transmit to Congress certain documents relative to that subject.

G.O. Washington

"Message and papers read and ordered to be committed to Mr. William Smith, Mr. Ames, Mr. Hillhouse (our own local congressman, who helped design New Haven's seal, laid out the Grove Street Cemetery, etc.), Mr. Venable, and Mr. Sherburne."

Messages "in writing" apparently promoted an economy of attitude and administration which we have lost as the federal government turned toward the printing press, the typewriter, and the copying machine. And our newspapers embrace 1,200 words-per-minute news reports.

Saturday, March 12, 1994
Editor's note

Driveway Sloping North

"Where are the snows of yesteryear?"
(The line's by an old French bard.)
Dear Villon, the snows from far and near
Still linger in my back yard.
The robin's around; the wild duck's northing;
The snowdrop is testing its mantle cold.
The squirrel has resumed his back-and forthing;
The willow yearns to turn green and gold.
But the roof's long shade and the lee of the hill
Have hardened me drifts I could leave in my will.
Where are the snows of yesteryear?
I've had them and have them. They're mine - up to here.

Saturday, February 3, 1979
Editor's Note

Know Biz And Show Biz

A show biz comment is evoked by a letter from Mayor Frank Logue rallying support for the city of New Haven's efforts to restore the Shubert Theatre as a music-theater center.

The project is one that should set many a New Haven heart to throbbing and many a toe to tapping in recollection of what the Shubert has been - and may be once again.

The city now owns the building. It has gotten some money from the New Haven Foundation to help in the planning work that must be done.

Its big target today is an" $800,000 "challenge" grant from the National Endowment for the Arts. Such a grant - and it won't be easily given - would have to be matched by locally-raised funds in at least the same amount over the course of the next few years~ Another application will be made to the state of Connecticut for help under the state Department of Commerce's "Restoration of Historic Assets Program."

The entire concept is one of great value to New Haven and its people if only it can be effectively developed and financed.

The Shubert has a history almost unparalleled in American theater. It was the starting place for most .of the significant dramatic enterprises between 1920 and 1960. They were 40 golden years. And though the old stage echoed first to the sounds of vaudeville and closed on a fairly unexciting sequence of re-runs, it is truly the only true claimant to the title emblazoned in its lobby: "The birthplace of' American hits."

Someday I'll do a column - one more - on the glowing succession of top Broadway-bound productions which opened there between 1940 (when I first began to come down from the steep second gallery to see rather than to hear the shows) and the late Sixties when the creativity and the economics of the' "big hit" era in American theater began to falter simultaneously.

The memory alone justifies the restoration of the Shubert. But beyond that memory lies the future promise of good things and good times for all New Haven if we can get the lights on, and the curtain up, at the Shubert again.

The mayor deserves everybody's backing in this effort.

"Hype"?

Saturday, October 30, 1976
Editor's Note

Expected - And Unexpected

As to the unexpected:

For nearly two years I've been writing these Saturday commentaries about the problems and the processes of newspaper journalism and the world of news reporting. They were dominant in my concern.

I've spent this week in another atmosphere, where I face the nearly unthinkable fact that the news doesn't matter. Or where it matters only as a frieze of newspaper headlines or flickering colorcasts on the edge of an arena of far more intense action - a hospital room.

Last Saturday my wife, hospitalized for what seemed a passing gastric upset slightly complicated by diabetes, was seized by a stroke. In the pit in which we struggle now the convulsions of the world of "affairs" are irrelevant. Can my finger in her inert palm penetrate the void into which she has been flung? Can my whisper of love and prayer in her ear call back from its wandering the sweet, vibrant spirit to which my own life is locked?

A newspaper wife puts up with many things. She is sometimes second fiddle to a news story or a deadline. She is always expected to subordinate private schedules to the flow of public news events. My lady has embraced this way of living.

Where there was skill she has always encouraged it. Where there was talent she inspired it. Where there was effort and hard work she supported it. Where there was disappointment or pain she soothed it.

Where there was kindness to be done she pointed the way. When there was cause for laughter, at the word or at myself, she helped me to see it, and we shared the laugh - which was often.

Now there is silence. Reaching. Doctors and Nurses. Prayer.

The news we chased for so long with zest and urgency, like

children after autumn leaves, has become a dim abstraction in the profound personal ordeal that fills so many hospital rooms.

Saturday, May 19, 1990
Editor's note:

Sad Signs And Symbols

NEARLY 14 YEARS AGO when I had been writing this column only a couple of years, I wrote from a room in St. Raphael's Hospital. My wife, Anne, was treated there for a stroke. It was a hard, sudden blow, and I wrote that our lives, spent mutually in chasing the news as it came, the way children were then chasing October leaves, had been transformed into silence and the prayerful waiting of a hospital room.

In a decade and a half of disability since then, there have been ups and downs. The good has far outweighed the bad because of her faith, her zest for life, her resilient spirit, her family concerns, her ability always to surround herself and her caregivers with love and good cheer . I've written occasionally about memories we shared of New Haven and the Fair Haven of our youth, of many a silver moon we watched through her window, of breezes and bright flowers in our yard.

Now the struggle has ended amid May's lilacs. The pain is gone. Things just recently shared are becoming memories. There is no kitchen editor to read and review this commentary with me at home before it is submitted to the Register.

Anne's final fourth-floor room at St. Raphael's looked out into the top branches of an elm tree striving against odds to best the hurry and fumes of Chapel Street. Each long day a pair of finches sported through the unfolding leaves. The male was red-headed, rosy-breasted and rosy-tailed: the female was more sedately reddish-brown and elusive. They moved in tandem arcs and circles, through swooping pursuits, nesting somewhere in one of the lower pine trees on the lawn.

They would have delighted Anne, a connoisseur of springtimes. So I spoke into her ear about them. There was no response. The blue eyes, so used to smiling, stayed closed. After 50 years as friends and lovers, the loss of that shared viewpoint, that other voice for my own thoughts, that other hand so ready to clasp mine in encouragement and affection, is the cruelest change.

But life's interwoven patterns, "sunrise, sunset," continuity within change, are there in the unfolding of the leaves and the flight of the birds. I think of the finch when his mate veered suddenly away into a bright blue afternoon. He chose a perch apart, high in the hospital elm, straining for balance, feeling the sun, testing the breeze - getting ready, when God's good time dwindles, to fly off in the same direction.

Saturday, August 18, 1990
Editor's note

Month Three

The June-grown grass is fragile green,
Silk threads against the graveyard clay.
Your name edged sharp in polished rock
Seems different from the name I say.
I water grass, pray, finger stone,
Walk down the hill again, alone -
To seek your laughter through the day.

Saturday, November 10, 1990
Editor's note

First Fall

This somber autumn, in faint color,
Leaves came down without a shout,
No roistering whirl, no clinging to the wind
In surging flight, defying hill and sky.
They fell silently in rain.
The maple you and I watched most
Stood green and summer-struck,
A suitor to the sun,
The leaves green in somber autumn,
Green as the day in May you died.
Then, in one long night
The maple tree was brown.
The leaves fell
Brown,
Rustling, settling, whispering where they used to whirl
The tree has come to terms with autumn,
And the snow - and you.
But how do I press hopes for spring
From somber autumn's brown, still leaves
That you saw green and growing?

Saturday, January 18, 1992
Editor's note

Remembrance

New bread, old song, a wave, a bird -
Shared beauty cleared our day of doubt.
A star at dawn, home pines wind-stirred,
Grace in a dance, child voices heard -
Unshared, such pleasure's now deferred.
Each crystal instant dims without
The luster of your smile, your word.

June 27, 1992
Editor's note

Anniversary Sonnet

How long we clung, contented, to that height,
Above the ocean's surge, out of the wind,
Flung there by stroke that smashed our old delight
In crowds and crafts and left us, somehow, pinned
In pain but still enwrapped as lovers, me and you.
Laughter and prayer embroidered happy days,
Even when Time tomorrow's hopes withdrew,
Your good hand and your smile gave God His praise.
But age erodes; it loosens every grip.
The noblest heart takes no firm grasp of stone.
On that far height new shadows crossed your brow,
Sweet sleep stayed longer, and I saw you slip
Away. What's left - old rapture in the bone -
Keeps you, and "then," the masters of my now.

Saturday, December 19, 1992
Editor's note

Listenings (for Anne)

Inside my house at midnight's high
I hear the clock's unyielding tick,
The pipe that gurgles in the hall.
Your lilac, leafless, scrapes the wall.
Inside my hide at midnight's ebb
I hear deep-set old bones and valves
And hidden ventricles adjust
Like whispers, doing what they must.
Inside my heart at midnight's gulf
I hear your voice, strain for your hand,
Then find the precipice of loss
Too broad for me to leap across.
Inside my head at morning star
The midnight murmurs all are stilled.
New birdsong gives the day its wings -
And I am left with listenings.

Saturday, November 1, 1980
Editor's Note

A long look at that First Amendment

Had enough election news and speculation? I have. The season's tight focus on politics was gratifyingly relaxed for me last Wednesday when the New Haven Division of the Anti-Defamation League of B'nai B'rith honored me with its First Amendment Freedoms Award - Connecticut's first. The testimonial was gratifying and words of acceptance were a challenge. Because I think the subject, more than the celebration, deserves your thought I offer here some excerpted remarks which express the evening's concern though they hardly express the sense of pride and unworthiness that came with the ADL's handsome plaque:

I do not feel - for your sake or mine - that it's appropriate to offer a repetition of my standard commentary about closed courtrooms, ransacked news files, jailed reporters, frightened news sources, and other recurring concerns of the free press. But the more I have matured as a journalist, and aged as an editor, the more I am convinced that the fundamental strength of the United States - the clearest, briefest statement of what our lives as free citizens are about - can be found in that First Amendment. Maybe we should touch upon that.

In an era of steady growth and centralizing power in government, the First Amendment is the key, I think, to everything that you and I want in life from Washington, or anywhere else, because - running against the modern tide - it spells out so simply but emphatically what government shall not do,

It guarantees your right to worship as you see fit. It permits you to speak your own free mind while free publication of opinion, free reporting, and free news gathering keeps you informed, And it permits you to assemble in a home, in a hall like this, on the New Haven Green, or wherever, to speak your opinion in groups as well as individually and to seek change wherever you think changes are necessary or desirable.

The most important aspect of the First Amendment is not just its tolerance for your opinions and beliefs, and mine, but its emphatic provision that government shall not interfere with them. This is the way the amendment reads:

Congress shall make no law respecting an establishment of religion, or prohibiting the free exercise thereof; or abridging the freedom of speech or of the press; or the right of the people peaceably to assemble, and to petition the government for a redress of grievances."

"Congress," let us remember, "shall make no law ..."

The exercise of First Amendment rights, however, can generate as much confrontation as good conscience among citizens shaped by our late 20th century tensions and suspicions. There is in many a constitutional grant that arises from the First Amendment that razor's edge, that fine line, which demands public consideration, understanding, and an element of flexibility if any, right is to be used and applied for the common good. And it is in this area that I have come most to respect the functions of the Anti-Defamation League of B'nai B'rith.

Free speech, free assembly, and even freedom of the press are not privileges, alone, of the rational people that you and I know. They are the right of every American - including a God-given quota of kooks, and a fair number of non-kooks who may simply have opinions and perceptions different from our own.

The ADL, in my newspaper experience, blows the whistles, rings the bells, lights the lights, and otherwise sounds the alarms - often gentle, rarely shrill - which relate citizen rights to general, practical truths. ADL asks questions and offers answers which contribute to public knowledge whenever a rights issue grows tense.

The American Nazi right to assemble and march in Skokie is not actually a question that permits much challenge - but it is a right that needs to be linked to fact and truth and related to the American Nazi history - and to world Nazi history - as the ADL insisted.

The right of individual citizens to possess arms, and even to join the Klu Klux Klan, is also assured by the First Amendment. But the Anti-Defamation League serves important public needs, and it asks people and political leaders the right questions when it challenges paramilitary training by KKK members, with their guns, in Connecticut or anyplace else.

These activities, plus the innumerable quiet explanations and illuminations it provides on Jewish belief and policy, make ADL a vital civic institution for America.

Such watchdog efforts are, I believe, going to be increasingly needed in the future from the ADL, the press, and the public, The First Amendment Freedoms which are our concern this evening face entirely new challenges in the future, in the probably unending battle against discrimination and in the ongoing defense of our freedoms in every form.

Congress has made no law, indeed, regarding freedom of the press.

But congressional inhibition has not been felt by courts, and judges, and regulatory agencies of government over the past 20 years. Proceeding from their concept of duty or mandate they have made deep incursions against the First Amendment, generally in the free press clause, often in the name of other amendments but more often in the name of nothing more than personal convictions about privacy, or secrecy, or bureaucratic convenience,

Now we stand at the threshold of an era when the publisher as a person, and his press as a tool symbolic of his opinion, and yours, may have to fight to stand free and clear of official interference of a new type.

Electronic news comes to you by television and radio through a web, and a maze, of bureaucratic regulation. It is beholden to bureaucrats for much that it does. And the airwave newscasters have achieved most of what relative freedom they enjoy 'by claiming rights that parallel the constitutionally guaranteed rights of the printing press. But change is afoot. The electronic data processing revolution is only in its infancy among newspapers and it has already opened new vistas, and raised new questions, for your daily paper in its old, free press function. Two examples.

Within weeks The Register and the Journal-Courier will be pulling down onto a Longwharf antenna all of their AP and UPI news of the world from a satellite 22,000 miles up in the sky. The volume, the speed, the economy make this process a marvel. But, the satellite is already regulated – its functions measured and governmentally authorized , rated, and licensed - in an official permission that the old-time reporter at the typewriter or the AP correspondent at the end of a cable or a teletype line never before asked, or got.

Within decades - in another change - at least some of the news you read in the Jackson Newspapers, and others, may be amplified and personalized for you on your home computer banks at the newspaper. Once again, an advance of incalculable value. But - television transmissions and such special call-up services are also highly regulated. Regulation is clearly defensible as electronic communication proliferates all around the globe's surface and out in space, as well.

Still, the picky-picky regulatory process, with its fat handbooks full of sub-paragraphs and penalties, is - in the end - quite unrelated to the magnificent simplicity of "Congress shall make no law ..."

And, for a moment's thought about the unthinkable, when nearly 2,000 newspapers and nearly 10, 000 radio and television stations look for their general news to that single news satellite in the sky, the flick of a single switch here on earth by any official hand, of friend or enemy, could produce an amazing result, could it not?

There may be a bit of exaggeration in this question - a little of Dr. Strangelove - but the possibility remains, the idea has its own logic.

The expanding wonders of electronic data processing in the 21st Century are shaping an information explosion - and official responses to it which will have an early impact, I believe, upon the traditions, the assumptions, and the protections afforded the print press since the time this nation was born in revolution and our constitution was written. With vigilance, I think, those invaluable, democracy-building protections - which, are not for the press alone and which involve the rights of every citizen to know and to speak - can be preserved.

Your Anti-Defamation League's First Amendment Freedoms Award, in that light, could not have been created at a time when its stimulation is likely to be more needed and its endorsement more gladly received.

Saturday, November 19, 1988
Editor's note

Coarsening Truth on Memory Lane?

The day John F. Kennedy died was for a while our contemporary connection to capital-H History. We asked each other, "What were you doing?" Recalling the moment when the commonplace in each of our lives coincided with an awful, unforgettable moment in world affairs bound us together. Now they're ruining that. As the entertainment industry subverts the Information Age for its mass audiences we are increasingly hit with cheap speculation, coarse revelation and the useless pseudo-documentation of tabloid television to explain what happened.

Old gossip is being revived after 2 ½ decades. Marilyn Monroe, Fidel Castro, the Mafia, the global underworld, the Russians, the FBI emerge in tasteless re-enactments. Prime-time prurience keeps getting in the way of the "search for truth" that is the claimed goal of today's strident baloney.

Still, the basic memories remain poignant.

Twenty-five years ago on this November weekend, my wife and I made the drive north to Portland, Maine, to a meeting of the New England Society of Newspaper Editors. The times were eventful. That summer Martin Luther King Jr. had given his still echoing "I have a dream" speech to 200,000 civil rights marchers on the Washington Mall. The Diem government was overthrown in South Vietnam. And now in the Dunfey Hotel in Portland, the newspaper editors of New England were orienting themselves to a world of change.

When lunch ended that Friday, Nov. 22, our minds were on Washington because we'd heard a talk by White House correspondent Les Carpenter. As the afternoon meeting began, there was a sudden stir in the lobby. Someone shouted to the podium: "Mr. Chairman, the president has been shot." Then came the word: "He's dying."

Our editors' group, like the nation, was plunged into a trauma that still haunts the American psyche. The meeting was dissolved in half an hour. Editors from all over New England scattered on the highways out of Portland, desperate to get back to the front pages they could not see or shape, guilty about the absence, fumbling as they tried unfamiliar dial settings on the car radio, frustrated as they rushed through town after town, going from day into darkness amid anonymous broadcast voices, uncertain facts, endless grieving opinion about a story we still cannot satisfyingly comprehend.

It was a time of sadness that became personalized within every citizen, a period of special trial for traveling editors cut off from the informative clack of their teletype machines and the comfort of their news crews about them. I phoned the Register but couldn't get the switchboard in the first glut of New Haven's alarmed inquiries. Meanwhile the bizarre story took shape - the president slain, a policeman killed, a sidestreet movie house in Dallas surrounded.

We editors all got home - but that nightmare ride, the radio constantly pouring out words of sorrow, confusion and speculation across a countryside where the lights did not seem to be lit, will never be forgotten by the news people who made it.

Late in the night I eased my pangs at the story missed by seeing the Register's Saturday morning front page put to bed in the composing room. Then it was a weekend for family circles. New Haven streets were quiet, the theaters empty, the bars and restaurants deserted, shopping left undone. The home television set was the focus of all concern.

I remember the phone call from my son at school in another state as he reached to the family for support amidst the numb grieving of his schoolmates. My wife and two other kids tried to touch him through the phone. My father, gathered with us around the tube, had an Irishman's love of horses. He kept his emotions tightly checked that dreadful weekend until the riderless black stallion - stepping high and fighting the bridle, black boots reversed in the stirrups that hung from an empty saddle - came into view behind the flag-draped casket. The cadence of the muffled drums beneath the single stride of all those marching men, the broken rhythm of the spirited steed's hooves upon the pavement in that ancient warrior display, my father's sudden sob are merged into a heart-scalding memory.

In killing the young president, those bullets - from Lee Harvey Oswald, the "grassy knoll," wherever - had wounded the nation and the world. With Kennedy, however illusory, there had come a sense of fresh intellect, youth, courage, fashion, fun in high places and mostly of promise, of looming possibilities. We were all made vulnerable, all diminished by the easy, instant destruction of such virtues. The public loss became a private one, and it has remained inexplicable, illogical, a mysterious and unacceptable injustice down the years - a news story never quite ended.

The current impulse is to cap such tragedy with sensation.

As the direct memory fades, the Kennedy story is being dug out and raked over again, seasoned with "maybes" and trivialized from one view or another as an audience vehicle sturdy enough to support a dozen commercials every 30 minutes.

The subject mesmerizes us. The sorrow still needs explanation and understanding. But we should let scholars and real reporters comb the evidences of that deed's doing, and we should await judgments more sound - and closer to being final - than the strident rehashings that have marked this anniversary so far.

We can't deny history if we can uncover it. But neither should we demean ourselves, or the decency of those tears we shed and shared in November 1963, by treating discarded theories and tawdry speculations as "new" research. The memory alone has a dignity imperishable for those who knew the day.

Saturday, April 3, 1993
Editor's note

History Hints At New Haven's Future

History tells us that the current concerns in downtown New Haven, the departure of Macy's and mixed opinion about the Taubman mall project - retailing atop the Oak Street connector - will eventually be solved, or substituted for, by local imagination and energy.

New Haven initiatives that are made appealing to investors from inside and outside the community have always been the source of local growth and prosperity. Nobody else will do it for us.

History also tells us that whatever help we get from Hartford, as the seat of state government, will be marginal. The political process that 30 years ago left incomplete the Route 34 connector - from our coastal interstate highways to the Housatonic and Naugatuck valleys - and that leaves the Coliseum with only half a parking deck today, is as grudging as ever. That being the case, the Chamber of Commerce is well advised to raise urgent questions, seek vigorous answers, and push in every possible way to revive shopping in downtown New Haven.

And while the effort's afoot, let's remember that hard times have hit before - and they've been overcome.

The first, and perhaps the worst, knock came long ago as the old colony tried to get its start. Adventurous George Lamberton, captain of the ship that brought settlers to Quinnipiack in 1639, had involved a small group here in efforts to trade for furs with Delaware River Indians. But the post they set up in southern New Jersey was destroyed by already-established Dutch and Swedish fur traders in 1641.

Then New Haven Colony leaders planned a cargo coup in

England. An 80-ton ship was built. Lamberton took command. Wheat, hides from the West Indies, and beaver furs were loaded.

In January 1646 the colonists were so eager to launch the venture that hardy seamen chopped and pushed through almost three miles of ice in the wintry harbor to reach the open Sound.

Wrote the New England poet, Henry Wadsworth Longfellow: "A ship sailed from New Haven/ And the keen and frosty airs/ That filled her sails at parting! Were heavy with good men's prayers."

But the ship and the bold gamble were lost. After two years, says the legend, in June 1648 a "ship of air" swept landward on a sunset wind and New Haveners - only 800 in all - said they could see the faces of the crew. "Then fell her straining topmasts .../ The masts with all their rigging/ Fell slowly one by one/ And the hulk dilated and vanished/ Like a seamist in the sun!"

Disaster was confirmed for the colony. Says historian Rollin Osterweis: "The loss of the 'Great Shippe' weakened the financial structure of the colony and played a significant part in its subsequent decline."

Next to that the Macy's move seems minor.

There have been other calamitous community events. Before and after the Revolution this was a thriving port. Ships carried wheat, peas, livestock in all directions. Wealth accumulated as Long Wharf became a focus of West Indies trading in sugar, molasses, rum, salt and fruits. In 1796 Ebenezer Townsend's "Neptune" took aboard South Atlantic fur seals, touched Hawaii enroute to China, then dropped home anchor in 1799. A duty of $75,000 was paid on its rich cargo of tea, cloth and tableware. But soon President Jefferson's embargo of 1807 and the War of 1812 brought the almost complete collapse of shipping in New Haven. The town survived.

In 1828 the Farmington Canal opened, moving boats from here to Northampton, Mass., by 1839. Links were envisioned to the St. Lawrence River and Canada and the proud local investors prospered. But by 1839 the Hartford and New Haven Railroad was running. The dying canal became a railroad bed - still visible between Hillhouse and Whitney Avenues. New Haven adjusted.

New Haven built fine carriages for the affluent as early as

1794. A century later five New Haven carriage companies took top prizes at the World Columbian Exposition of 1893 in Chicago. In 25 years their factories were empty shells as automobiles from the Midwest tooted through town. Other work was found for thousands of New Haven artisans.

In meeting each of these challenges New Haven and its people had to find new directions and fashion new, co-operative ways that would renew purpose and prosperity locally.

They may have drawn much inspiration and even financial support from outside. The factors forcing change, in fact, came almost always from the outside. But the constructive responses were rooted in New Haven's internal grasp of opportunity. Macy's going or Taubman's coming is ours to shape.

Connecticut Hall at Yale, *1750. Nathan Hale's dormitory. Rebuilt 1952.*
Photo: T.S. Bronson.

Saturday, April 9, 1994
Editor's note

Arnold's Treason Still A Puzzle

For more than 200 years, Benedict Arnold has been one of New Haven's mystery men. What made a busy local merchant and patriot-hero turn traitor after such courageously fought battles for American independence?

The question was raised again on Tuesday when Arnold's latest biographer, Clare Brandt, came here to deliver the New Haven Colony Historical Society's Pitkin Memorial Lecture. She talked about her just-published, 300-page study, "The Man in the Mirror, A Life of Benedict Arnold" (Random House, $25). The book explains Arnold and documents his remarkable life, but even in the careful details of Brandt's account, he remains an elusive, contradictory personality.

Arnold was born in Norwich in 1741, the son of prosperous parents. An earlier Benedict Arnold had helped found Rhode Island. He was enrolled at a good grammar school. But his Puritan mother died when he was 14 and his merchant father was overwhelmed by drink and debt. So, schooling done, he was apprenticed to his brother, a Norwich apothecary.

At age 21 in 1762, Arnold came to New Haven and set up shop as a druggist-merchant. He married Margaret Mansfield in 1767. They had three children. No home body, Arnold spent some months each year on merchant voyages to the West Indies, Canada and England. Amid excitement like the Boston Tea Party, New Haven organized a militia company in 1774. Arnold was elected captain.

When the fighting broke out at Concord and Lexington in 1775, Arnold mustered his militia on the Green. As cautious town fathers paused to debate, he demanded, and got, the keys to the powderhouse. The event is still reenacted annually by the Second Company, Governor's Foot Guard. Arnold marched out of this city to Revolutionary celebrity. But his hot-tempered clashes with officials gave hint of the unending future clashes he had with soldier comrades, the Continental Congress, and eventually with his British overseers.

The "man in the mirror," says historian Brandt, faced history as a "master of self-delusion." Arnold, she says, saw in his glass a man whose course was always right, whose critics were always wrong.

Arnold plunged into the Revolutionary War with gusto. After Concord he and his troops joined Ethan Allen's Green Mountain boys in the heady capture of Fort Ticonderoga in New York, with its valuable cannons. Later, with Washington's backing, he led a thousand men up Maine's Kennebec River through three months of ice-crusted misery to reach the walls of Quebec at Christmas. With a musket ball festering his leg, short supplies and troops, he managed a masterly retreat that stalled British hope of invading the colonies from Canada.

He outfoxed the king's better armed ships on Lake Champlain in a foggy spring encounter. Then, in April 1777, he and Gen. David Wooster drove off a British attack on Danbury. That fall in the long battle for Saratoga he galloped heroically at a Hessian redoubt, sword swung above his head. But his horse fell dead at the barricade and crushed the leg Arnold had so badly injured at Quebec. That was the general's last charge for the cause of American freedom.

Off the field Arnold had always been a headstrong administrator. Ethan Allen's men hated him at Ticonderoga. Other generals resented his pride and resisted his opinions. He was charged several times with mishandling supplies and funds. He reacted so insultingly that some critics won findings of defamation against him. Such trials were conducted within the Continental Congress - where Arnold simultaneously made new enemies with his repeated petitions about higher rank, more money, his claims of seniority, and his right to resign if not properly promoted.

In 1778 mercurial Arnold - disabled by his wound and by

controversy - was put under wraps. He became commandant of the city of Philadelphia as field strategies faltered and the war drifted toward stalemate.

His first wife had died only two months after he left New Haven in 1775. Relatives had reared his three children. So in the "city of brotherly love" Arnold wooed and wed vivacious Peggy Shippen. She was 19 years old to his 37, the daughter of a wealthy Loyalist family with strong ties to the British. She dazzled Arnold. They lived stylishly in a watchful city. Very soon the commandant was charged in Congress with manipulating ship permits in the port and conspiring to corner the market on key commodities.

A trial was ordered. And within weeks Arnold was talking to the British about ways to capture West Point - a blow that might end revolution. Always eloquent, he wangled appointment as the West Point commander. Then, when carrying maps and plans made by Arnold, the British major, John Andre, was captured outside New York City. Arnold fled to British protection in Manhattan. His first military mission for the enemy, and his last fight, was a raid that sailed him past this city to burn New London in summer 1781.

Later that year Arnold retreated to England on the ship that carried Gen. Cornwallis home after his surrender at Yorktown. The war was over; Arnold was 40. He was installed in a mansion - and avoided socially. He tried to start over with a shipyard in New Brunswick in Canada. When it failed in 1791 he and his wife, with five sons and a daughter, returned to a small house near London. He died there in 1801.

At the Philadelphia trial he spoke grandly of "the blood I have spent on defense of my country." But by then, says Brandt, he had also been "transmitting intelligence to the enemy for the past eight months."

The motto on B. Arnold's timeworn street sign in the New Haven Colony Historical Society, a bit sad in hindsight, says: "Sibi Totique" - "For himself and for all." Biographer Brandt thinks Arnold lived only by the first two words - and lost his way.

Saturday, June 14, 1986
Editor's note

A Forgotten Waterfront Fire

The bright, modern Long Wharf area today puts New Haven's best foot forward at the water's edge and in sight of interstate traffic along 1-95 and 1-91. Fifty years ago the tract from Water Street to City Point was, as I remember it, mostly swamp reaching back from harbor mud flats to the trackage around the New Haven Railroad's station. There was a rickety industrial fringe, the outmoded Belle dock and the Canal dock, two or three railroad spurs that served those docks, and - its bad smells isolated by stretches of marsh grass and bullrushes - the Sperry & Barnes meat packing plant.

Even earlier, 100 years ago, there was a Sperry & Barnes meat plant closer to the docks and the water at Long Wharf. And a century ago next week that place went up in a spectacular, stubborn, fat-fed fire that was big news in The Evening Register of June 17, 1886. The following are excerpts from that old news story. Said the Register:

Dense masses of mingled fog and smoke hung over Long Wharf this morning, almost obscuring the blackened walls of Sperry & Barnes' packing house. Two fire engines, steamers Nos. 2 and 4, had kept their valves running all night long, while the weary firemen stood by the hose, relieving each other by turns. This morning at 7 o'clock the men who had worked during the night were relieved and another gang of men kept the fires burning (under control) and the streams playing on the greasy flames during the day.

The fire did not spread during the night. It was still confined to the packing and storage rooms on the second floor in the rear half of the building.... The mass of lard and pork in which the fire was embedded was covered over by bricks which had fallen from the floor above and the roof, making it difficult to put on an effective stream. It is thought that the fire will smoulder away for several days yet....

The employees of the firm, or a large portion of them, were on hand this morning. They had been ordered to report for duty to begin the work of clearing away some of the debris in the outer portions of the building. The north half of it is utterly ruined.... The front walls stand intact. The rear walls and interior portions are pretty badly damaged. The total loss is estimated today as being over $400,000.

"The firm's greatest loss," said Joel A. Sperry this morning, "is really in having our business interrupted. It will do us inestimable damage. We expect to rebuild as soon as we can get at it. Of course we must wait before doing anything until the insurance companies get things settled."

"Have you any theory about the origin of the fire other than was mentioned in the Register yesterday?"

"No, I can't account for it. ... One thing I do know, and that is that it is pretty hard for me at my time of life to go to work and build up again anew.... It was an awful blow to me."

Various theories are vented by different persons to account for the fire, but most of them conclude with the assertion that after all the fire was quite unaccountable. It doesn't seem likely that the fire was set, and it doesn't seem probable that it caught from the smoke house....

The harbor waters caught big supplies of lard and grease from the rear of the building and some of it was washed up along shore at various points south of Long Wharf. Wherever such collections were found in large quantities, men were at work with boats, improvised rafts, coal hods and wooden scoops in fishing out the stuff and collecting it in barrels. They had hopes of realizing immense sums for the sale of the grease....

A good many local butchers complain that they could not get enough meat yesterday to supply their demands. Strong, Barnes and Hart's storehouse and supply house is located below Brewery Street on the wharf, and the fire engines with their many lines of hose cut off railroad communication (with suppliers). This morning the switching of trains on Canal dock was interfered with by the fire engines, and the hose had to be uncoupled with the stream stopped to enable (freight) cars to pass....

That the police and fire department are shorthanded was shown yesterday. Chief Hendrick remarked that the close budget for the fire department was such that he would have no authority to employ extra men, even though the firemen should be disabled and exhausted.... The police, though not having so severe duties to perform, had a great deal of hard work and were thoroughly tired with battling the crowds of people who crowded to the scene, some for plunder and some for the purpose of seeing the fire .... An alderman is reported as saying last night that there were a hundred policemen. He, of course, had not examined the payroll.

This morning a fireman went home after his long term of service at the Sperry & Barnes fire. He was an object to behold. His clothes were covered with lard and mud, and his face was blackened with smoke; he appeared hardly able to walk. Where there was a bit of clean space on his face a deadly pallor could be seen. Many firemen were made sick by breathing the thick smoke of the burning hams and lard, and had a large fire broken out elsewhere last night the department would have hardly been able for duty.

This old news story is a reminder of other days - when most of New Haven's food was grown and prepared locally, when horse-drawn steam pumps pushed water through fire hoses, when working hours were unlimited. The news from a yellowed, 100-year-old Register front page is a reminder, too of the way your daily newspaper records today what is tomorrow's history. In this case it also emphasizes the difference between yesterday's marsh-edged, back-of-the-tracks Long Wharf and today's upfront showpiece for the city.

Saturday, March 28, 1987
Editor's note

A Brief Register History

A morning Register was published here for six months in 1846, so Monday's morning "new" Register is not without precedent. The morning edition was started when the old three-times-a-week Columbian Register became the daily Register 140 years ago. After a half-year test - from January through June - perhaps because there were a couple of other morning papers, perhaps because the publishers preferred daytime work - a new nameplate proclaimed The New Haven Evening Register in the first week of July 1846. And that decision held until now.

We move on Monday to another morning Register, tailored this time to a more specific measure of reader needs and community service. Next week, bright and early each day, the proof of that design will be on the presses - and in your hands. At this historic shift, as the Register becomes New Haven's only newspaper, a look at where we've been may help readers as well as newspaper folks to ponder where we're going.

New Haven business pressures, created by President Thomas Jefferson's embargo on shipping during the British-French war and by the general decline in coastal commerce linked to our own War of 1812, had a key role in Joseph Barber's launching of the Register. He was a Jefferson supporter in a conservative community where the Federalists had much other newspaper backing. There was a role for defenders of the administration, and the Register seized upon it.

On Dec. 12, 1812, the Columbian Register's first weekly issue was published, and it built an early following. By 1826 the paper had grown enough to need new quarters, and Barber was busy enough to bring in his nephew, Minott A. Osborn, to assist him.

When Joseph Barber stepped down in 1835, Minott Osborn

took over with William A. Baldwin as partner. Thereafter the Register moved innovatively to hold its place on the local news scene. On Aug. 20, 1840, the paper began to publish three times a week. On Jan. 1, 1846, it became a daily - and tried the morning publication mentioned earlier. That July afternoon publication resumed; the paper was called the New Haven Evening Register; and the Columbian Register's name was kept for a weekly paper that went by mail to the country areas around New Haven.

The Evening Register, in those pre-Civil War days, cost $5 a year, consisted of a standard four pages dally, and carried as its page motto a quote from Thomas Jefferson: "Equal and exact justice to all men, of whatever state of persuasion, religious or political."

The Register began to receive occasional telegraph news dispatches before the Civil War, and it reported that struggle in terms often critical of Republican President Abraham Lincoln.

In 1866 William A. Baldwin retired. Minott A. Osborn brought his son of the same name into the company that year, and in 1868 they completed a brownstone-front office building, marked "Register Building," on Chapel Street below Orange. In 1875 the business took in more shareholders and in 1877 the elder Osborn died - a full half century after his start with the Register. Robert W. Wright, Judge Samuel York and William Parsons became major stockholders, with the Osborn family still represented in management.

In 1879 the new owners launched a Sunday Register - in the face of much criticism of such anti-religious activity on the Sabbath. In 1884 Norris G. Osborn, recently out of Yale, became editor; he held that responsibility for 25 years. That same year the expanding paper moved to a new building on Crown Street. In 1886 the first Linotype machine was purchased to move the paper toward speedy typesetting and larger circulation.

In 1896 John Day Jackson and his Yale classmate, Samuel York Jr., became part owners as the Register rode out a new period of financial shakiness. Jackson became general manager. After courses at the Sorbonne in Paris, the University of Berlin, and Harvard Law School he had worked for the Washington Times, the New

York Evening Post and the Journal of Commerce. A sophisticated and dynamic journalist, he bought out his classmate in 1905 to become the sole proprietor of the Register.

In 1925 he also acquired the Journal-Courier as a morning complement to his major evening paper. When he retired in 1958 he had been a journalistic force in Connecticut for 63 years. Two sons, Richard and Lionel S. Jackson, succeeded him as co-publishers. The Register expanded its suburban coverage, developed specialized departments and added new presses, and the news staffs of both papers were enlarged greatly in this period. The company also embraced the new printing technology that brought such great mechanical change to the newspaper industry.

The 1929 building at Orange and Audubon Streets was replaced in 1981 when Lionel Jackson moved operations to the present Register building at 40 Sargent Drive in the Long Wharf area. A sweeping single-story building, first used by Gant Shirtmakers, it has immediate access to Interstate 95 and 1-91 and is strikingly adapted to efficient newspaper operation.

In 1986 the Jackson family's three-generation involvement in newspaper ownership ended with sale of the Register and the Journal-Courier to Ingersoll Publications Inc., a growing nationwide newspaper group. Lionel S. Jackson Jr. retains a role as publisher of the New Haven paper, with Thomas Geyer, former president of Ingersoll, now leading the operations as editor and chief executive.

This weekend the Ingersoll ownership, which has pre-Revolution ties to New Haven through the family of its chairman, Ralph Ingersoll II, takes a major step of its own by converting the Register to morning delivery as New Haven's only daily newspaper.

Names and dates like these are merely signposts in a longer, fuller story. But they provide a background for readers who are also interested in and involved by the change.

Saturday, February 7, 1981
Editor's note

A Reform -- And A Remembrance

A few years ago my wife was gravely ill. Felled by a massive stroke she could not walk or speak. In that difficult time for both of us a small package was delivered one day to her hospital room. It contained a music box which played the familiar theme from the movie "Love Story." The thin, sentimental tune was the first music we heard, or took time to hear, in a period of deep personal crisis. It has ever since been close to Anne's bed, and its small, private sound has become special to us as a symbol and a signal of abiding affection and hope.

We played it again the other night -- sadly.

When you open the music box there is fixed inside the cover a small hand-written card from Ella Grasso.

As aftermath to the governor's own gallant struggle I have checked the headlines of that time in1976 when she sent the music box to us. They were busy days and nights for her. She was beginning work on her budget for the coming year, she was preparing for a Washington session with President Carter and other governors on the problems of the Northeast, she was leading an attempt to reorganize much of the structure of the Connecticut judiciary, and she had just been listed as one of the 10 most influential women in the country.

Yet Ella Grasso could reach across that flow of events and the governor's busy schedule to share with two shaken acquaintances a message of endearment and faith, a song for the ordeal at hand. The gesture was typical.

She matched a sharp intelligence with a constantly warm heart. She was up to the hard daily demands of running a state, of giving firm leadership, of being political, realistic, disciplined, accountable, pragmatic. She could occasionally throw a partisan tantrum. But the message inside the music box was, in essence, the message she sent everyday, in every action, to all Connecticut:

With Love
Ella Grasso

Connecticut has always reciprocated. And today the sorrow is genuine and deep as the state mourns a leader, a lady, and a Connecticut-lover.

Saturday, June 25. 1988
Editor's note

An Extended Hot Spell

The hottest summer I remember was the summer of 1943 in Abilene, Texas. I'd been drafted into the Army Air Forces. Having left my wife and New Haven in a January ice storm, I went through a comfortable "basic" in Miami Beach hotels, trained as a cryptographer at a Hudson Valley prep school, was assigned to first duty at Abilene. We arrived, unsuspecting, amid Texas bluebonnets in the thin grass and early summer breezes in the mesquite shade.

But there was hardly a tree on the base. Even then the two or three multistory buildings of Abilene 10 miles away floated like a mirage on shimmering afternoon heat waves. By June there were days when we put our twill fatigue shirts on the baking earth to insulate our hands for the obligatory pushups. In July there were days too hot for any exercises on the ground. By then the spare grass had turned to straw. The soil had surrendered to the season, its surface crackled and fissured, the cracks opening wider in parched stress under each day's bright bronze sun.

The temperatures were not unbearably higher than those reached here in New Haven, but they were persistent, unyielding. In those days - before air conditioning had made the "Sun Belt" seem affluent and genial - West Texas was still a harsh, dusty place, even for steers and rattlesnakes. Our own tarpaper-covered barracks smelled of bubbling pine sap and sweat. We went to bed hot after the lights went out. We arose warm and sticky for morning formation in the dawn. And a bouncing, open-windowed bus trip to town only added the twang of Texas voices, the clump of high-heeled cowboy work boots, a barroom's immediate noise and a future headache to the inescapable heat.

So, a week like the one we are ending brings sweltering Abilene to mind.

That hot climate and the company we shared are interlocked in memory.

There was 1st Sgt. Chamberlin, with a knife-edged press to his pants, natty creases sewn into his tightly tailored shirts to resist the wilting the rest of us endured. He was a regular Army man, proud not to be a draftee, a muscular stud whose sharp commands got obedience, a "shack-up" master driven by the warrior tradition to keep a woman in town. Each day his immaculate departure at the post's sunset gun, his full-strength whistle blast for sun-up roll call, expressed within its narrow margins his sense of calling and of duty beyond self.

There was Master Sgt. Dewey Shurtleff, from country Colorado, who kept the squadron flying almost single-handedly, the way other mechanics-minded Americans kept our armies moving to victory in World War II. Custodian of our unit's "tech orders," Dewey knew every part of a P-39 fighter plane, every repair and replacement process. With only one after-hours window open in the "secured" headquarters shack, an electric fan blasting, Shurtleff poked his way night after night through Air Forces technical manuals, identifying airplane troubles he found along the flight line. His brow dripping, his neat fatigues soaked by the sweat of exhaustion - and exhilaration - Dewey had a love affair with the machine that kept Air Forces planes flying all over Texas and in any weather.

There was Cpl. John McCulley, blond, tanned, Texan - a handsome youth until you looked into his troubled eyes. He said he had an IQ of 157, a top-level intellect, but he bitterly dropped out of Officer Candidate School. He told me he had been a reporter for the San Antonio Light, but he hated newspapers and their skinflint publishers. He had a withdrawn Southern belle wife and baby in town. McCulley would work all day, shower and dress, intent on catching an early bus home. Then, from the back of the barracks, someone would rattle the dice against a footlocker. McCulley would waver and yield. The bus would be missed.

"Snake eyes!" he would pray, blowing on the cubes in his hot fist. "Eighter from Decatur," he would cry, bouncing the dice in a kind of rapture. "Baby needs new shoes!" The sweat would drip, the fierce eyes glitter, the hidden bottle emerge from the barracks bag, the bones knock again and again on the footlocker wall. With darkness the buses would start to return from town. McCulley, lost in longing and loathing, would collapse on a cot, cursing his luck.

There was Lt. Martin Cohen, gangly and smiling, from the Bronx and NYU, a personnel officer. I put out a mimeographed squadron paper called the Peashooter (the P-39's nickname). He oversaw it. I took exception to a camp order that all soldiers must authorize automatic deductions for insurance. The editorial headline was "Insurance Or Castor Oil?" Lt. Cohen let it pass. The Peashooter became the biggest thing on base for a day. Unit officers called special formations to say the National Service insurance was essential for combat-bound troops; buy it now.

At night in the unventilated mimeograph room, Lt. Cohen said, "I'm transferring out to Georgia." "Was it the Peashooter?" I asked. He said no. "These are National Guard officers called in from a Colorado unit," he said. "They think alike. They'll never understand me. I'm glad to move." He added: "They'll probably never understand you either, corporal. But an enlisted man doesn't need their understanding." We shook hands that night and I never saw him again. As it turned out, the base commander was right about the value of the life insurance. I still have it.

At the hot season's end we were all assigned to a damp, cooler airfield near Alexandria, La. Fat cows grazed in green fields nearby. The old P-39 was being replaced as a reconnaissance flier by newer, faster, photo-equipped fighter planes. New units were being organized for new campaigns.

The men of the squadron, burned by the Texas sun, harder in body and smarter as soldiers, a little older but hardly wiser, shook hands and exchanged the home addresses that nobody later remembered. The squadron broke up.

A brief hot season in a now-distant passage on the way to war and back ended for me 45 years ago as it began, without warning and without grieving.

But when hot days and nights pile up, I remember Abilene.

Saturday, July 25, 1981
Editor's note

Summitry And Sympathy And Strikeouts

An editor s job is a constantly shifting set of assumptions and obligations. It varies with person. It varies with the newspaper. And it's a matter that seems to be of interest to the general pubic as well as to journalists. People always used to ask me, as I know they ask our Executive Editor Bruce Reynolds: "How did you get your Job?" "What do you do all day?"

You won t get a specific answer from either of us.

But B.H. Liebes, a. professor of journalism at San Francisco State University recently reported on answers he had gotten from 108 editors in a national survey:

"Among the guideposts on the path to the managing editor's chair, these signs appeared most prominently:

" - Staying put with one paper.

" - Having previously occupied middle-management positions such as city editor, news editor, or assistant or associate managing editor.

" - Having a college education.

" - Achieving the position before the age of 50.

As to the job's content and the specifics of what an editor or a managing editor does, Prof. Liebes produced this outline from the bulk of his replies:

"When the editors were asked 'what, takes up most of your job time' they invariably listed staff problems, morale, personnel, hiring and recruiting and supervision of news play.

"Some representative comments:

"Pleading, threatening, leading, driving, fixing something, applauding, questioning, warning and trying to think of more creative solutions. Few managing editors can accurately tell their wives what they did today.'

"Responding to mail, publisher's requests, local phone calls, public appearances, labor relations.'

"Meeting with readers.'

"Meeting with staff members.'

"50 percent news, 50 percent people.'

"50 percent management and 50 percent personnel problems."

"Consultation with staff. It is astounding how many chats are necessary and how much time talking requires.'

"Other duties also mentioned frequently were budgets, liaisons with other departments, meetings, dealing with syndicate salesmen, 'reading my papers and other papers' and critiquing (the work of staff members)."

Busy enough?

A summer without baseball has produced some good baseball stories. Among the season's best with a local angle is the current week's piece in The New Yorker by Roger Angell.

It's about Smokey Joe Wood of Marvel Road, fabled Boston Red Sox pitcher and later Yale baseball coach, who is now 91. It's about Joe as he watched Ron Darling's climactic Yale game with St. John's University in mid-May. It also features surprisingly, as a sort of Greek chorus shouting rah-rah grandstand support for both Darling and

Smokey Joe, none other than New Haven's Richard C. Lee. And that's probably the biggest novelty in the piece.

I've never thought of the ubiquitous Lee as a sports fan. But here he is in, of all places, The New Yorker sports feature, urbanely presented as the arranger who brought together writer Angell and Joe Wood and the man whose amiable Yale Field chatter about the game and Ron Darling are woven into a classic baseball yarn.

It's a piece for the scrapbooks: Smokey Joe Wood's because it captures the nostalgia and the pungent immediacy of an unending affair with baseball by a player who had a couple of the game's greatest seasons and then lost out to injury. Ron Darling's because, to quote Angell: "Someday - perhaps years from now when he, too, may possibly be a celebrated major league strikeout artist - it may occur to him that his heartbreaking 0-1 loss in May, 1981, and Walter Johnson's 0-1 loss (to Smokey Joe Wood) at Fenway Park in September, 1912, are now woven together into the fabric of baseball. Pitch by pitch, inning by inning, Ron Darling made that happen. He stitched us together."

And Richard C. Lee's scrapbook, too - because Angell has exposed him in a new light, as just another suffering fan in the grandstand. In a season without baseball it makes baseball in New Haven a particular pleasure.

Saturday, November 15, 1986
Editor's note

As The News Scene Changes

Change is in the air for The Jackson Newspapers these days. There are personnel changes and procedural reforms, and in the news department work is beginning on page prototypes for the new morning Register, which is scheduled for delivery by March.

"But what will I do," readers ask me, "without my Journal-Courier in the morning and my familiar Register at suppertime?"

That question, of course, is what kept the Jackson family publishing two newspapers in New Haven for the past 50 years and long after this market had begun to meet all the standard measurements for a one-newspaper community.

It's a question that the new ownership here, the Ingersoll Publishing Co., hopes to answer by producing a "new" Register, a paper designed to deliver effectively, in one improved package, all the things that faithful readers and steady advertisers have found in the Journal-Courier and Register on a regular morning and evening basis.

Cities with two newspapers are fewer and fewer in the United States. In 1923 - before radio or television or the growth of modem advertising - there were 500 American cities with competing daily newspapers. In New Haven at that time there were four dailies - the Register, the Journal-Courier, the Union and the Times - all under different ownership. Thirty years later, halfway to today, there were 91 cities with competing -newspapers. In New Haven the Register and the Journal-Courier survived. Though they were still produced in separate buildings by separate staffs and printed on separate presses, both were owned by John Day Jackson.

Today there are only 31 communities in this country with

competing daily newspapers, most of them metropolitan in size, many of them facing the loss of one or more papers in the foreseeable future. Despite great technological advances in the production and printing of newspapers during the past two decades, radio and television and other modes of advertising limit the once almost unbounded reach of newspaper ad markets. And professionalized staffing, using higher-quality tools, and responding to higher expectations among our readers are all factors that keep the news "product" labor-intensive and costly in many ways.

For at least a decade every newspaper specialist looking at the New Haven situation - stalled circulation figures in an area of slow population growth, a constantly expanding delivery area with congested traffic patterns, plus other demographic measures - has said a single daily paper would best solve the internal publishing problems while better serving the newspaper readers, too.

The change is just beginning. Having made the decision to put out one daily paper for this region, management now must examine all the familiar features of the Register and the Journal-Courier. We must explore useful or informative things that will be new to our newspaper as a "package," weigh questions of value and appeal, consider what is essential and what is least necessary, try to get a sense of what the readers think about such change, and encourage input all along the line from the staff and from the public.

The next three months will be crowded with such planning and testing. Concurrently there will be a need to reorganize and invigorate a work crew that has had to combine the excitement of new times with the hard realities of staff reductions and changing work assignments.

We will be consulting with our readers in organized focus groups - by professions or interests and individually - as the new format takes shape and as a single daily newspaper for New Haven is laid out. We recognize faithful readers' concern for finding the old satisfactions and some sense of familiar presentation in the new paper as it begins to reach their homes at its new time. At the moment we have a bushel basket full of ideas and suggestions but almost no single, specific decision about the newspaper that will emerge from such choices.

As I noted at the beginning, editor groups and staff committees are having their first tentative skirmishes over the content and appearance of various parts of the paper. We see such changes as ways to share a bigger, better, livelier and more personally useful newspaper with all of our readers. We'll be talking to you about the plans and proposals as we move forward.

Losing something good has always been part of the recognized price of progress. Suspension of the Journal-Courier after 230 years in New Haven doesn't come easy. It had a role in taking this community into the American Revolution, and it has been a vital observer and participant in almost every other local development of any importance.

In the November issue of the Yale Alumni Magazine an article by Bernard Heinz tells of the building of Yale's Connecticut Hall, still on the Old Campus. President Thomas Clap invited Benjamin Franklin here for the dedication and an honorary degree in 1753. Out of that visit came New Haven's first newspaper, which Franklin launched as the Connecticut Gazette in 1755. Franklin's partner James Parker ran the paper, then turned it over to Thomas Green (who started the Hartford Courant in 1764). Later Franklin's sister's son, Benjamin Mecom, was in charge. The Gazette's direct link to the Connecticut Journal and New Haven Post-Boy, founded in 1767 by Thomas Green, is traced through its type and adornments, which were part of the original Ben Franklin import from London in 1755.

Franklin, who was the crown's deputy postmaster and manager for all the provinces in North America before the Revolution, said in ordering his press and type: "... There is a University (in New Haven) and a prospect that a Bookseller's Shop with Printing House may do very well."

He was right, of course, and he was unsentimental. It is on such solid business judgments· that newspapers begin - and end.

Saturday, March 19, 1988
Editor's note

Cause And Effect - And Spring

Down in the rushy glen below the hill on which I live in Bethany, the last ice is going from the brook. It forms a thin crystal shell, lace-edged, on black rocks as the water tumbles below them toward Long Island Sound. The peepers are already there in the frigid mud, half out of hibernation but slow to sound their springtime pipes as Bethany's native Indians might have heard them in times more simple.

An ancient process is afoot this last weekend of the winter. I can observe it any morning on my way to work in the city. The water follows its primeval course through the stone and down the hills. It is hemmed in, along with state Route 69, by the West Rock palisade on one side and what is left of the Ice Age western highland on the other. Near town it adjusts its natural flow to the human burdens we have imposed upon the land, factories where there once were minor waterfalls, office buildings on the sandy flood plain, homes and blacktop everywhere that swampy nature can be made to retreat.

Through seasonal coincidence the West River is just now being corseted the length of Westville by a flood control project. It puts the stream between sloping, stone-paved banks and contoured green places to tame it when the rain is heavy. At this same time West Haven's two mountainous landfills - like corks wedged into the river's mouth to cause the upstream flooding - are being pushed and petitioned toward closure by citizens who resent their mean condition and the environmental mess that results.

In a changing season this is all a study in cause and effect.

Self-effacing Sanford Brook on my eastern boundary rises in

Cheshire and quietly gurgles down through Bethany and Bethany Lake into Lake Watrous and Lake Dawson, the stepped reservoirs of the New Haven water supply system. At Dawson the slender Sargent River, draining westerly slopes, comes down from the old Sperry mill pool and Glen reservoir, goes under the Litchfield Turnpike. It joins the Sanford to fill Lake Dawson and the water authority's domed storage tanks. Then, merged, the country brooks slip over the spillway as the West River.

Drivers on the highway from Waterbury can follow all this clearly when the leaves are down. Small streams feed the system from upper Woodbridge. Birds on their timeless flight paths, and bird watchers, attend the water lovingly as it widens out at Konold's Pond and then moves, unthreateningly narrow, through the flood plain that is now the Woodbridge industrial park. Just before the West Rock tunnels the West River is a backyard's length from the road. Near the old Pond Lily plant it moves closer and its newly structured banks - firmed and bermed and spread with wood chips - stylishly express its late 20th-century formalization.

It is this stretch from lower Woodbridge through lower Westville that is being engineered today, a paternal government's answer to the flooding - once or twice in a quarter century of factory floors and motel parking lots, "low-risk" residential construction and adjacent street traffic. The private expense of such experience is now being matched by the public expense of preventive measures.

Following the river down into central Westville, as I do on my way to the Register via the Boulevard and City Point, you ride Whalley Avenue where it's built on what geologists call the "gravel shelf' of the prehistoric river bank. The stream moves along trippingly, but safely shallow, past housing projects and Blake Street factories. Then it curves to the right, crosses beneath Whalley Avenue near Fitch Street and enters Edgewood Park - a park because it was once part of the river meadows.

From this point the natural course of the West River takes it between wide marshy banks where cattails and decorative swamp grasses flourish in a three-mile reach to the Sound. This wide tract should be the flood absorber that would quickly draw off and soak up the river when overflow threatens or takes place. But almost at the edge of Long Island Sound the drain has been blocked. From the old river bank on Central Avenue at Derby, just beyond Yale Bowl, an unnatural, stiff-profiled ridge rises against the southern sky - the bleak West Haven landfills. Two adjacent mounds of refuse, garbage and paper and plastic and metal and wood, reach a hundred feet into the air' and smother the marshy acres with urban waste.

What was once for native Americans and Puritan colonists a flat, water-embracing and water-absorbing landscape, bringing earth and sky together, merging the river with the sea and keeping both in balance, has become in the past 50 years ugly, oppressive and - as the people who live near it know - nearly life-destroying.

The West River is choked beside these mounds, squeezed into grim channels, so overloaded that it floods in Westville when there are freshets in the hills. Still, it pushes through. Eventually waters that started deep inland as rain and mist and brooks, where small frogs sing in their springtime mating, mix with the Sound's salt tides.

This day or two before another equinox is reached, that is a progress worth remarking and celebrating. Like the grass that may be greening next year on West Haven's draggled mesas in the marsh, it reaffirms old hopes. Our human hand is often heavy on the land. But the river rolls along, evading and resisting what we do to it, intent as always upon the tryst with spring.

A thought for Monday and the new season, from Henry David Thoreau:

"In a pleasant spring morning all men's sins are forgiven. Such a day is a truce to vice.... Through our own recovered innocence we discern the innocence of our neighbors. You may have known your neighbor yesterday for a thief, a drunkard or a sensualist, and merely pitied or despised him, and despaired of the world. But the sun shines bright and warm this first spring morning, recreating the world, and you meet him at some serene work, and see how his exhausted and debauched veins expand with still joy and bless the new day, feel the spring influence with the innocence of infancy, and all his faults are forgotten…

"You see some innocent fair shoots preparing to burst from his gnarled rind and try another year's life, tender and fresh as the youngest plant."

Saturday, May 21, 1988
Editor's note

Checking The Information Flow

Freedom of information in Connecticut was a seminar subject for Register news staffers the other day. It's a subject that needs regular review because our own reporter turnover - which brings many new members onto the staff - and the turnover among public officials or agency workers often keeps people uncertain about their rights, or their duties, under the law. When reporters brush up on the statute they are able to ask the right questions in public offices and, equally important, to remind officials responsible for open meetings or open records about the kinds of access they are expected to provide for all citizens - including news gatherers.

Connecticut has one of the best of all state "sunshine" laws. It keeps most conflicts about information out of the crowded court system, thus avoiding the procedural delays that frustrate understanding and solution when information is withheld. It provides for relatively timely hearings, with penalties for serious infractions. And it is founded on a forthright legislative intent, with only a few stated exceptions, to keep written records open and accessible and to hold all Connecticut governmental meetings as public meetings.

Despite these strengths, the law benefits by the kind of review and restatement just given it here at the Register. In the 13 years since it was enacted in 1975, immediately after Watergate, the demand for totally open government has not been boldly undercut but it has more than once been quietly resisted. The natural needs of our democratic system are based on full citizen understanding of official activities. The natural inclination of even the best bureaucracies, surrounded though we are by our own New England town meeting tradition, is sometimes to question the reasons or the rights of citizens who ask inconvenient questions.

So Connecticut needs to keep reminding itself, and its elective or appointive public servants, that locked files or closed meeting room doors are not the way we want to do public business.

The FOI law's fundamental simplicity, says Mitchell Pearlman, executive director and general counsel to the state Freedom of Information Commission, is its strength. The law states essentially that: (a) All records are public records for the use of the citizenry; (b) Every meeting starts as an open meeting, which means any citizen is entitled to know it is being held, to attend it, and to find out what happened at it.

These major assumptions are, of course, defined and hedged in by a full 18 pages of single-space typescript. These pages outline how the law applies and what exceptions may be argued by those in charge of records or in charge of meetings - what Pearlman described as "a lawyers' full-employment act."

Though newspapers and other news-gathering agencies have an obvious interest in Connecticut's FOI law, it does not serve just the interests of the press. The fact is 70 percent of the complaints brought before the Freedom of Information Commission are brought by individual citizens who don't like the way things have been done in their informally run hometown or even in their professionally managed major city. Since disputes between public agencies are also considered, complaints from newspapers, or television and radio news operations, amount to less than one-fifth of the 250 cases handled by the FOI Commission each year.

What the press does most importantly, though, is to keep fresh for itself, and for officialdom, a regard for the law's original concerns and its constantly changing potential. We check to see that meetings are properly announced and publicly posted in advance, and we try, to give just one instance, to dig out such things as the performance evaluation of the highly paid school superintendent when his board of education keeps it under: wraps. The kind of refresher session held by the Register and the questions asked illustrate the range of concerns:

What about an agenda? We sometimes have no idea what is going to be done. (An agenda should be available for all regular meetings. A special meeting needs no agenda, but the special subject to which it is limited should be posted 24 hours ahead.)

What about a one-party caucus? When 11 out of 12 members of the board are of one party, they often reach decisions in a closed caucus. (The biggest loophole in today's law. Knockdown, drag-out politics are OK in a caucus, and there's no way to get a record of such decisions under FOI law. The political party isn't a public agency.)

What about the boards of ethics that have been created in some communities? Does the law apply? (The state's Ethics Commission observes confidentiality in its considerations. The local ethics boards are not covered by the state's exemptions. Their records should be open.)

There were other questions in the same vein - almost all dealing with current issues in the public offices and agencies where news is made today.

Analyzing precedent set by the commission or the courts in the past helps reporters and editors determine approaches for the future.

A man-in- the-street disdain for freedom of information discussion is one of the first things that surfaces for me after I write a column like this. I can predict that at least once in the week to come some genial reader will say, or write, that the flow of public information is not a matter of personal concern - so when will I get back to the nostalgic recollection that readers like best?

But having been a reporter for so long, and having sat as a member of the Freedom of Information Commission for five years, I consider this kind of commentary a duty every once in a while. In New Haven and in every town surrounding it, there are at this moment real issues, significant decisions, high-cost commitments being affected by things the public wants to know and things that elective and appointive officials don't want known - at least completely. The freedom of information law is the basic key, and the fundamental crowbar if need be, in opening up locked files or unsealing closed doors.

The public in general needs to recognize it for the democracy-serving tool that it is. Journalists, in particular, need to keep themselves informed of both the current challenges and the possible opportunities that are found in a law so essential, so important to everybody's right to know. If you've gotten this far, I consider your time well spent.

Saturday, September 14, 1988
Editor's note

Catching Up With Summer's Passing

On the season's thin edge between summer and fall there are hot-weather leftovers to be disposed of in this column as well as in other places. Today's comment touches several things that have been too long in my "current" file.

Most timely, perhaps, is a reminder of what newspaper readers should look at in a political poll. After tomorrow's initial debate between Bush and Dukakis the figures are sure to proliferate - and the arithmetic, or the meaning, of each poll is up to you.

Most of the time, remember, the meaning of a poll begins to grow stale the moment it is taken. So consider every poll a possible signpost but not a solid prediction. The inherent problem with any poll is that it represents a tiny sample of opinion in a tight period of time. The pollster's art is the projection of large numbers from small ones. There can be differences in the way random samples are determined among voters - who is questioned. There can be differences in the way a poll is conducted - for instance, whether the pollsters call back to get the opinions built into their sampling plan, or whether they discard a call if the person is not there. There can be differences in the way questions are asked, in the sequence of the issues raised, in the response they hope to elicit.

The randomness of the poll itself has a weakness. Since only 55 percent of the voting population has been turning out in U.S. elections, nearly half the people a pollster calls may have no intention of voting. The polls try to guard against this fact but it persists.

To read a poll best today, see if you can find out how the same poll reported things last week or last month. The uniformity of method gives the figures some continuity. To form an opinion on the polls, watch all the polls. Where there is consensus among several you may have a real trend. Where there are contradictions, someone is usually wrong. The problem with polls as news is that they often are commissioned as neutral reports but given partisan interpretations once released.

Finally, all polls are subject to almost immediate revision except for the poll the voters themselves initiate on Election Day.

In a burst of boosterism I suggested late in July a couple of strolls that could emphasize downtown attractions for city visitors. Reader Orpah Blazier of Fair Haven begged to differ:

" ... I moved to New Haven in 1927 after graduation from high school and was thrilled with the city. I loved to walk across the Green after dark, watching the stars play hide-and-seek with the city lights. Now I seldom venture part way into the Green and even feel nervous sitting on a bench in daylight. There was a good mix of department stores in various price ranges in the center. One could easily hop a streetcar, or later a bus, to go home after an afternoon of shopping or an evening at the movies.

"On your voyage of discovery apparently you didn't travel from Church Street to State down Chapel. That is the Ninth Square and will be renovated - but how long has it looked like a bombed city while other buildings in other places are razed for more office space? ... There is a serious parking problem, but has anyone ever thought of rapid transit? No one without a car can enjoy a weekend downtown because there is no way to get there.... But the biggest disgrace is the homeless situation. That problem is not new, and planning would benefit the whole picture. It is difficult to see why it takes the city so long to complete a job, why there are so many vacancies in public housing when the waiting lists are so long and so old ....

"The youth of New Haven is the hope of its future. Are we concerned that a portion of our future citizens are being denied a home life, good education and worthy role models (because they are) growing up in motels and shelters?

"I, too, appreciate New Haven and hope it can retain its charm, but I am distressed by what I see and hope some way can be found to reverse some of the current trends and to plan better for the future."

Reader Blazier is right to express impatience. I was right, I think, to express hope. At the end of the 20th century almost all cities like New Haven, and their people, are on a frontier where old ways have died and new ways have not yet been prepared or funded. Finding solutions is our toughest challenge.

The cry of "banzai" was heard again this week outside the Imperial Palace in Tokyo. It saluted the dying old man in whose name so many Japanese, with the same cry on their lips, killed Americans and themselves in World War II.

Hirohito ruled for 63 years as a symbol. When I was a boy he was divine, a descendant in unbroken line of the Shinto sun goddess, and in the old newsreels Japanese averted their eyes, and some even turned their backs with heads down, when such superhuman splendor passed in a royal cortege. When I was a soldier, he was the celestial proof to his troops that Japan could never be defeated, the embodiment of cold privilege for the brutal generals and the avaricious industrialists of the empire he had inherited. To die with the emperor's "banzai" on his lips was a soldier's highest honor. For the past 40 years, as Japan was resurrected, Hirohito has been in eclipse, an emperor without empire, gentle, academic, a laboratory scholar aloof from his people.

When they shouted "banzai" in Tokyo this week there was poignance in wishing so old and weary a man "ten thousand years." But through the far Pacific, in deep seas and in a thousand strange burying grounds from Guadalcanal through Malaysia and Korea and Manchuria, there must have been a stir on the breeze, an unheard groan, at the sound of that foolish word and the carnage it recalled. Nobody would begrudge an old man good will at the time of his dying, but for some "banzai," with all the evil it excused, is not the proper word.

Saturday December 18, 1982
Editor's Note

Christmas-Time At The Crossroads

SEVEN MORE DAYS to go! As the shopping stampede moves into its last hectic week there is no way to recapture the old time Christmas prominence of downtown New Haven. But didn't it once have a convenience and a community efficiency we can still admire?

I hear family members and friends and associates discuss their exhausting travels. "I went from the Connecticut Post in Milford to the Hamden Mart ...Bradlee's in East Haven to the Amity Center ... Maybe the Naugatuck Mall or Meriden would have it ..."

And I recall the busy crossroads at Church and Chapel Streets 50 years ago. In 1932 whether you came from Hamden, West Haven, East Haven, Westville, Fair Haven, the East Shore, Cedar Hill, Newhallville, City Point - wherever - your trolley crossed that corner. Within two blocks of the intersection you could buy anything you might possibly need.

Hamden's Magic Mile was then a lovely slope of apple orchard rising from Dixwell to Mix Avenue. And the only significant retail operation between New Haven and Milford on the Post Road was Wayside Furniture, then an experiment - and some thought a gamble - on selling to customers with cars.

Downtown's merchandising temples, Malley's and the Gamble-Desmond department stores, stood side by side across from the Green. Gamble's was a crowded, slightly dowdy emporium in the old style - its reputation for quality still exemplified in its grand French Empire architecture. Malley's, wide windowed and sleek, epitomized style and gracious regard for both tradition and merchandising smartness.

A few steps down Church Street was Savitt's jewelry and J. Johnson & Sons, clothiers, and Longley's mens' store, and further down - where Macy's now turns its back on Church Street - was the Sears Roebuck store. Facing it across the street was the Alling Rubber Company, an outdoorsman's paradise - piled ceiling high with boxes and bundles of real flannel, wool, and leather goods in that day when plentiful clerks on ladders could search the stock, and the stockrooms, for your halfsize. Or get it in a week.

In the retail concentration at the Church and Chapel crossroads Christmas was, at least in the week before the holiday, a hurly-burly for grown ups and a wonderland for children. Malley's "toyland" was in the basement - and Santa Claus heard childish whispers from his ice-palace throne while gnomes and brownies distributed - for a small admission price - mystery packages of games or books.

Gamble-Desmond's, as I recall it, did very little with Santa, perhaps for lack of space. But Shartenberg's big store on Chapel near State devoted its cavernous fifth floor to him and to a cast of Yuletide characters. In my memory there was a very large "fishpond" full of intriguing packages. A pretty attendant gave you a fishing pole and then "hooked" the package of your choice. There was also a rollicking pirate who'd let you reach into his Treasure Chest for the same fee. And long before Mickey Mouse and Disneyland, there were Mother Goose characters and an Uncle Wiggily bunny to afflict shy children with their noisy affection.

Kresge's and Woolworth's, and Grant's and eventually Newberry's - all "10-cent stores" jostled each other between Church and Orange on one side of Chapel. On the other side was an array of "lingerie" and shoe stores, with an occasional "haberdasher" for dressy males. Centered among them was the Loomis Temple of Music where you could buy everything from sheet music to a harmonica or a piano. The next block was dominated by the big five-story Shartenberg store. Across the street was Besse-Richey's clothing store, the bustling lower priced Stanley's department store beside it.

Facing each other on Chapel near the corner of State were two treasure houses no New Haven child of the time can shake from the collective Christmases of memory.

Rohan's toy store stood packed and overflowing beside Shartenberg's. It was an unbelievable melange of toy soldiers and porcelain dolls, of Bavarian wood carvings and British cast-iron vehicles, of games in a thousand boxes, and engines, and wooden blocks, and long-tailed oriental kites.

There were sleds and wagons and bicycles and electric trains - all in a space not much wider than a couple of modern supermarket aisles. Above the counters were super-structures piled high, like the wall shelves, with more boxes, stuffed animals, and various gimcracks. And if something particularly out of reach was needed the tallest man in the store, Mr. Rohan himself, was summoned to take it down.

As a boy grew older there was Bassett's - the "oldest hardware store," they said, in Connecticut. It was agleam with cutlery, and canvas and leather for the wilderness camper, magnificent knives in a hundred sizes, flashlights, the first pair of snowshoes I ever saw, telescopes, binoculars, barometers, compasses, a dream of adventure in each cabinet and counter. And there were aged, polite male clerks - who knew the uses of everything - to place on a green felt board whatever treasure you asked to see. The narrow shop, with entrances on Chapel and State streets, was dark with age but aglow with bright metal and polished wood and the special grace and utility that still marks most things called "hardware."

In that block there was Loft's chocolate-scented candy store, a bakery window always full of cream cakes, a cut-rate druggist's, and, on each of two corners, one of those last, fragrant outposts of what had really been a man's world - a tobacco store, the drawers and counters full of allurements we now see as addictions, a blue gas flame ever ready in a chrome fixture to light up a customer's "smoke."

A little off Chapel Street, on Orange Street at Pitkin Alley, was Judd's Book Store - a fabled, two-floor repository where the clerks were really bibliophiles and librarians. Its broad central staircase was inevitably crammed at Christmas with books that overflowed its shelves and tables. The manager - fitted with bifocals and crisp, loud opinions - seemed always to be calling out book recommendations to favored customers. The place was an intoxication of stories to read and strange worlds to ponder, from London's yearly edition of "Chatterbox" to the Tom Swift adventures.

Between Temple and College the shops on Chapel Street became what today's marketers call "upscale." Hamilton & Company, address: "upper Chapel Street," a general store for the well-to-do, stood beside the old Quinnipiack Club, now site of the restaurant New Haven. Nearby was Wylie's on-the-Green, a fine china shop filled at Christmas with table settings in holly and evergreen. S.H. Kirby and Sons had windows full of silver plate and full tea services to back .up Wylie's dishes. On the corner across from the Hotel Taft was, for years, the Mary Oliver candy store - and west on Chapel Street from there marched the exclusive and expensive haberdashers and custom tailors who served Yale's gilded youths.

In this grab bag of impressions from Christmases past, grist for a dozen more columns and side-street safaris stands untouched. But when contemporary planners wax eloquent over the way they would mix - in their model urban centers purveyors of food and of fashion, sources of trivial fun and serious centers of profit, places for art with places for commerce, places for people to look and lounge, to sit, and sample, to work and to buy, I think of Church and Chapel in the Christmas-tides of my childhood - and of the streets around that community rendezvous.

The trolleys have gone, with their tracks. The life-blood of old downtown went with those tracks, though we didn't know it in our push for progress at the time. The business, the sociability, the prosperity that was riding on the trolley's passage in its iron-rigid course has been scattered far and wide by the combustion engine, the rubber tire, and the "flight from the city," which is a phrase that encompasses American dreams and ideals as well as deficiencies.

Whatever we eventually do with downtown New Haven's College Street entertainment district, or the empty Malley's building - or even with the North Haven Mall - will have to be shaped to the wheels and the roads, the transportation habits and the selling-and-buying modes that come naturally to the future's customers. Nostalgia won't help.

But in the 20s and the 30s the single central crossing of those trolley tracks beside our Green created a community economy, an efficiency, yes even an ambiance, that a professional planner might envy and that kept New Haven vibrant at its heart. Though it all took shape untrammeled by public finance or civic supervision, and though it flourished purely on the profit motive among big and little entrepreneurs - who would have preferred being called shopkeepers - what a place it was for Christmas shopping!

And, in fact as well as memory, what a place it was for the magic Christmas spirit, too!

Saturday, March 22, 1980
Editor's –Note

Considering Good News - And Bad

"I am tired of hearing only the dark side of the news. I think it is important 'that equal time and emphasis be given to the lighter side. This constant tearing down process is debilitating and needs more of the positive and assuring to help balance things out and bolster our morale. A constant diet of bad news gives indigestion among other things. It also is self-defeating in that it destroys our confidence and can produce a state of mass depression and an 'Oh what's the use attitude.

"It can also produce a guilt feeling which cripples our ability individually and collectively to function constructively and resolve our problems. People who feel good about themselves can cope with most things; whereas people who lack self-esteem cannot. This is true of nations as well.

"I would like to hear more about the good in man - the things that uplift rather than push down, the things that bring a chuckle, that make you feel hopeful and glad that you're a member of the human race. Maybe this type of news won't be sensational but it will bring a glow to our hearts.

"So, enough of self-defeating rhetoric. Let's think positive. Let's be grateful and proud of our country and ourselves and let's join in building a great future for ourselves and our country with the help of the media. We need to be uplifted."

Gertrude Gutkin of Hamden
in a letter to the editor

"We real journalists, too, have made a good thing out of ... relentlessly seeking out and exposing all the (non-media) corruption we can find, and chronicling all the discontent and divisiveness that nimble energy can seek out or manufacture ... The no-exit America in which we are now trapped together has been poisoned and left almost helpless by the self-contempt we journalists have engendered in it ...

"After all, to have written anything positive about our country - its generosity, good humor, inventiveness, energy and essential loveableness - would have made us seem naive. Only a crook, or a Norman Rockwell, or some ignorant lout of a farmer would be so crude as to do a thing like that. And now, just look what's happened to us ... Is it really essential in the name of truth that we be superficial, and destructive, and bitchy-ironic, and morally superior so long and so relentlessly?...

"The country I see when I look up from newspapers and TV is still, in spite of it all, energetic, smart and tough, and has a powerful sense of inward unity. The country I see, if it could get over the induced idea that it's inherently evil, could do just about anything it pleased; defend itself, curb inflation, have a renaissance of good feeling. But the America the media show me is not at all that way..."

Dick Dabney, Washington Post writer
in an article on our Forum page

When journalists sit with their consciences, which is a more common occurrence that you might think, they often ponder judgments like those printed above.

One of the oldest and most persistent criticisms of the press is the claim that we ignore the "good news" and revel in the bad. It's a claim that's easy to make because most of the things that are good in life are relatively routine: happy marriages, loving children, honest merchants, helpful neighbors, conscientious public servants. As the old song says: The best things in life are free.

But by their very nature such "best" things are also commonplace, familiar, and unsurprising. A chubby baby's smile, the smell of fresh-baked bread, a meadow in the moonlight uplift the heart. But they are not quite within the dictionary definition of "news" as something which commands attention because it is a recent event of special interest.

So newspapers from their beginnings have stressed the unusual, the novel (the French word for news is nouvelle), the event which is dramatic, informative, or scandalous as well as the event which is significant. The result is a flow of news today which often does seem heavy with crisis, with conflict, with disaster, pain, and trouble.

It is the glut of 1980 news reports - instantaneous, unending, globe-girdling - immersing us day after day in the hectic uncertainty of the whole world's problems, which leaves people disillusioned, uncomfortable, sometimes resentful, and often hungry for some report that "will bring a glow to our hearts."

Newspapers like The Register try to meet that hunger.

We select and label good news on our daily Upbeat page. We devote lots of space to weddings, and sports, and good things to cook or eat. We try to dig out interesting and affirmative features about the goals and accomplishments of our readers. On tilts editorial page - where we make our modest recommendations for a properly-run world - we salute' monthly some unsung citizen service for its goodness. On our adjacent Forum page we look for balanced commentary, for reassurance as well as reform in the public issues discussed.

On a column-inch basis we have shown, several times, that there is really more "good" news than bad news in your daily paper. But it's true that larger headlines, and the facts that most dramatically demand your interest, are found with the reports of trouble and disaster - because that is the tradition and the nature of news in this late 20th Century.

And if our readers mix in their minds the newspaper's broad detail with the narrower, more tightly focused excitements of electronic news by radio and television, they may well come up with a feeling that nothing gentle or smiling is permitted to surface in the flow of current events.

It's also true, in my opinion, that despite the rising public question about negativeness in the news, our American traditions aren't basically linked to "good" news.

American newspapers helped create this country by creating, before and after 1776, the climate of open criticism in which King George Ill's edicts were rejected and his troops repulsed. In the new republic, to use a phrase of James Madison, the newspapers were seen as the necessary "censors of government." Their first and most valued function was not the publication of good news, but the exercise of free speech and free opinion in ways that would protect the people from errors or excesses in government,

The young people who have been recruited or volunteered in the service of 1980 news gathering see strong reflections of the "censor" role in the Woodward-Bernstein reporting of Watergate, in the flap over the Pentagon papers, and in other investigative forays by the press. Even in assignments to our suburban towns they are energized by the conviction that there are things worth probing for beneath the routine surfaces.

From the prestigious Pulitzer Prizes on down, award after award in today's American journalism asks of applicants as one general criterion: What significant result, or administrative reform, or change of public policy grew out of this reporting? The standard is not whether the news was good but whether it was bad enough and effectively enough exposed, to enforce change.

That being said in explanation as much as defense, let me add that the concerns expressed at the top of this column must be dealt with effectively if the American press is to remain free.

In the Third World countries - in Africa, Asia, the Middle East and Latin America - there is already a formal U.N.-linked insistence that the Western concept of uncensored, questioning news does not fit the concept of government-serving and society-building good news appropriate to an emerging socialist nation. That insistence is slowly drying up access abroad to independent opinion and uncontrolled news.

The last thing we need is to have that conviction - which already threatens the free global flow of information - linked to a sense of distrust or dissatisfaction with the press among the

American people.

Newspapers, for the most part, mirror the attitudes of the community. The social disruption, the political struggles, and the deep divisions over personal and public morality in the Sixties and Seventies have been reflected in news reports that expressed suspicion, complaint and controversy.

In a period of stronger unity and better feeling more affirmative perceptions should begin to emerge in the news. The surge of good spirit and cheerful patriotism that closed the Winter Olympics demonstrated this. And news gatherers were the first to chorus this message and to analyze it.

When the American majority is confident about our national purpose and national progress, that confidence is reflected in the news columns of your daily paper. Until then, it is not evasion to say that "good" or "bad" news depends not so much on what the press tells the society as in what the society tells the press.

Yale President's dwelling, *Hillhouse Avenue, 1871. Built as a Victorian mansion for railroad pioneer Henry Farnam, it became Yale Georgian in 1937.* *Dana Collection.*

Saturday, July 22, 1995
Editor's note

State FOI Law Healthy At Age Of 20

The Connecticut Commission on Freedom of Information celebrates its 20th year of operation this month. It plans a formal "birthday party" in the fall.

The good news is that it continues to serve as a model, nationwide, for an effective state agency that can work on behalf of open public records and open public meetings.

The bad news is that the FOI Commission tangled with Gov. John G. Rowland over campaign questions hinting at spousal friction just before he was elected in 1994.

The hope is that the commission and the governor can enjoy the mutually comfortable relationship that has existed with other Connecticut governors since Ella Grasso was an enthusiastic advocate, and even a legislative pathfinder, for Connecticut FOI law at its beginnings in 1975.

Designed to speed public information processes and, where possible, to bypass lengthy court dockets, the FOI Commission has always been apolitical and quasi-judicial in its approach.

After 20 years, its record of citizen service is solid. And Rowland's own demonstrated capacity for reasonableness and practicality suggests that suspicions, if they do exist, need not be permanent.

An FOI clash at election time was not everybody's goal.

The Hartford Courant, pursuing a news story, claimed that Middlebury police refused it access to facts on an alleged complaint by Rowland's first wife.

The paper petitioned the FOI Commission a month before the1994 election. Rowland, who has since remarried, claimed that a verbal argument in their home, a domestic disagreement within the circle of family privacy, was all that took place. He noted that the Hartford Courant was opposing his election.

The Middlebury police chief justified withholding the record because, he said, there was no crime involved in the complaint. After a hearing, and with the election looming, FOI Commissioner Dean Avery of New London recommended release of the police report. The full commission concurred. That order was enjoined in court. There were other legal motions. And with the police report still undisclosed, the issue now awaits a judge's decision, perhaps later this summer.

Meanwhile the term of Dean Avery expired. He was not reappointed. But the governor has since named three new commissioners. One of them Frederick Hennick of Naugatuck, was an FOI commissioner for four years previously, and had stepped down voluntarily in 1993. So his return to the commission is hardly a radical change in its direction.

The judge's decision, when rendered, should illuminate the debate over the Middlebury police file, and if we're lucky - and there's no appeal – it might also dissolve any lingering personal feelings.

Though this case, like many of the commission's significant cases across 20 years, involves a complaint by the press, the widest role of the FOI Commission has been as the agency that assists individual citizens to get information they need and use for their individual purposes, usually in their home communities.

That function provides the common ground on which commissioners and governors have consistently met to support and extend the accessible records and the open-door meetings basic to our tradition of free government.

Preserving Freedom of Information is not just a Connecticut challenge. Here's what Paul McMasters of the Freedom Forum's First Amendment Center at Vanderbilt University wrote in the current issue of the Bulletin of the American Society of Newspaper Editors:

"Increasingly, local law enforcement and emergency response personnel are prohibiting or denying photographers and reporters reasonable access to accidents, fires, natural disasters and crime scenes ... The public still has to depend on handouts, the press on leaks, for most news about the deliberations of Congress ...

"The Securities Exchange Commission and the Federal Communications Commission, chafing under the strictures of the Sunshine Act (proposed closed hearings) ... As for the courts, the Judicial Conference of the United States, which made decisions affecting open government at its meeting in March, conducted its own business in secret sessions.

"On state and local levels, the fight for open meetings never ends ... No editor needs another job to do, but keeping records and meetings open has to be job No. 1. If we fail to fight as file drawers and government doors slam shut, then we may as well close our own doors and go home."

Connecticut's FOI Commission-based experience is dramatically better than that of most states or the federal government. But, after 20 years of FOI Commission progress, citizen vigilance and official cooperation and accountability remain the public's best guarantee of good government, in Hartford or Washington.

Saturday, September 23, 1995
Editor's note

Award Honors Townshend Role In City

When Doris and Henry Townshend received the Seal of the City Award for community service on Thursday, they were saluted for their decades of personal effort across a wide range of New Haven needs and concerns.

Both have been involved with numerous groups working on economic, educational, or social programs for this region. Harry Townshend ran twice as a Republican candidate for mayor in the 1960s. As a contrast, one of his most unusual hobby-based projects was creation of a larger-than-life model squid for the Peabody Museum. Deb Townshend's thorough and information-packed books, "The Streets of New Haven" and "The Streets of East Haven," her history of old Fair Haven "A Journey Through Time," and the family record she has called "Townshend Heritage" are each lively contributions to an understanding of regional history.

The New Haven Colony Historical Society's award went to them as a distinguished wife-husband team who, while involved in contemporary community endeavors, have also done exceptional work in the preservation of the old places and the old practices from Connecticut's past.

Apart from the honorees' deeds, individually and as a "dynamic duo," one of the things that most impressed me about Thursday's celebration was the equal liveliness of past Townshend generations here in New Haven. About them "you could write a book" – as Deb Townshend did.

The first local generation took root in 1739 when Jeremiah Townsend, 27, and his brother Ebenezer, 23, arrived from Boston. They had descended from Thomas Townsend, who settled at Lynn, in the Massachusetts Bay Colony, about 1638.

Jeremiah was a barber-surgeon and wig maker. He served wig-wearing Yale professors and scholars and lived to the age of 93. Brother Ebenezer, meanwhile, became a prosperous ship owner in the city's West Indies trade.

His son Ebenezer Jr. built the fabled sailing ship "Neptune." It left Long Wharf in 1796 with Ebenezer III in the crew, harvested a cargo of seal skins in the South Atlantic, rounded Cape Horn and traded them in China for silks, teakwood, tea, camphor, chinaware and other precious goods, then came home after 30 months at sea and a trip around the world. The ship's investors shared great profits.

Two of Jeremiah's grandsons, Isaac Jr. and William Kneeland Townsend, were merchant tailors big on London imports. About 1830 they built at Chapel and College Streets a brick building, the Townsend Block, which still shelters Claire's Corner Copia at that comer.

When central trading collapsed in the War of 1812, some of the Townsends moved west to New York and for years "conducted the entire commerce" of Lakes Ontario and Erie with their fleet of vessels. Another, based in Sandusky, Ohio as an operator of lake boats, became president of that city's first bank and a founder of the first railroad west of the Allegheny Mountains. A third Townsend, working in New York, was the first president of the Continental Bank which became the Chemical National Bank - which now in 1995 could be merged with Chase National to become a megabank.

Isaac Henry Townsend, who entered Yale at 15 in the class of 1822, was later Yale's first professor of law. In 1854 banker James M. Townsend, a curious man, had Benjamin Silliman of Yale analyze oily skim from a pool in Pennsylvania, then sent Edwin Drake to examine the site. In 1859 Drake drilled the world's first oil well there.

Charles Hervey Townshend, born in 1833, was a sea captain during the transition from sail to steam. He made more than 200 crossings of the Atlantic, his ships always the biggest and fastest vessels under U.S. ownership. After marrying here in 1871 he became a harbor-side farmer and oyster grower - and even sent a flat-bottomed Fair Haven sharpie to France to show French aquaculturists U.S. methods.

It was Charles Hervey who changed the family name from Townsend to Townshend, with an "H," after research in England convinced him this was the ancient and original spelling.

These few boughs and branches from the family tree are typical of the lively role many other Townshends have played in New Haven - as, in effect, they put a seal of their own on the city.

Incidentally, today's Seal of the City Award features an image embossed on parchment in antique red sealing wax. It uses the municipal seal designed in 1784 by Ezra Stiles, James Hillhouse and Josiah Meigs.

The seal shows, in Stiles' words, "the harbor of New Haven, a ship at the entrance, and an Ionic pillar entwined with a Grape Vine." Under the ship is inscribed "Mare Liberum" for freedom of the seas. The words "New Haven" and "Connecticut" in Latin are on the circular border.

The 211-year-old seal, now priceless in its symbolic uses, is preserved at the New Haven Colony Historical Society.

Saturday, December 22, 1984
Editor's note

Far Away And Years Ago

Forty years ago this week, during World War II, I spent a soldier's Christmas in the Philippine Islands. The following is an excerpt from the mail dispatch the Register published about that 1944 holiday so far from home.

THE PHILIPPINES, Dec. 25, 1944 - It's funny to be sitting here by the warm Pacific, writing about Christmas under a great horizon-rooted cumulus, with my belly full of turkey and my two-bottle beer ration empty at my feet - particularly when I know you won't read a word of this until (if the mails are good) close to Valentine's Day...

In Europe, where there are more familiar scenes, Christmas may have been a time of poignanace and regret for the soldier away from home. But here in the far Philippines it has not been a time of conscious regret, or too strong nostalgia, for any of us. Waving palms and warm surf, two months without mail, and a shortage of generated power, which deprived our squadron of even Armed Forces Radio programs, left the men anesthetized to the season's memories.

There were exceptions to this numbness, of course. The 19 year-old boy who made himself, and us, a Christmas tree by tying a spiral of small branches to a tapering tree limb, wrapping them in green palm fronds, and decorating it all with string, frayed manila hemp, seashells and chewing gum tinfoil had not lost the magic feeling of Christmas. Nor, in another way, had the slightly graying man who spent the afternoon crating a beautiful, vari-colored conch shell for his children at home ....

The holiday began, as it does everywhere, on Christmas Eve. A few musical soldiers who had sounded tentative carols during the week came out in strength as the late island twilight faded.

One by one others gathered round, and by the time the darkness had really crept in from the ocean and the Big Dipper started up the sky there was music in the air....

"The First Noel" and "Silent Night" and "Jingle Bells" and "White Christmas" rang out in the soft night, and over the steep palm-crowned hill behind us shone a westering star as bright as the one the shepherds watched.

Even our Southerners in these warm islands talk of the snap in the yuletide air at home and the sparkle of snow in the moonlight. But here there is no snow to hide the tropic green. Instead, in the palm top above the singers, a small blizzard of fireflies swirled like phosphorescent snowflakes that never reached the ground.

When the songs had all been sung over, the Japanese lighted our Christmas tree for us. On the hill the warning siren screamed three times, and up and down the beach the ack-ack men shot off their three lingering flares. Steel helmets were placed handy as the singing went on. But in a little while it stopped; the guns on the point several miles away were putting up too good a show:

Unseen Japanese planes in the air were met by fountains of shells, blood-red tracers that arched up from both ends of the airstrip as if some prodigious juggling twosome were passing each other an endless stream of fiery balls.

Sometimes in the darkness, as these two streams unite, there is a golden flare of gasoline in the cross fire, and a Jap plane goes down... But tonight the planes stayed off, the crimson fountains dwindled and died, the single "all clear" siren blast came from the hill, and we were left alone to sing a little more.

The western star still shone above the ridge. The fireflies twinkled in the palm. The last few voices closed their song: "The hopes and fears of all the years are met in thee tonight."

At midnight there was a Mass for Catholics in an abandoned Filipino church now used as a GI mess hall. A bright red supply parachute hung behind the altar for decoration. Two dozen candles provided illumination, for the celebrant and the soldiers and the holiday-decked Filipinos who came to greet the Child....

In the morning it was Christmas, and soldierly gifts were passed around - a pack of paper matches, a bag of moldy tobacco, a roll of toilet tissue. But the day's sensation lay in a gesture of fellowship by our officers. They took over the holiday kitchen police.... At noon the officers arrayed themselves behind the aluminum pots and trays, and the chow line opened.

Ice-cold grapefruit juice, the first cooled drink we'd had in two months, splashed into the cups. Our cooks had wangled the small cake of diamond-precious ice from an elaborate Seabee mess down the coast. Then the turkey, almost a pound per man, was heaped on. Mashed potatoes, dressing, giblet gravy, corn, stewed tomatoes, hot biscuits, apple pie with cheese, steaming coffee, and hard candy followed.

We plunged into it and came back for seconds.... But this wasn't quite the end. All week there'd been rumors that one, 10, 20 bottles of beer would be rationed out to every man. And now, as the after-dinner lassitude settled upon us, we were electrified by the news of the beer's arrival. Like forty-niners heading for the hills, we rushed for the chow tent. And over the counter, warm and sawdusty, came two bottles of Milwaukee's best.

Some buried it. Some hung it in the shallow well. Some drank it right away. They all came out the same in the end, for it didn't cool. But to the long-unslaked palate it tasted ambrosial, and it added a final festive touch to the day.

Now the bottles are empty. The KPs have been dismissed. The night that must move across us, and China, the vastnesses of Asia, and the turmoil of Europe (and though I didn't know it then, the blood and ice of the Battle of the Bulge) before it comes to you in East Rock shadows, is rising from the sea. The fireflies will soon be out again. The ack-ack batteries already are alert.

Christmas is over. The wise men search on, for a prince and the promise of peace.

In the season when this reaches you, may your Valentines be many!

Saturday, January 5, 1985
Editor's note

Facing A World Of Change

So we took the U.S. out of UNESCO. As an idealist who believes that "the parliament of man" is a better concept that any battle plan, I'm sorry to see the United States turn away from even one aspect of United Nations involvement. But as a working journalist I've spent nearly a decade watching, and protesting, as UNESCO, the United Nations Educational, Scientific, and Cultural Organization, made foray after foray against the idea of freedom of the press.

When the United States finally withdrew as a member last Monday it made sense to me. Our government is the largest contributor to UNESCO - about $50 million a year. But most of the agency's activities are hostile to goals we and our international allies support, and some UNESCO policies deliberately flout and frustrate American efforts. Our withdrawal at the end of 1984, and the promised British withdrawal at the end of 1985, testify to UNESCO's operational failure to give fair hearing, or equal consideration, to Western democratic arguments about world problems.

UNESCO's Third World leaders have been persistent, and sometimes devious, in their refusal to reject, or even table, moves toward a "new world information order" which was first blueprinted by the Soviet Union in the '60s. At conference after world conference the new "order" has been pushed by UNESCO officialdom as well as by the Iron Curtain bloc and Third World dictatorships. In its essence the new "order" places all news reporting under official controls, makes the "good" of the government and the "stablility" of the populace an essential news objective, and makes hazy provision for the licensing of all reporters - not only within a country but among many nations with different standards.

Such regulations would end the kind of free news flow existing today. The United States sets a world standard, for open access, but our press is vigorously imitated throughout the countries of western Europe, in Canada and many of our hemispheric neighbors, in India, in Japan, and in various other places. The kind of global news exchange that exists, however inadequately, today would be totally throttled. The substitute in UNESCO's "new world information order" would be the kind of censored, delayed, hard-to-assess "news" we get from Moscow.

Critics of the U.S. pullout say we should have stayed in so we would keep fighting to "reform UNESCO from within." But in the news controversy I know best, we have spent about a full decade trying to "reform," restrain, and reshape the Marxian- socialist determination that news gathering must be a function controlled by government, that reporters must be held to standards set - and licensed - by officialdom, that clear information about disasters, wars, injustices or simply official mistakes must be approved before it can be generally circulated.

At the moment UNESCO supports these anti-freedom concepts insistently.

Walking out of UNESCO is the most effective way of showing Americans believe such policies are not foundation stones for freedom anywhere.

And since the UNESCO fat cats - philosophy aside - spend 70 percent of their budget on Paris headquarters activities and hardly 30 percent on education or research or cultural backup elsewhere in the world, the loss of U.S. dollars may have some persuasive effect.

I don't think they want us out of UNESCO permanently.

Paper becoming obsolete? Canadian pulp and paper makers, forecasting development trends, say computers only increase the paper work:

" ... The wide application of computers and word processors tends to increase the use of paper. One of the most significant developments in the widespread use of computers is the tremendous increase in the amount of data processed and made available. The end product of computer applications is usually a printed report, so that rather than replacing paper, the computer has increased its use. Furthermore, new methods of composing and printing, again using computers and electronic processing ... will maintain or improve the competitive position of the print medium. It is said that we are at the beginning of the communications revolution. If that is so, then the use of paper, still the most effective means of communication for many purposes, can be expected to expand."

Hard rolls and raspberry twists: My children wonder if I can live without them. I wonder too. But there is no choice.

They closed the Westville Home Bakery this week, and some of the small things, the earthy pleasures that stand up to a lifetime's steady savoring, are gone.

Whoever said that man does not live by bread alone had not been to Westville. For some 20 years the rolls and the twists - simplest of the delicacies shaped to old Vienna's highest standards by the skilled and fastidious Westville bakers - have been a part of Sunday's goodness in our house. The ovens and the frosting bowls produced much richer delights for me and my wife, decades of birthday cakes; holiday tortes of richest hue and deepest, densest flavor and lightest texture; berry fillings; whipped cream in ridged, snowy drifts; intricate confectionery flowers; gingerbread houses.

But if they had a touch of the ethereal (not counting calories), there were always simpler alternatives. The basic elements, fire and the good earth, were encapsulated as fragrant air and risen flour within the golden crunch of those hard rolls. The sugared, crisp flakiness of the pastry twist, a fruit-flavored zephyr, was kept real and fit for mortals by the innocence of raspberry's imperfect seeds.

The kids are right. How can one do without such small, such primal glories? And we didn't even try to freeze a few.

There will be other hard rolls, of course, as there are other bakeries. But taste buds so respectfully tempted can make a day, and keep tolerable a week - and for a long time they did. Whatever the passing of the Westville Home Bakery does for my waistline, what will it do to my palate? Or even my psyche?

Saturday, March 15, 1986
Editor's Note:

James Madison's Birthday

National freedom of information day will be observed tomorrow. It won't be earthshaking. James Madison's birthday was selected only a few months ago by the Society of Professional Journalists, Sigma Delta Chi, as an appropriate date for public observance of the way that a free flow of facts serves American democracy. So there are few organized forums around which supporters of freedom of information may rally tomorrow.

With time, perhaps, the observance will become more structured, the important message better stated. In the interim it's worth your while to give the First Amendment in the Bill of Rights a little thought - not for what it does for the press or religion, but for what it does for the individual American's freedom to make crucial personal choices. Article I says:

"Congress shall make no law respecting an establishment of religion, or prohibiting the free exercise thereof; or abridging the freedom of speech, or of the press; or the right of the people peaceably to assemble, and to petition the government for a redress of grievances."

That is a power-packed paragraph. When it says Congress shall make "no law" it puts religious belief, and personal opinion, and peaceful assembly and petition (or protest), beyond the easy reach of officialdom. It rejects the coercive control of mind and person that was central to Great Britain's rule of these colonies. And it opens our country and our society to remarkable achievement, and exceptional personal satisfaction, on the part of every citizen.

The freedom of religion and assembly are, by themselves, subjects big enough to fill a book. The idea of a free flow of information - this weekend's subject - is the source of much of the vitality and the democratic success for which our country is known today. The press as the critic of wrongdoing, as the "censor of government," is a concept that has been at work in American affairs from the War of 1812 to the recent fall of Ferdinand Marcos in the Philippines.

James Madison's birthday, March 16, is an apt time for such newsy consideration because he was the principal architect of the First Amendment. Born in 1751, four years before the Connecticut Gazette, the Journal-Courier's predecessor, had its New Haven start, he was the fourth president of the United States and in his second term when the Register was founded here in 1812. Small of stature - 5 feet 6 inches tall - weak of voice in an era when speech making was prime leadership talent, Madison nonetheless, by his intellect and his persuasive powers, was "the best informed man of any point in debate," according to his Virginian colleagues.

Madison, Alexander Hamilton and John Jay collaborated in writing "The Federalist Papers," which became the standard commentary on the proposed Constitution for newspaper readers during the Constitutional Convention of 1787. He argued energetically for "people power" in terms still understandably modern - and the thrust of his thinking was always toward broad popular government as opposed to the limited elitist goals of some contemporaries. About freedom of information, Madison said:

"Nothing could be more irrational than to give the people power and to withhold from them information, without which power is abused. A people who mean to be their own governors must arm themselves with the power that knowledge gives. A popular government without popular information or the means of acquiring it is but a prologue to a farce or a tragedy, or both."

Such sentiments, 199 years after Madison expressed them, have helped give freedom of information its vital role in American affairs.

"Eternal vigilance," though, is still the price of freedom. In Washington national security, personal rights of privacy and other reasons are constantly put forth as new reasons for curtailing, or "reforming," laws that generate a free flow of information. Here in Connecticut a model freedom of information law creates official critics and currently rides a seesaw of frustration as lawmakers first widen its concepts and judges then question its breadth. In federal or state situations the cautious citizen, remembering Madison, should never stop at "Why?" but always ask "Why not?" in any argument over the release of official information.

Finally, in any examination of freedom of information, there is the role of the press itself. The First Amendment Congress addresses these words to reporters and editors:

" ... Every journalist bears some responsibility for the fate of the First Amendment. People judge the credibility and fairness of the media according to the diligence with which we do our jobs. They believe that, if we are careless about little things, we cannot be trusted to be accurate about the big ones. Most people form their views of the press according to how often their local newspapers and radio and TV station's:

"Misspell their names; misunderstand news about their business; display insensitivity or inaccuracy during a family tragedy; fail to tell all sides of an issue they care about; refuse or neglect to publish information readers believe important or get the facts wrong.

"A Gallup poll done for the First Amendment Congress showed a positive correlation between those who have had bad experiences with the media and those who favor more regulation of the press."

Ways of getting public information have proliferated since James Madison's day - as have the public problems about which we must inform ourselves.

Saturday, April 2, 1988
Editor's note

Journeying With Pain

In the winter of 1936 I wangled a first date from the girl who became my one-and-only. She was beautiful beneath that evening's early-risen moon, rosy-cheeked in a cranberry colored coat and a black hat. I walked on air as she picked a less smitten path through snow-banked streets to the Orange Street bus on our way to the movies. My heart still skips at the memory.

The show was at Poli's Palace, the grand Church Street theater that made Depression-time escapism easier with its baroque marble balustrades, glittering chandeliers and acres of rich carpeting for 50 cents a seat. The feature film was "Ah, Wilderness!" by Eugene O'Neill, a movie with Walter Huston as its fatherly star, a first-rate Hollywood production crafted to follow the O'Neill play's great success on Broadway.

The story was all sunshine, a smiling study of family affection and first love, full of gingham, white picket fences and turn-of-the-century nostalgia - a tale that Cupid might have chosen for the occasion. Its mood of untroubled beguilement stayed with us for years. We were new to each other and to Eugene O'Neill -- but I pushed, successfully, the vision of that loaf of bread, a jug of wine and "thou beside me singing in the wilderness, Ah, wilderness were paradise enow!" So - we went to the movies again.

Two decades later we sat in the Register's reviewer seats at the Shubert - a wedding, a world war and the births of three children behind us. Again it was Eugene O'Neill's genius in the spotlight, this time in one of the greatest but darkest of American dramas, "Long Day's Journey Into Night."

Everything bright and promising in the earlier play, including a setting during the same years in the same New London house, was transformed by 1956 into tormented, unredeemable anger and pain. Love's cheerful understandings had, in O'Neill's new focus, turned to ashen, anguished accusations drawn from the struggle within his own family. He offered us, unflinchingly, a fragile, pious, morphine-addicted mother; his father, an oldtime matinee idol, domineering and vain and miserly; his eldest brother, a self-destroying sot; the younger son bedeviled like O'Neill himself.

The play was, and is, a theatrical experience that can be excruciating in its demands on all who confront it, including the audience. But its brooding sadness and lacerating language, its personal grief and mutual guilt, its awful realization of failed affections, lift it to the highest levels of tragic drama.

We saw it that night in 1956, shared its agonies, strained for ways' to express its meaning and impact in a pre-Broadway review - and once again O'Neill had left a mark on our lives together.

Both of those plays are now being performed for the Yale Repertory at the old university theater on York Street. The distinguished company, directed by Long Wharfs Arvin Brown in "Ah, Wilderness!" and by the original 1956 director, Jose Quintero, in "Long Day's Journey," celebrates the 100th anniversary of Eugene O'Neill's birth with local performances through May 21. Then the linked performances move on to New York's First International Festival of the Arts.

The tribute to our greatest American playwright is significant because the two family plays have never quite been linked in this way. One, as O'Neill said, painted life "the way I would have liked it to be." The other was so emotionally draining that he sometimes had to be helped to bed after working on it.

Though both themes, the bright and the dark, comedic and tragic, remain vibrant in our personal memories, old Time has also left its mark in our house. My wife's illness means that I must now see these new productions in the theater for both of us, then tell her what fresh perceptions another staging has given us to share.

The newspaper angle in all this is the fact that Eugene O'Neill was a cub reporter in New London, working for the defunct Telegram, when he first turned to writing as a profession. The more-or-less "local" angle is that he was a recuperating tuberculosis patient at the Gaylord Sanitarium in Wallingford when he decided that play writing would be his life's serious pursuit.

His biographers report that O'Neill, sick and sanitarium bound in December 1912, got off the train at New Haven with his father and a nurse. Always alert to dark omens, he watched a baggage truck with three coffins roll across their path. "My God, what a reception," she remembered his saying. He was 24 then, with 41 more years to live.

Eugene O'Neill was born on Oct. 16, 1888, in a hotel at Broadway and 43rd Street, New York. His father, James O'Neill, was a successful actor who played from city to city in heroic melodramas of the day. His mother was the convent-educated daughter of prosperous Midwestern stock. She and her two sons traveled with their "star" and his troupe, maintaining family constancy despite the burdens of one- and two-night stands most of the year. Their release came in the summertime when for many years they spent at least three months, without travel, in a home facing Long Island Sound at New London. The old house still stands.

It was in this house that the mother withdrew into infirmity, the actor-father struggled with age and fading magnetism, and the two sons -- high-strung and intelligent -- wrestled separately with the demons of childhood and manhood. Over and over in O'Neill's work there are echoes of the strife and strain and humor, love and resentment and fear, that he first pondered in the Monte Cristo cottage.

Four times a Pulitzer Prize winner, once a Nobel awardee, O'Neill now has his most lasting links with academic scholarship here at Yale. The only honorary degree he ever accepted came in 1926 from Yale, and when he died in 1953 his literary papers were left to the university.

The Yale degree hailed O'Neill "as a creative contributor of new and moving forms to one of the oldest of the arts and as the first American playwright to receive both wide and serious recognition upon the stage of Europe." That 60-year-old citation explains this year's celebrations, too - and the laughter and human anguish they renew in O'Neill's impassioned terms.

Saturday, December 29, 1984
Editor's note

Living By The Bells

Bells and St. Nicholas at Christmas, bells and the New Year's coming are symbols we all share. The bells in this report written for the Register 40 years ago, in 1944, marked off the hours in simpler lives, in a Filipino village just beyond the Pacific battles of World War II (And after this - I promise no more war stories for a while.)

Somewhere in the Philippines - I've used up quite a few words in recent months telling you about the sounds of war - the noises of planes, of guns ... the hot-foot bounce and rattle of jeeps, the smooth 90-octane swoosh of amphibious ducks, the rasp and ramp-thud of LST and barge come in to shore, the thunderous clank of bulldozers carving out a strip - and when the strip was done, the mounting predawn roar of airplane engines warming up....

But in the quiet of this little guerrilla town, (San Nicolas in northern Luzon), behind the lines of the beleaguered Japanese, our small air commando group has stepped out of this century....

Bells still measure living in the outer Philippine provinces. At the close of the long dreary night shift they break the sunrise stillness; they sing at 7, and at 8, they call the students schoolwards....

And all through the day, and the night, as the bells punctuate village activities, there are other quiet sounds like echoes from the Middle Ages.

Over this village looms an ancient church - a crumbling (Spanish) product of the 17th century ... fronted by a mossy, walled court. The thick old wall, made of flat, heavy bricks covered with scaling mortar has crumbled away in many places. And through its ragged gaps each early morning comes a herd of dancing goats, black and brown and white and spotted ... Their small, mincing hooves pick delicately at the time-worn wall as they bound like frisky pagans into the garden stillness...

Then their barefoot herder, bamboo crook in hand, speaks softly to the old goats, and with a muffled clatter of hooves (they move) to greener fields outside the town. The kids caper down the road with small, proud steps like children learning ballet, and after them through the village they haul the hesitant day.

At the end of the square the great hand-pump - big enough to keep a 5 or 6- year old swinging up and down steadily – begins to creak, and the women and girls come down the road, like Rebecca, with water jars upon their heads. The village stirs, and the 7 o'clock bells confirm the day. A few children, an old man or two, and many matrons head toward Mass as the belfry men pull sure and vigorously on their ropes....

As 8 o'clock approaches the boys and girls come barefoot from the houses. A barking mongrel herds an old sow and her brood through the hedge ... The school bell rings. And the pupils troop in to their desks, bare feet leaving dusty imprints on the polished wood inside the door.

The town is quiet again. Until noon there is only the sound of a passing GI truck or jeep, the creak of a two-wheeled ox-cart, the sweet simplicity of children's schooltime songs, and from a nearby yard the heartbeat-constant thud, thud, thud of a woman pounding corn.

Her mortar is a scooped-out, knee-high tree trunk, her pestle is a 4-foot hardwood pole, polished with years of use. Through the window you can see her lift the heavy rod before her, rise on tiptoes, drive it down on the corn, lift it, rise, and drop again. A soldier ponders coded messages and through the deepest concentration her beat continues, the pounding as strong and unchanging as the village bells.

At noon the clapper swings against metal in the school yard. The angelus follows from the church tower. Children's voices echo in the roads beneath the banana trees ... A bustle prevails all through the hour after noon. Then the 1 o'clock clangor from the steeple rolls across the roofs, surges through the glassless windows, ripples down the sharp-stoned narrow streets, beyond the bamboo stockade and the gate that guards the mountain entry to the town - and spends itself in the sun-burned fields.

When the bells cease, the instant hush is heavy. Only Americans stir the silence now. Filipinos squat on their high smooth floors of bamboo or mahogany, talk softly and rapidly among themselves, or they stretch out on a hard, cane pallet and wait for the sun to soften its white-hot stare.

By 3 o'clock the major heat has passed ... Children gather in the school yard. Teacher's bell clangs and a new class starts to sing ... Then, at 5, the church bells peal once more. At 5:30 school bells ring. At 6 the day is tolled away. The light ends as the light began, with bells. In the soft dark the water carriers come again to the pump, slim and perfectly balanced little women with long, strong black cigars clutched in their teeth ... They drift back down the roads by twos and threes ... In the houses cocoanut oil lamps flicker for awhile. Then they fade one by one. The quiet of generations of rural living rests over everything.

In our communications building where faint clicks and chirrups link us to the warring world, a monastic quiet prevails. The radio operators are locked behind their earphones; the code clerks cloak themselves in alphabetic concentration. The gurgling croak of a tree toad in the bamboo marks the midnight watch.

As the moon floods out from behind a cloud, a rooster stirs ... A long, jubilant crowing shrills through the town - but the message center clock says only 2 a.m. The rooster shuts a disappointed eye. San Nicolas sleeps on.

Generations of Filipinos, old Spaniards, Japanese and Americans have been a part of this stillness. In the morning the bells that all have heard will ring again, and their sound - for us - will prove a truth we like to hear proven: that wars in point of time are short.

Ring in the new, they say once more. But never quite: Ring out the old.

Saturday, April 7, 1984
Editor's note

Logistics, Learning, Language

Trekking into China later this month, Ronald Reagan will demonstrate his presidential role - and make headlines while his Democratic competitors are slashing at each other here on the home front. But the news coverage of such a journey demands attention to logistics.

Associated Press White House correspondent James Gerstenzang recently spent 12 days, and traveled 23,630 miles, to help negotiate arrangements from Honolulu to Peking on behalf of the print reporters who will cover the Reagan trip. Broadcast and photography specialists also accompanied the scouting party which included White House communications people, Secret Service agents, military aides, and the troubleshooters from AT&T and ITT who will set up the essential news links between China and this country.

Gerstenzang's share of the costs was $6,200 - and there was a 707 planeload of others to split the bill. His job was to contribute to a compact 5,000-word report - for official use only, not for news distribution - covering everything from the way reporters will be fed and housed, to how dispatches will be sent (by telephone but probably not via portable computer terminals).

When the trip is under way we'll all draw fact and opinion from the news flow. The scouting trip is only one reminder of the work and planning that's behind the "spontaneity" of a global summit meeting.

Five weeks at Wilbur Cross High School went into the Register education series by reporter Lynn Tufts. Though the news reports were concluded a week ago, discussion of them continues at many levels in many parts of the community.

Reporter Tufts' six-part series was directed more toward questions than solutions. Its narrative look at the things students do in the classroom, and the things they think about their hours in school, expresses more community challenge than conclusion. It documents the gap between the conventional concepts of self knowledge and growth that teachers and administrators are working to accomplish in our schools and what unskilled learners, uninterested and bored students, and a few of the genuinely alienated see as a lack of connection to their own lives and goals.

The reporter spent five weeks at Wilbur Cross, sitting in on some 40 different class periods, sharing lunch and corridor time with the students on occasion, talking to teachers in their classrooms and in their cafeteria. She did an extended stint in the library observing study habits and talking with pupils and staff about the approach to book learning in that environment. And, of course, she did a lot of background reading, and thinking, about the condition of education today and the general public expectations - or disillusionments - that have risen around it.

Lynn Tufts' presence at Wilbur Cross was known in advance to the teachers and was announced to the students. After a few early hours of self-consciousness all-around, she came and went almost unnoticed.

Teachers were concerned about gaining understanding for themselves and their students - and their mutual needs. Some of the kids continued, to the last, to be suspicious, not of the reporter but of the idea that their opinions about education and school operations should be of public interest.

The series, at the moment, is - like a stone dropped into a pond - still sending out ripples. It will take a while to judge community response, longer still to seek and get community action. But as a recent reporter assignment, it was one of the most unusual.

Saluting a public-spirited citizen in a recent column I said she "presently chairs" a state commission. I meant that she chairs the commission at present. But reader Murray Warner of Madison caught that as error.

The basic meaning of "presently", noted Mr. Warner, is not "now" but "soon" or "in a little while." Example: "Since baseball's being played, spring will presently arrive." It's one of those words that can trip you, now or later.

Bergen Evans' Dictionary of Contemporary American Usage says that "presently" as a word meaning immediately, or in the present, "has been regarded as obsolete since the 17th century but has been revived as a vogue word."

The Harper Dictionary of Contemporary Usage says that the esteemed Oxford Dictionary traces back to 1485 the use of "presently" in the sense of "at the present time". However, it adds, "the sense of 'in the near future' soon becomes more popular."

There are stylists who ask why use the word at all - especially, as I did, to indicate "now." If a person is NOW chairing a commission why not say simply: she IS chairing the group. My excuse is that in the same sentence I had made reference to a former commission chairwoman and I wanted to differentiate present from past.

In the Harper Dictionary, discussing "presently" in the sense of "soon", author Stewart Beach comments: "It is utterly unnecessary to use 'presently' under any circumstances. It's pretentious." Novelist Herman Wouk says: "This is a barbarism like 'momentarily' and" 'hopefully.' Let's fight it to the death."

What I wrote was understandable, but casually worded. If the urge to use "presently" comes upon me again, I will, and should, think twice.

Saturday, February 27, 1988
Editor's note

Modes Of Communication

Using worn-out phrases, Tom Walton, editor of the Monterey (Calif.) Herald, had a little recent fun. Have at it:

"When it comes to clichés I've got tunnel vision, a chip on my shoulder and an ax to grind. I'm madder than a wet hen. I won't try to pull the wool over your eyes. Sometimes I worry that I'm swimming upstream on this one, that I'm up the creek without a paddle, bucking the tide as it were, and chasing a red herring.... If I had all my oars in the water, if my elevator went to the top floor, if I had all the dots on my dice, I'd concede that maybe we're beating a dead horse here. I'd just let sleeping dogs lie and find other fish to fry.

"Let's hang clichés out to dry. Make them twist slowly in the wind. Let's get on their case and send them to that final roundup, that great cliché compactor in the sky. Let's lock them up and throwaway the key! Let's nip this time-honored tradition in the bud. At least it's something to chew on, if only we'll sink our teeth into it.

"The stakes are too high; we must not be left at the starting gate. If our feet are set in concrete on this, we'll all be dead in the water, deep-sixed by our inability to come to grips. Sure it's a lousy job to gang-tackle clichés wherever they hide and expose their warts to the hard light of day - especially if it's between a rock and a hard place. But I'm happy as a clam to do it. It's a tough nut to crack, but one day we'll be rid of these thorns in our side - Good Lord willin' and the creek don't rise - and then we can really live high on the hog.... Our language will at last be pure as the driven snow. You catch my drift?"

Right on! Tell it like it is.

Saturday, July 7, 1984
Editor's note

Old Shade And New Elms

THE ELM TREES ON THE GREEN have been New Haven's pride and challenge for more than two centuries.

A month ago the Garden Club of New Haven - as part of a larger citywide "Project Trees" restoration effort - planted 58 elms on the Green to replace trees damaged in the March ice storm. Members are still seeking private pledges, suggesting elms as personal memorials or even as personal Christmas gifts, to renew the city's greenery. Participation in such plantings, it seems to me, is a remarkable personal opportunity as well as a public contribution. How better could a husband and wife, parents and children, friends - for $1,000 - give something to the community that would reward givers, plus two or three coming generations, with a gift of life, of shade, of natural beauty and civic grace?

Our "City of Elms" didn't get its title haphazardly. It was created, quite consciously, by earlier New Haveners who chose the elm as the most desirable of city trees.

Nearly 300 years ago, in 1686, first mention of elms on the Green came with a gift of two trees which an admiring member of the congregation planted before the home of the Rev. James Pierpont.

Two hundred years ago in 1784, when our old town had just become by formal state charter the City of New Haven - there was a planting of elms along Temple Street, through the center of the Green. These trees augmented 250 buttonwood and elm trees which had been planted around the perimeter of the square in 1759.

And exactly 75 years ago, in 1909, a couple of tree-generations of elms having given the city splendid shade and a rich tradition before they declined, civic leader George Dudley Seymour was campaigning in The Register for continued attention to New

Haven elms.

"It 'seems to me," wrote Seymour, "that we should lose no time in fully replanting the old Green with elms, since the elms planted 100 years ago and more by the Hon. James Hillhouse and his associates are dead and gone, or doomed to die."

Three quarters of a century ago downtown New Haven was different from the city we know. Traffic was no problem; it was mostly trolley cars or horse carts. The commercial pace was slower. There were still a few fine residences along the Elm Street side of the Green. But, if there is a gap between now and then, one of the great community constants has been the elms.

George Dudley, a "city beautiful" crusader, titled his series of Sunday Register articles: "The Rise And Fall of the 'City of Elms': a Campaign Document Urging Spraying of the Elms and the Employment of An Expert to Begin Replanting and the Systematic Care of All City Trees."

Seymour's proposal, as presented to the community in the pages of the Register on March 21, 28 and April 4, 1909, was above all systematic. He provided a history of the city's elm plantings, giving James Hillhouse credit for the great tradition. He dealt at length with diseases of the elm and the silviculture most conducive to good growth. He supported a shade tree association and a city-employed "tree expert."

"We regard the trees as works of nature and able to take care of themselves, rather than as plants needing constant attention and intelligent care, all the more because they are struggling for life in city streets instead of growing in the open in the forest.

"When I came to New Haven in 1883 I was struck by the fact that the trees all over the city were mutilated by horse bites, which not only disfigure and deform trees, but lead to their certain decay and death. Even the colonists of 150 years ago seem to have understood this as we are told by Jared Eliot, who saw the Green in 1760, that the trees planted the year before around the Green had been protected against the 'ravages of beasts.'

Citing Henry T. Blake's "Chronicles of New Haven Green,"

Seymour recounts the first recorded elm tree planting in 1686. Two trees were set out by William Cooper as a gift to the Rev. Mr. Pierpont whose house "stood about where Temple Street enters Elm .... One of them was still standing almost in the middle of Elm Street, in front of the Bristol residence until cut down in 1840." Minister Pierpont's 1680 house was replaced in 1800 by the Bristol house, which was replaced between 1908-10 by the present Ives Memorial Library.

The "great planting" on the Green, under the leadership of James Hillhouse, came between 1784 and 1796.

The most famous of New Haven's elm-y wonders - the lofty Temple Street arch in the Civil War era - was the result of Hillhouse labors. Said Dr. Leonard Bacon in 1786:

"He brought from a farm of his own in Meriden, and planted, partly with his own hands ... the famous colonnade of Temple Street."

Says Seymour: "The last considerable planting was done in 1839 when 150 maples and elms were set out by order of the common council on the upper Green - which up to this time had remained nearly bare of trees."

After Seymour's 1909 series of Register articles, which were part of an orchestrated drive, the City of New Haven did hire its first superintendent of trees, and a shade tree association was formed under the leadership of Prof. Henry S. Graves, director of the Yale Forestry School.

It is that heritage, renewed 75 years ago, that New Haveners are called upon to refresh again today. In the words of George Dudley Seymour: "Our citizens are alone responsible for the neglect of the trees and they are alone able to reclaim them."

This year's "Project Trees" has a goal of about $100,000. Some $40,000 is already in hand; there is more than $50,000 to go if the complete plan is to be realized. The goal is to spend about $500 per new elm planting and to have another $500 for maintenance and care as each tree matures.

Gifts are tax deductible. The address for Project Trees is Box 6242, Hamden, 06517. For inquiries, phone 288-0819 or 776--6088. Keep an elm in your future - and ours.

Saturday, May 24, 1986
Editor's note

Poppies And Remembrances

They put more memory into Memorial Day back in the era when I began to pay attention to holidays. Fifty years ago in Fair Haven an afternoon march augmented the citywide parade held downtown in the morning. It was a small but neighborly processional.

The St. Francis Parochial School Drum and Bugle Corps provided the music. A hundred or 200 people mustered on Blatchley Avenue at Grand beside the maze of tracks and switches in front of the block-wide trolley barns. Members of Philip J. Brady Post 107, American Legion, gathered in the pride and slightly paunchy strength of men less than 20 years home from "the war to end all wars." There was a thin platoon of still-smart veterans of the Spanish-American War in their "Rough Rider" uniforms. And Sons of Union Veterans in patriotic garb clustered around the big "open" Buick or Hupmobile in which rode, waxen and fragile, one or two of the octogenarians who still survived from the Grand Army of the Republic.

These were old, old men, reed-voiced and shaky but often erect and determined in the iron Yankee way, wearing the romantically slouched campaign hat or the more formal peaked and slanted cap of their youth. By 1936 those Civil War vets were 71 years removed from the dim battlefields on which they must have fought, or drummed, as rosy-cheeked young boys. They sat stiffly in the May breeze to salute through a haze of neighborly applause as their car rolled by, the sons of Union Veterans marching beside them like ghosts of their comrades passed.

We looked at those symbols of honor and commemoration as the climax of the parade. The suffering in their war, and the innocent springtime decoration of graves Blue, and Gray, North and South, which had prompted this formal holiday, underscored the ceremony we owed them and each other.

Down Grand Avenue the drums and bugles led the marchers to the bridge on the Quinnipiac River. Here, with few words, a large floral wreath was dropped upon the waters to swirl in the eddies around stone footings and then to drift gently, a ring of bright tribute to those lost at sea, downstream and into the distant Sound.

"Counter ... march!" came the order in front of Roland T. Warner's hardware store, and back up the slope to Clinton Avenue went the columns, off Grand's sunny commerce into the shady residential heart of the old oyster town. The parade passed beneath tall trees, by wide-porched houses where flags were flying and families waved. At Clinton Avenue Park there was another pause near the great old central oak, now gone. There was another wreath, a reminder on solid earth of the sacrifices made in many wars by neighborhood boys, the memory of their individual promise and pluck burnished along streets where they once ran and played.

Again the drums and bugles set the cadence, down Chatham Street to Rowe, wheel left at Rowe. Soon into view came the high-picketed fence of the Fair Haven Union Cemetery. Inside the old burying ground the ceremony was deliberate, even reverent, as hand flags fluttered on the graves. There was a speech by some distinguished citizen, a few muffled words from the hardiest of the Civil War vets, a brief prayer, the comradeship of the rifle squad's three-shot volley. Then the sound of "Taps" floated out, leaving each of us solitary and sad beneath a sun moving west as cemetery trees cast longer shadows and the breeze grew cool.

That was Memorial Day in 1936 - pretty much what it was as it began in the grieving springtime peace of 1868, when the Civil War was over, Abe Lincoln dead and the South destroyed.

Equivalent community tribute was noted by the Register in 1936 in Westville, West Haven, Hamden, the Naugatuck Valley, North Haven, in all the old shore towns. Most of the marchers had also paraded earlier past 50,000 spectators in New Haven's three-mile grand parade from Whalley and Sherman to Howe, to

Chapel, to Church, to Grove, disbanding on Tower Parkway.

There were speakers, all veterans, for every class in every school in New Haven the week before Memorial Day.

Even more strikingly, on the prior Sunday, May 24, Yale's Sprague Hall was jammed for the city's traditional evening memorial service. The commander of the 169th Infantry, Connecticut National Guard, gave the address. There were readings:

Gen. Logan's Order establishing Memorial Day, the Gettysburg Address, the World War I poem "In Flanders Fields (the poppies blow ...)." An orchestra and a "patriotic choir" of 30 voices led the audience in: "The Star-Spangled Banner," "America," "Tenting Tonight," "When Johnny Comes Marching Home," "Keep the Home Fires Burning," and, among seven other tunes, the Soldier's Chorus from "Faust" and "Nearer, My God, to Thee."

The program and the songs, I guess, show the difference between 1936 and 1986. Twelve songs and recitations - we were a self-entertaining people then, not just an audience. Today, after new wars, we are swamped by intense high-decibel sounds and sights, our wheels and wings move us restlessly, and our old sense of neighborhood is submerged in the vagueness of the media-made global village.

We can't turn back. But the focus of ordinary people on memorial action and memorial thought is what makes those old times glow. Commemoration says as much about the future as about the past. So, this weekend, try to remember!

... If ye break faith with us who die,
We shall not sleep, though poppies grow
In Flanders fields.

(The weekly Editor's note commentary was named Wednesday as first prize winner, best column of its kind in Connecticut, at the awards meeting of the state chapter, Society of Professional Journalists, Sigma Delta Chi.)

Saturday, May 30, 1987
Editor's note

On Garlands and Memorials

We're ending a memorial week. Our Memorial Monday was followed in midweek by the reception rites for the sailors who died on the frigate Stark in the Persian Gulf. And soldier dead have been remembered - and their graves decorated - more frequently on today's date, May 30, than on the activity-packed last Monday in May, as is the current practice. There is a move, in fact, proposing that Congress take back the 30th as Memorial Day so the country can get away from the recreation-driven, highway-oriented weekend observance that leaves so little time for true memorial. I'll second that motion.

The first national Decoration Day was observed on May 30, 1868. Gen. John A. Logan, commander-in-chief of the Grand Army of the Republic, issued military orders about grave-decorating ceremonies to be held in conjunction with the discharge of the last troops who fought in the Civil War. The springtime honoring of soldier graves actually had started in the Confederacy during the war. Fighting done, the natural poignancy of such community grave decoration held national appeal for agrarian Americans in search of healing and new hope.

In my boyhood, 60 years after the first national observance of Decoration Day, there were still alive a few fragile veterans of the Grand Army of the Republic. They rode in the Decoration Day parades that, each May 30, were the highlight -and single public purpose of neighborly processionals to the nearest major cemetery.

Ex-soldiers came to the schools a day or two before the observance - World War I or Spanish-American vets in my experience - to tell children personally about their comrades who had died for freedom's ideal. And on the big day, as official wreaths were placed and the soldier graves were each marked by a small American flag, grown-ups and children also brought flowers and plants to place before the family gravestones, for deceased mothers and uncles and grandparents, after winter's leavings had been raked away.

The speeches, the flags on the May breeze, and the sound of taps at some time during the day in almost every cemetery paid reverent tribute to youths who often had died in places far away. At the bugle's sound men removed their hats, children froze in motion, women wept. But there was community connection also in the flowers and the prayers offered on Decoration Day at the family burial plots.

The loss of such connection in this restlessly mobile era probably helps minimize our memorial feelings. We might do better to take a step back, to duck the weekends filled with travel and trivia, and to concentrate on a single day of remembrance for the war dead and their civilian neighbors in their shared "gardens of stone."

Memorial Day parades in Fair Haven half a century ago assembled at Grand and Blatchley. They proceeded to the Clinton Avenue park, a make-do village green, before dispersing amid speeches and flowers in the cemetery behind the highsteepled Congregational Church. There was one short countermarch - when the parade, passing the Pequot movie house and the wooden post office, went downhill on Grand to the Quinnipiac bridge by Roland T. Warner's store.

There - as in this week's tribute to the sailors of the Stark - the loss of Americans in unknown seas for reasons hard to state was grieved as two or three bright-blossomed wreaths were dropped upon the river. In those times before the gentrification of Fair Haven and its river banks, there were clamshells piled at the landings and small mountains of Japan-bound scrap iron on the polluted sand. The fragile wreaths, spinning in the rushing currents around the bridge foundations, seemed aimless on the water. But they were intended, we children knew, to float downstream to the harbor, to the Sound, out to the deep Atlantic, and to the far comers of the earth wherever Navy men sailed and died - and waited for some signal of remembrance from home.

Such symbolism holds lessons for a lifetime.

Lighting the charcoal in the grill as a standard Memorial Day rite, I stepped from the lawn's bright sunlight to the shady porch. Reflected in the wide window beyond I suddenly saw my long-gone father's image. He wore the shirt and summer trousers I had donned that morning - but there in the glass, his age upon him, I saw the familiar rounding of the shoulders, the set of the head with its silver hair, the angular reach of the arms, the hands with their stiffening fingers, the foot and ankle moving cautiously on the stone flagging.

Startled, I laughed at the old boy and waved. My father waved back, laughing silently too. Then I was alone - with the confirmation that time had used the same matrix in aging both of us.

I observed something similar at the recent funeral of an old associate. His son, who moved away some 30 years ago, said a few words to the gathering. Then, as he turned back from the lectern to his pew, he became his own father. The tentative hunch of one shoulder, something of the trouble in his eyes, the way he stepped from the altar - all were precise reminders of movement I had seen many times before in his dad.

In this season of remembrance, a flower placed on a grave just so, a hand that moves across the brow in a certain way, a fleeting smile may echo generations in the bone or in the blood. A memory carried in the mind and heart is often, also, a deeper memory in the genes.

Such patterns of instinctive remembrance, as indefinable as love, are common in our private lives. They haunt us in the present with our past, and with the gift of sudden, mortal insights.

As an extension, the public function of remembrance - and a Memorial Day's basic justification - is to honor ceremonially our best shared hopes as they were and are and will be. To preserve and renew memorial patterns is each generation's challenge - "lest we forget." I think a Memorial Day can hold far more meaning than a memorial weekend.

Saturday, August 10, 1985
Editor's note

One Way The War Ended

When the Pacific war ended in 1945, between the dropping of the A-bombs and the arrival of the USS Missouri in Tokyo Bay there was an interval in which even a tentative peace had to be negotiated. The first meeting between victors and vanquished came when a Japanese delegation on its way to Manila landed at Ie Shima, off Okinawa. This is the mail dispatch written by the undersigned and published in The Register 40 years ago.

IE SHIMA, August 1945 - When the two white surrender planes of the Japanese alighted on this busy chunk of coral several afternoons ago there were few among the thousands of sky-scanning soldiers who could not feel history being made .... Men who had pushed (and not always without a great "Why?" in their hearts) through, the grime and heat and mud, the strange splendors and the bitter dying of a thousand Pacific islands, suddenly saw and literally touched a peace they had never quite been able to conceive, despite its inevitability if they were to live.

As two Jap planes circled overhead we stood erect in the August sun and watched their flight - the foxhole forgotten, the helmet untouched, the great coral airfield thronged with men, the oil-bright guns unaimed.

This is a midget island. If New Haven were superimposed on it, Fair Haven and Spring Glen and Beaver Hill would all slide off into the sea. And like all such islands, it gives the impression of being lower than the horizon, of being in the center of blue-sea saucer, with the Pacific sloping up on all sides of the sky.

At first the planes were just a sound in the hostile north. Then a flight of silver P-38s took tiny shape. And among them were the Japanese and their escorting Mitchells. Around the western rim of this bowl droned the planes, far-away black specks that might have, been a casual, unpatterned flight of swallows but for their sound. They moved in a wide horizon arc and then began to swing in from the southwest. As they moved closer, the tremendous hope that lay in all our hearts in August was hung in the sky. Men who had watched the planes of the Army Air Forces cavort and flourish through four years of war now saw caution on the wing. It was not so much a flight as a procession. The twin-tailed Lightnings, as supple as song when unleashed, flew straight on course above, below and beside our reined-in B-25s. The Japanese planes themselves, pale ghosts of the vicious Bettys that had flashed over many an American runway in the past, seemed suspended in space.

Sweeping wide across the island the formation came back again at a lower level, and the first of the B-25s peeled off and dropped to the runway. Twice after that the two white enemy ships moved over the field. Then the first one circled low and pointed for the strip. Several thousand feet above, P-38s and 51 s and 47s hovered like watching hawks. Offshore the destroyer which stood guard at the end of the strip scuttled through the sea, tracing a white wake behind the Japanese shadow. At yardwide intervals along the runways and taxiways stood our guard troops. And behind them by the thousands were the soldiers of the island.

The strange white ship, marked with the green crosses of surrender, glided smoothly down. There was the thud and lurch of rubber on coral (a good landing, though), and the slow-seeming air speed of the plane became hurtling ground speed. Almost before the first had stopped, the second Betty drifted down - the same dreamlike quality clothing all of the wonderful, terrible realities it symbolized.

High overhead, tiger-tense and ominous, floated whole squadrons and even groups of American fighter planes. In the lower foreground the remaining Mitchells of the honored escort group prepared to land on an adjacent strip. The Navy's "cans" cut proud white furrows in the saucered sea. And on the land were sunburned Americans, many thousands of them, squinting sunwards, each with a deeply personal stake in what the white planes carried.

The enemy ships were reunited at the runway's end. Led by an MP jeep, they turned and taxied back to where the giant American C-54 waited, poised for its flights to Manila. For a matter of moments they stood there alone in the sun, strange and inscrutable. The door of one was opened. A three-step ladder touched the ground. And the Japanese descended.

They were, to an American's eye, typical. Squat men in field green, they wore knee-high polished boots of brown or black and grasped the ornate swords of the samurai that swung - curiously long and oversized - from hip chains. There was an admiral in spotless white among them, and two or three civilians, one weirdly informal in sports coat, tan shorts and knee-high white stockings. An American officer gave them brief instructions. Then, as an island-full of eyes stared at them, they picked up their bulging briefcases, grasped their swords and moved toward the American military men waiting beneath the wing of our huge transport.

Flashbulbs flared. The warrior formalities were dispensed with as swiftly as possible. The Japs were conducted into the plane, and one by one they vanished within the silver shell. Within minutes it soared up over the sea, climbed to the quiet heights above Okinawa and turned south as it dwindled in the distance. The crowd watched it fade Philippine-wards, the final decisive flight in a war that had started so bloodily in the air.

(The next day) ... as twilight faded and the first star came out, the big-tailed Bettys rolled northward down our runway, slid out over the seas and - without circle or salute - headed directly into the darkness stealing down from Japan. These ghosts of war were frail and flimsy now, and even their big engines were dwarfed in the drone of the night-loving Black Widows which had the escort honors.

Flanked on all sides by the red and green lights of American fighters, the white symbols of defeat sped home across the sea.

Defeat, we saw - after all the blood and banzais - was a small, uneasy clump of men standing beside an outmoded flight machine, their hands still clasped on the bright, senseless sword of their ancestors. It was an unpleasant sight, but not an unhappy one. After that, no shot was fired.

Saturday, July 20, 1985
Editor's note

Putting Aside A Reunion

We were tent mates. This means that in World War II in the Philippines we felt we had enough community of interest and outlook to share the 12- by 12-foot ground space of an Air Force two-man tent -- and that when community of interest wore thin we had enough tolerance between us to accept whatever else might come.

Our association was totally coincidental, in the military tradition. Some time a year or two before our Philippines landing Nick and I - he in South Bend and I in New Haven - had both received those greetings from the President of the United States which launched a draftee into military service. A letter, in that sense, brought us together.

And now a letter - the kind that old comrades know is inevitable - brings news of farewell. On a sunny morning at summer's start, in a house by the Indiana lake he loved, Nick, in the words his widow wrote: "had eaten a good breakfast, seemed very happy, walked out in the yard and was doing his usual puttering. About 10: 15 he fell to his knees ..."

Ralph C. Nichols, stalwart Hoosier and proud grandfather, one-time cryptographer with the 343rd Airdrome Squadron of the Third Air Commando Group, retired at 64 last November. We had hoped to see each other when the rhythms of retirement had been mastered and he and his wife, Virginia, were ready to travel.

Now I will never quite know the man who emerged behind the youth who waved goodbye as the homebound planes took off in Japan - and who became a husband and father, an expert in industrial sales and personnel work, a Rotarian, a deacon of his Presbyterian church, a supportive foster parent to children in India and Brazil and other places. The Nick in my mind's eye is still my tent mate, a perky 23-year-old who needled me for being 28, a bit of a dude who preserved a stiff-peaked "50 mission" garrison cap spotless in his mildew-prone South Pacific barracks bag, a cheerful sybarite who would shower three times a day if he could and who liked to smoke a Filipino cheroot during the quiet moments when he was writing to his girl, a hometown booster of South Bend's major institutions - the Studebaker car factory and Notre Dame University, a soldier who took his code room duties seriously but aspired only to be a civilian.

The memory of war, when soldiers grow old, has two aspects. There is an ambivalent sense of its madness and futility, and at the same time a recognition that war's best moments can be glorious in their evocation of individual sacrifice for a common cause. Secondly, there is the cherished comradeship.

When World War II veterans celebrated V -E Day last June, or D-Day in Normandy a year ago, and when they turn to the 40th anniversary of V-J Day in August, the outlines of history are focused for them in personal terms. They remember themselves as the youths they were, poised between the dream and the nightmare of war in a strange place, observers of death's random reality. Their lost agileness and endurance and idealism is renewed in the memory of soldiers who were their contemporaries and friends. At Omaha Beach or at Guadalcanal, no matter how stiff the gait or how grizzled the hair of old soldiers and sailors, their eyes look out on things that young men saw and kept fresh in aging minds and hearts for four decades.

That was the common ground that Nick and I might have firmed-up if we had the chance.

Compatibility isn't carbon copying. Nick was a talker. I was a reader. He was a big fan of the squadron baseball I ignored. He liked comfort but pushed himself physically. I always doubted my own durability. Once on a training bivouac in Carolina lowlands the squadron was marched far in intense humid heat. At a "take five" break, as we gulped salt tablets, I looked at Nick. His heavy twill fatigues were dripping and inside them every inch of his body from scalp to soles was erupting in a sullen purple heat rash. After the medics put him in the shade they asked, "Weren't you hurting?" "Sure," said Nick and shrugged.

We saw some action together. Our C-47s dropped the paratroopers who recaptured Corregidor. The tanks that helped take Manila ran on gasoline delivered (in explodable 50-gallon drums) by cargo planes using Quezon Boulevard for a runway. Nick and I, a third cryptographer and a radio team, were loaded in among the high octane barrels, and our message center on the highway helped keep the gas lift going. In northern Luzon we leapfrogged tattered enemy lines in the mountains to set up an air strip first guarded by guerrilla Filipinos. From there our P-51s went against the Japanese on Formosa and monitored rescue missions in the busy combat waters north of the Philippines.

At that base the natives showed skill in building bamboo frames and floors for our two-man tents. Nick chose and coached the young man who could build best, and we had solid, dry, and relatively clean quarters for the only time overseas. When I got a letter telling me my wife had borne a son, Nick trekked to Laoag City to find a dozen black Filipino cigars as tokens. Later, on the little island of Ie Shima, off Okinawa, we pondered news of the atom bomb and Hiroshima and Nagasaki. We huddled for a week under a blown-down tent, soaked and leveled by a Pacific typhoon. And finally we watched two white surrender planes from Tokyo land on our air strip with an imperial delegation on the way to capitulation in Manila and war's end.

After homecoming from Japan we both moved casually, through 30 years of Christmas cards and rare phone calls, toward a reunion that was not to be.

Nick was active with veteran groups, so he had a military funeral. I'm glad, in a way, that I didn't hear the bugler blow taps. When the war ended I had a son and a few more discharge points so I took an earlier plane. But Nick's going-home grin beside the snow-powdered Japanese air strip on far Hokkaido - his last full-arm wave of fulfillment and happiness - was what stuck with me that day. It's what comforts me now, as we accept the finality of another parting, the folding of another tent.

Saturday, July 4, 1981
Editor's note

'Quiet Dust' And Vibrant Company

In Grove St. Cemetery today a muffled drum and a mourning bugle salute the signers of the Declaration of Independence in a memorial exercise that is more festive than it might, or first, seem.

There is discreet celebration at the grave of Roger Sherman, that sturdy New Haven enterpriser who was our delegate to the Continental Congress and whose plain name, confidently written, graces the original Declaration parchment. There follows homage at the grave of Gen. David Humphreys, Son of the American Revolution, whose organization sponsors today's observance nationally and has developed it since 1952 from a purely local tribute to a countrywide exercise that takes place wherever a signer of the Declaration of Independence is buried.

Flags and fireworks are the traditional marks of the Fourth of July. But the Declaration is the root of Independence Day.

The Sherman ceremonial was a Register conception, developed as an alternative to the outlawing of fireworks, after a conversation between Managing Editor Roger A. Connolly and William Prendergast, then a reporter and an amateur historian who wrote the column "Our Connecticut" for this newspaper.

The idea has bloomed in the ensuing 30 years. New Haven is proud that it originated at the grave of Sherman. Newspaper people are proud that it had its roots in thoughtful local journalism. Bill Prendergast had a hand in today's planning, as he has done for three decades. And Roger Connolly, who died, ironically, on the Independence Day weekend of 1953, has been represented as a participant each year by the Second Company, Governor's Foot

Guard in which he was a captain.

The Declaration of Independence defined the American grievance against unrepresentative rule, the cruelties of class, and the greedy domination of kings, and it laid the foundation for all of our constitutional liberty. So an annual salute at the grave of the New Havener most personally linked to that bold document is the least we can do to justify the light-hearted triviality of so much else that is done on the Fourth of July.

And if there is a place outside of Philadelphia and Independence Hall better-suited for such salute than the Grove Street Cemetery - anywhere in the country - I'd be surprised.

Almost everything memorable in the flesh-and blood history of New Haven - and, by extension, of our country - is briefly touched in these 17 acres so close to the center of our city . Almost every stone and grave marker reflects in some way the pilgrim passage of our American ancestors over 150 years.

Emily Dickinson, the poet who made lyric the dry wit and practical insight of the New England Yankee said of an Amherst burying ground:

"This quiet dust was gentlemen and ladies,
And lads and girls;
Was laughter, and ability, and sighing,
And frocks and curls.
This passive place a summer's nimble mansion,
Where bloom and bees
Fulfilled their Oriental circuit,
Then ceased like these."

And in an almost Dickinsonian turn of phrase New Haven's 19th Century historian of this cemetery, Ellen Strong Bartlett, wrote about those old New Haveners who came to rest in this pleasant "neighborhood of death."

"An afternoon stroll, particularly in the blooming spring or in the leafy summer re-enforces the sense of neighborliness and of things shared across the generations. Up and down the streets we find that remarkable catalogue of special names and special deeds that make the place a distillation of national as well as community history."

Starting at Roger Sherman's grave on this Independence Day, the deeds, the decades, and the records of public dedication run away in all directions and in all degrees.

The Who's Who is impressive:

Eli Whitney, the inventor of the cotton gin and the man whose rifle was built from the first interchangeable parts of the industrial age.

Charles Goodyear, who discovered the way to vulcanize rubber and thus put the world on soft-rolling wheels.

Naphtali Daggett, the crusty Yale President emeritus who was pummeled and stabbed by British troops when he tried to hold them off with a blunderbuss at Allingtown hill during their invasion.

Noah Webster, in the grave lot next to Whitney's, the compiler of the first dictionary of the American language - an insistent scholar. The apocryphal story says that when his wife came upon him flirting with the housemaid she remarked: "Mr. Webster, I am surprised." Noah replied: "My dear, it is I who am surprised. You are astonished."

Ithiel Towne, the great church architect who built the first truss bridge in the world at Lake Whitney. He died in 1844. Next to him E. Wight Bakke who died in 1971 and is memorialized for his Twentieth Century honing of the new management skill of arbitration ..

Admiral Andrew Foote, who created a steam-run navy after the Civil War.

Out by the gate, Yehudi Ashmun, whose energy created the colony of Liberia in Africa and whose Colonization Society foresaw before the Civil War the beginnings of today's search for black identity and ethnic pride.

Jedidiah Morse, Yale scholar and the father of American geography.

Samuel W. Johnson who envisioned and helped establish the country's first Agricultural Experiment Station in this city. Out by the Canal Street wall Theodore Dwight Woolsey, Yale's 10th president, and A. Whitney Griswold, its 16th.

Josiah Willard Gibbs, the strange, reclusive, far out thinker who in 1858 discovered the laws of chemical equilibrium - an Einstein for his time.

James Hillhouse, the man of practical politics, a U.S. senator, the tree-lover who made this the Elm City, the organizer who made the New Haven Burying Ground - this Grove Street Cemetery - a workable entity after others had floundered in its planning.

Eli Whitney Blake, inventor of the stone crusher that made possible Connecticut's traprock industry and launched our American faith in hard-surfaced roads leading everywhere. The great five-foot cube of stone upon his grave is almost a denial of the chips and nuggets which made his fortune.

Pert Margaret Mansfield, first wife of Benedict Arnold. Margaret was helpmate to the impatient patriot who heard the news of Concord and Lexington and demanded the keys to New Haven's powder house. It is useless now to speculate, but his shame at West Point - rooted again in impatience - might never have emerged if Margaret Mansfield had lived and tempered his hot spirit.

There are so many others: Yale President Ezra Stiles who watched and chronicled the British. invasion of New Haven from his town's highest; steeple; General David Wooster, one of the Revolution's primary warriors; Hiram Bingham, pioneer missionary to Hawaii; David Humphreys, Yale 1771, Washington's youngest and smartest aide, a renaissance man for a revolutionary time; Joseph Earl Sheffield who founded Yale's scientific and engineering school; Benjamin Silliman; the wife of Jonathan Trumbull, the artist; the widow of Samuel F.B. Morse who invented the telegraph; and out at the back of the burial ground, Ann Gerry, the widow of Elbridge Gerry who signed the Declaration of Independence for Massachusetts.

The roster is filled with names that made Yale into a great university. And there is the other long roster of family names - Woolsey, Dana, Day, Dwight, Winthrop, Farnam, Trowbridge, Townshend, and many others - that gave New Haven an Athenian grace in a frontier nation and serve it still.

On any day, not just today, impressions and emotions are tripped by a visit to this "summer's nimble mansion." The obelisks push high the pride and power of old families vying with each other in the cemetery block opened when Cleopatra's Needle was a world wonder. There is a cast iron monument or two, laurel and ivy and boxwood for the shady places.

A stray student, perhaps from the Law School, reclines in study under a tree. There are the inevitable joggers - prompting wonder, presumably, among these silent watchers from an earlier time, when all energy and muscle power were needed for each day's physical demands. The bell on the Egyptian gate still tolls for the rare burials or public ceremonies. The city birds make city music and the street sounds are muted by the wall and the grilled iron fencing.

Look what we've got! goes the civic-booster jingle for today. From the burial ground we hear the cheery counterpoint: Look what we've had - as part of what we've got!

Frederick Brewster Estate, *1910, Whitney Avenue at Hamden town line. A 66-room mansion, razed after the owners died and the landscaped estate became a park in 1963.* *Photo: Jack Stock Studio.*

Saturday, August 26, 1989
Editor's note:

Encore Music In Woolsey, Hall

The news from Poland this week has been full of excitement and grave challenge for the Polish people. Once more they are on the verge of something that looks like freedom. But for 900 years Poland has ridden history's roller coaster, plunging from self-rule into the depths of tyranny, then throwing off the shackles once again. The Polish land, mostly a vast sweep of plain between the militarist Germanic kingdoms and the empire-hungry czars of Russia, was without natural defenses. Despite long heroics, the Polish people know that eternal vigilance and endless struggle are part of liberty's price for them.

The headlines and current speculations about Poland's course reminded me that 50 years ago, in 1939, that country rode another loop on time's roller coaster. And that crisis on the eve of World War II was given personal impact in New Haven by the presence of statesman-musician Ignace Paderewski for a concert in Woolsey Hall. I attended his concert. Before that I wrote a Register Sunday feature story about the fabled patriot and performer who was returning here at the age of 79.

Paderewski came in triumph in 1939, as he had from the time of his first New Haven visit, in 1891 when he was 31. He traveled in a private railroad car, wore a top hat- in the grand style of European aristocracy, slept most of the day and partied when the music was done, insisted upon a darkened concert hall and a heated concert stage in all seasons.

For the Register's feature I had talked with Rudolf Steinert, whose father, Morris Steinert, organized the New Haven Symphony and brought the Polish virtuoso here for his first appearance. He was then the toast of Edwardian Europe and a sensation in New York. The Steinerts, who ran a music and instrument shop, were agents for all Paderewski's New Haven appearances.

Rudolf Steinert recalled that they once entertained the youthful Paderewski at an after-concert supper in Praeger's Cafe on Chapel Street. The party was an all-night affair as he remembered it in 1939:

"Several prominent New Haveners were present, among them Justine Ingersoll, the brilliant daughter of a former Connecticut governor. Paderewski was extremely gay and light-hearted and as usual dominated the party with his personality and wit. About 2 or 3 in the morning he expressed a desire to play billiards. The company set out to gratify this wish at the old Harmony Club in Elm Street. On their way through the Green, Steinert recalls, high spirits infected both Ingersoll and Paderewski and they indulged in an impromptu, leaping dance through the center of our downtown square."

The other side of Ignace Paderewski when he came here in May 50 years ago was his standing as a Polish patriot. His mother, the daughter of a Siberian exile, died before he was 3. At that age Paderewski watched the czar's Cossacks drag his father out of their country home to jail. During World War I he had been the official Polish emissary to the United States. And when a democratic Poland was established by the Versailles Treaty in 1919, Paderewski became the first premier of the new state.

But politics had less appeal than the piano. After a year in government he returned to the concert stage. And after decades of grand musicianship and poplar adulation, his 1939 concert tour was given special poignance by his age and by the sense that the peace and freedom of Europe were crumbling. That March Hitler had dismembered Czechoslovakia, and Poland had by then been high on its roller coaster for 20 years. A sense of doom was widespread.

On Thursday, May 18, 1939, my best girl and I got to Woolsey Hall early. Among other admirers we stood hand-in-hand to watch the musician-patriot - high-hatted, long-coated, the famed red-gold hair now a silver aureole - as he stepped from a limousine and was escorted through a side entry. He was pale and fragile, but not feeble. (We were as fulfilled as today's rock fans on Mick Jagger night at Toad's Place.)

Inside the hall, a full house was abuzz. The grand piano was at stage center, simple in its challenge. The platform door opened. An honor guard moved in cadence to place the flags of the United States and Poland behind the piano. Then Paderewski entered to waves of standing applause. After many bows he turned to the piano. The hall went dark.

It was a night for musical romantics. He played Haydn, Mozart, Beethoven's "Appassionata" sonata; evoked the Polish spirit almost tearfully in a ballade, nocturne and mazurka by Chopin; then turned to a Shubert impromptu and Liszt's transcription of Isolde's Love Death theme by Wagner. Perhaps his playing was affected in part by fingers eight decades old, but the performance was electric.

Register music critic H. Earle Johnson wrote of the "laciness" of the old man's sound: "The audience was loath to leave the hall or permit the artist to close his recital"

The Register Page 1 headline that night said: "Chamberlain Offers New Peace Policy~ Says Germans Should First Abandon Force." The next day's headline: "Rome-Berlin Alliance Invincible, Says Duce."

A week after our concert, a crowd of 15,000 gathered in New York on May 25 to hear Paderewski play in Madison Square Garden. The piano remained untouched. He had a heart attack in his dressing room and never again played in the United States.

Almost three months later to the day, on Aug. 23, 1939, the Hitler-Stalin pact, dividing up Poland, was signed. That done, German tank divisions rolled against Polish cavalry on Sept. 1, 1939. World War II began on those open plains. The Polish people were shackled anew by communist chains made in Moscow.

This week, as Poland stirs, the shackles are being broken and faint notes from an old patriot's fingers echo in Woolsey Hall.

Saturday, November 18, 1989
Editor's note:

Edgerton - A Partnership Park

Now in its 25th year as a city park, Edgerton - once the fabled Brewster estate on Whitney Avenue at the Hamden town line - is beginning to come into its own as a public treasure and a public responsibility. For a long time, it represented a memory of the Gilded Age, a place where beauty and luxury had been maintained at costs beyond the reach or the inclination of municipal taxpayers. But over the quarter century since 1964, when the grand Tudor-style mansion was leveled as directed in the will of Frederick Brewster, the 22-acre park behind the high wall has become a popular recreation center. Nestled into the Prospect Street ridge and surrounded by urban populations, it makes a sanctuary for bird lovers, tree lovers and garden amateurs, a delightfully "special" enclosed place for musicales or big picnics or other gatherings that draw grace from its lingering formality.

Edgerton today is a popular park. The police department's horses are stabled there. The privately organized Edgerton Garden Center Inc. uses its carriage house as a base for a wide range of education-linked flower and vegetable gardening activities while it works in partnership with the New Haven park department to maintain and improve the grounds. Using public and private funds, the partners completed recapping and repointing of the Whitney Avenue side of Edgerton's wall - a massive restoration that cost almost $500,000.

And this week the mailings have gone out to residents of greater New Haven from a newly established restoration fund committee. The committee's long-term goal is a fund that will keep Edgerton action-ready into the 21st century. Its immediate objective, working with the city's Cultural Affairs Commission, is a $250,000 project to restore the fountain and the once balustraded small plaza that stood in front of the great house and still provides a central focus for activities inside the park.

The Brewster house was completed and occupied 80 years ago in 1909 - a palatial English manor house built to a scale that was becoming obsolete as its owners moved into it. Frederick Foster Brewster was the son of a wealthy man who had reportedly struck it rich in the California gold rush of 1849 and who capped that good fortune by becoming, with John D. Rockefeller, one of the ten original investors of the Standard Oil Co. The house at Edgerton, on the edge of town, was Brewster's gift to his bride. She was the daughter of John B. Fitch, a prominent carriage maker whose own home was on Hillhouse Avenue. Margaret Fitch and Frederick Brewster were married in 1908.

Their lofty stone house had 66 rooms, turrets and chimneys massed around its steep slate roofs, and dozens of fireplaces, with those on the main floor almost 6 feet tall. Italian marble and Belgian marble, gold-leafed ceilings, a room with embossed leather walls, Venetian glass chandeliers, grand corridors banked with flowers and plants from the hothouses - these are among the remembered details of Edgerton.

The staff numbered about 25. It was augmented when there were parties for 200 or 300 guests. Even when the dinner parties were small, the Brewsters followed a formal protocol, a footman behind the chairs of every two guests. There was a gate house, a carriage house as big as most city residences, a steam-heated greenhouse, meticulously kept gardens, sweeping and decoratively planted lawns - all within the high gray stone wall. Brewster's wife was said to have chosen the wall over its alternative, a string of flawlessly matched pearls.

In his final years, Frederick Brewster left Edgerton to the city for use as a park. By then operation of the mansion was costing him about $100,000 a year. A careful businessman as well as a sentimentalist, he had seen the dilapidation that public handling too often brings to cherished homesteads. He decreed that the home be kept as it was until his wife died, then taken down, the site to be leveled and replanted and made a natural part of the grounds. He died in 1959 at the age of 86. Margaret Brewster died at 76 in 1963. The next year, Edgerton became the park it is today.

The fountain design and renewal that is the object of the fund drive being launched this week is Phase 2 of the park's "restoration master plan."The Whitney Avenue wall was Phase 1. Even without its mansion, Edgerton is listed on the National Register of Historic Places. It is, says the fund brochure, "a superb example of 'Country Place' architecture with its delightful mixture of long and short views, wooded and open areas, and inviting walkways." Designed by Robert Storer Stephenson in the style of 18th-century English landscape gardens, Edgerton Park "was cleverly conceived to keep the sights and sounds of the city out. ... The belt of trees planted along the top of the east wall (Whitney Avenue) ties Edgerton to the top of East Rock Park so that the visitor inside is unaware ... of any break in the forest from the edge of the dell to the top of East Rock. This visual elbow room is a rare treasure in today's environment. "

Edgerton has spent a quarter century growing away from its beginnings in privilege and its deeply personal ambience. In the next decade or two, given good maintenance and an imaginative adaptation of its beauties to civic needs and purposes, it can become an exceptional park. It doesn't offer a bleachered athletic field, a bustling playground or a pleasant woodland drive by car - all standard attributes for an urban park. But Edgerton captures serenity as a public resource, and it does that uniquely in New Haven.

A place that uses its wall to enfold, to reach out and soothe quiet-seekers can become a park to inspire pleasure and relaxation, new group understandings and new personal insights, for a cross section of citizens from every street and neighborhood in New Haven and in surrounding towns.

The Restoration Fund of the Edgerton Garden Center Inc. is

a notable way of bringing private and public initiatives together in a no-strings partnership with the park department. It deserves all the dollar support we can muster in behalf of the community heritage that Edgerton represents.

Saturday, January 7, 1984
Editor's note

Past, Present, And Future

Election year uncertainties were pushed to their uncertain zenith with the Jesse Jackson visit to Damascus the other day. It may well be downhill, as far as dramatic news goes, the rest of the way to Election Day.

Jackson briefly upstaged the president with the release of Navy Lt. Robert Goodman. Then he was matched by the old soft shoe routine from an undeclared Republican candidate as Ronald Reagan saluted his success and swept him into the White House for some credit sharing. The five other Democratic candidates had a less easy time swallowing Jackson's achievement, so they endorsed it faintly while attacking Reagan for making it possible.

The Journal-Courier has reported 48 presidential elections since the first one in 1789. The Register, founded in 1812, 23 years after the first vote, has covered 42 presidential elections. Neither has ever reported an Election Year launching quite like the Jesse Jackson coup of this week. And that's why reporters and editors with a sense of the old and the new take so little for granted in politics - or most other human affairs.

The way we were came to mind again the week with the passing of Catherine L. McCrann who was the personal secretary to John Day Jackson. She was Catherine in the obituary but for some 40 years on Orange Street she was Miss McCrann in the formality of the publisher's office. John Day Jackson greeted all his employees as "Mr." or "Miss" and even his closest aides and managers were unaccustomed for first-name treatment. Miss McCrann was his office major-domo.

In Miss McCrann's days that office was the humming powerhouse for a sole proprietorship. Mr. Jackson, as publisher and editor and one-man board of directors, (and honorary member of the pressmen's union) kept - into his eighties - a schedule that would drain 10 of today's M.B.As. He carried the operating budget in his head, the accounts receivable in his coat pocket, notes for a week's worth of editorials in his vest, an estimate of last week's circulation figures on his hip and there was an unending string of orders to be given or reports to be solicited from department heads.

Amidst a welter of other activities by a man of wide outside interests, Miss McCrann managed these newspaper assemblies and professionals. She would signal by telephone that it was time to don a jacket and hurry down to see the boss - or she might stave off too early an arrival if some colleague was being hauled over the coals by the publisher. This was a withering ordeal, best unwitnessed, because Mr. Jackson's meticulous courtesy at such times was surpassed only by his icy logic and by the powerful vibrations of disbelief, disappointment, and disapproval he could marshal around an errant employee.

Miss McCrann was herself a majestic figure, nearly six feet tall. She was isolated by the august nature of her job from the easy give and take of others in the Register "family." She cultivated reticence in dealing with members of the staff, and familiarity was the least of her concerns. But she had a presence of her own in the publisher's office and she was able to communicate it despite the boss's mood.

The senior editorial writer, Alden W. Smith, and I were seldom on the carpet, but on occasion as I moved bruised from such official encounter, there was unspoken reassurance and even some support in the way Miss McCrann could announce to Mr. Jackson the arrival of his next appointment.

Once I heard the publisher give her a torrent of instruction about things that still needed doing on some project afoot. He was always eloquent in detail. As secretary to one of Connecticut's primary men of affairs she embraced detail, and her workload was mountainous. Miss McCrann listened to his catalogue of urgencies and replied: "I'll do what I can in the time we have available."

There was no remonstrance, no resentment, in her firm and businesslike tone, simply a reminder that action isn't always as easy as words. The publisher in his turn listened and, by saying no more, acquiesced.

I learned much about discretion from Miss McCrann. Behind a poker face she enjoyed a joke. She was a keen observer, realistic and precise. She spoke her mind plainly. She disdained small talk. In a couple of decades of almost daily association with me she never once made personal reference to anything we might have mutually experienced or observed in the publisher's office ..

Little took place there that demanded secrecy. John Day Jackson ran two growing newspapers with enthusiasm and skill. He trumpeted his opinions and proposals with vigor on the editorial page. As a man of wealth he conducted much other business through his own singular efforts and those of his secretary.

As a woman of independent thought and substantial intelligence, Miss McCrann, for her part, made loyalty to those efforts her primary attribute. It is typical of her service that I have had to pay her tribute with words as much about her boss as about her. Nothing absorbed her more than the Register except, perhaps, the devoted attention she gave her mother and father, her brothers and sisters and their families.

When I think of unflagging energy and fealty, of what a good personal secretary could be --and can be -- I think of Catherine L. McCrann.

Later this week George Keeley, photographer, and Pat Keating, Naugatuck Valley correspondent, were buried on succeeding days. Both were fabled.

Pat was born to be a bachelor and a gay blade in the old, best sense - courteous to all womankind, gallant with the men. Dozens of news people who trained under Pat during years of command in the valley have held position of responsibility on the Jackson Newspapers. Secretaries and switchboard operators remember his gifts of flowers and candies in holiday time and his unfailing politeness in conversation. Others who became ill or infirm were themselves always remembered with get-well wishes and Pat's kindly prayer cards.

Too busy in Naugatuck to accept promotion in New Haven,

Pat Keating made a routine town correspondent's job a key assignment.

George Keeley was the second staff photographer to be hired by the Register, back in 1925. With the redoubtable Terri Altieri as his partner, (George endlessly and affectionately mimicking Italian-born Terri's fractured English) they set a standard for roving photographers, covering almost anything that happened almost anywhere in this state in a day when news services took no photos.

Outgoing, quick-witted, athletic and tireless, George Keeley in his heyday would have ranked high in any contest for the best recognized man in Connecticut. He introduced governors to publishers; he mortified young reporters by calling out their name to the General Assembly or to an altar full of priests; he asked judges to look his way during swearing-in ceremonies.

Any downtown photo assignment for irrepressible George was an unending series of shouts, waves, introductions, wisecracks and advices to old acquaintances who crowded every block. And he took good pictures within the sideshow he created around him.

Personal rapport with the newsmakers, personal respect for the news, and the willingness to chase a story endlessly were things Pat Keating and George Keeley shared. Reams more could be written about either. Both made significant contributions in yesterday's newspapers to my journalism generation's best memories of the way we were.

The way we were - in 1984 - has been the most overdone news story of the year's first week. The ceaseless commentary has even begun a run on George Orwell's novel at the book stores.

The irony is that Orwell was satirizing society's directions in 1948, not making a prophecy. The doom year he chose, 1984, was hardly more than a casual reversal of the year in which he was writing. Today's superficial excitement, however, refreshes a proper public concern about ways to protect ourselves and our individuality from technology.

Writing in The Quill, magazine of The Professional Journalism Society, the University of Kentucky's Michael J. Kirkhorn has a few upbeat speculations about Orwell:

"What would he have thought of us? First, he would have assured us that we have not been overtaken by 1948 ... Orwell might have complimented us on doing a fairly good job since 1950 of retaining democratic institutions and protecting our rights and for not destroying ourselves in the process.

"He might have been amused and alarmed by our trembling over the supposed imminence of his invented totalitarianism. Our quavering he would have dismissed as the silliest sort of peeking under the bed of history ..."

That is not a dismissal of Orwell but a dismissal of much of the past week's calendar-turning interpretation of "1984".

Saturday, April 15, 1989
Editor's note

Printing from Another Place

Advertising inserts, those loose parts of the paper that may drop to the driveway or porch if you're not a careful picker-upper, have become a basic part of the modern newspaper. They vex some people, to be sure. We had a letter to the editor the other day from a reader who'd like to buy a paper without inserts.

But most readers consider them a way of holding the nearby shopping centers comfortably in hand, an easy source of bargains and comparisons with clear and inviting illustrations of almost everything available on the local market. And the price-cutting coupons among the inserts can, if used, far exceed the value of the Sunday paper. Last Sunday's Register included about 20 separate advertising inserts. The total coupon value, if you were able to take advantage of everything offered, was $71.85. Where else can you find that much loose change for the plucking?

Preprints began to develop about two decades ago. Color printing on newspaper presses was then less advanced than it is today, so the glossy print job was one justification. Marketing methods were also changing as locally based merchandising gave way to nationwide chain operations in everything from groceries to clothes to hardware and home supplies. A single advertising insert simultaneously distributed to a dozen New England newspapers can move large inventories - ceiling paint, lawn chairs, snow shovels, shirts - through huge regional warehouses at a swift pace. Retail prices based on dollar volumes can be tracked and reprogrammed almost automatically. The insert has thus become an essential marketing tool.

Today, preprinted inserts account for one-third of all the ads in newspapers. But because non-newspaper presses do the printing, the inserts provide only about 10 percent of newspaper advertising revenues. The retailing industry is the source of 87 percent of all insert placements, so these preprint packages do today what a walk through downtown once did.

When viewed in terms like these, the insert clearly isn't going to disappear as part of your newspaper. Some advertisers are testing links between day-to-day "run-of-paper" ads and the weekly inserts. Like so many other aspects of "newspapering for the '90s," the preprint faces further development and change. But it's not going away. Continuing to shuffle and choose among those loose pages will payoff for most readers.

Saturday, February 28, 1987
Editor's note

From Sunset To Sunrise

The death of a younger colleague is depleting to an old-timer. There is sadness in the loss of talents that might have matured richly, in the recognition of developing judgment and insight now denied a future, and - for a senior - in the removal of youthful hands reaching for a torch not quite relinquished. Ed Petraiuolo, who is being buried today at 28, will be remembered by his newspaper peers and sources for his love of a lively party, his leadership in newsroom debates, and for the way he organized curiosity and cheerfully focused intelligence to find what was happening, and why, wherever he went. He'll be remembered among older friends for the direct and kindly assumption that he and they had common understandings to share.

My discussions with Ed were hardly ever personal. They involved things in the news - the Shubert, the Green, the local banks, Science Park or City Hall, The Palace and the Maritime Center, and these newspapers themselves. The issues were part of the news routine - and in that sense "professional" concerns. Yet every subject led to a discussion of people, of human needs and personal motivations, the reasons for which somebody chose this course of action or that, the unfolding connections and the past collisions that might explain a present controversy.

Ed enjoyed speculation and nuance, the whisper about profit made or calamity coming, the cranky calumny. He had hometown instincts. He liked to ponder old political alliances, new business maneuvers. He was a zestful questioner who could challenge you to justify a conclusion with which he didn't quite agree. Ed mixed camaraderie with courtesy in following his deep impulse to discover what made people tick and to record them, accurately and fairly, in their news-making roles. He was just hitting his stride as business editor. Then cancer struck. He resisted gallantly, talking when it was hard to talk, dredging up the old élan in spurts for as long as he could, working almost to the end.

A news person's paradise is full of unforgettable old friends from newsrooms of the past - editors and oddities, poets, tough-talking idealists and legendary bad spellers. In so personal a pantheon for those who knew and admired him, Ed Petraiuolo now takes his place. Dedicated as a citizen, a warm companion, good-spirited, probing, accurate, fair: his legacy as a reporter is his example.

Saturday, August 13, 1988
Editor's note

Front Streets And Back Streets

Community spirit for New Haven is better measured by the way the city's people feel than by the way its buildings look. Who'd argue with that thesis? Not I.

Two compassionate readers, Timothy and Elizabeth McGinley, responded critically to my column (July 30) touting four quick ways to see the newest investments in downtown vitality for New Haven. They suggested, instead, some sociological studies, mostly after dark. Begin at the YMCA, they proposed, and move out Dixwell Avenue to observe the inner city's problems of street crime, drug abuse, bad housing, high infant mortality and so on. Their letter (published Aug. 6) urged others to confront local need and to pray that "the vitality and generosity of Leeney's New Haven" reaches those in the rest of New Haven.

I've never quite viewed it as "Leeney's New Haven." But I've spent a lifetime here. I've enjoyed the old town's advantages and pleasures, the stimulating interplay of art, education, business energies and workaday bread-winning that, most of the time, have had a scale and a style that embraced all citizens.

I've seen homegrown civic leadership strained and diluted, over time, by absentee ownership, and then through the loss of many thousands of the industrial jobs by which workers and their "bosses" once brought shared goals in the factory to bear upon shared goals in the community where they all lived. On the "up" side, however, I've also seen some new corporations contribute imaginatively to a resharpening of community conscience.

I've seen how thriving neighborhoods can decline into mean streets full of alienation, threat and moral deprivation as well as physical poverty. I've seen decade after decade of elected officials struggling with constantly reshuffled federal subsidies to maintain the tax base, to entice new investment that would ensure employment and guarantee local payrolls, to thus provide all New Haven's people with effective public services and a pleasant, productive place to live.

I don't shrug off pain in the old town. The problem is that my civic-booster tips about ways to view New Haven's newer places - as symbols of continued confidence in our city's potential - and our correspondents' darker view of people in pain behind whatever facades we erect are both part of the same unending urban challenge.

Community prosperity and good human services are interlocked. You cannot have the latter without the former. Ideologues may argue for shattering "the system" that won't separate them. But meanwhile, apartments in the arts center or along the Quinnipiac, town houses on Temple Street, rentable office space at Long Wharf, clean streets and a well-kept central Green all have a direct effect on our community potential for educating children, for dealing with drugs, for nurturing personal health and for building hope among all our citizens.

So I'd encourage New Haveners, as the McGinleys do, to explore our people problems - but without the risks of sidestreet rubbernecking at midnight. Our newspaper regularly reports the pain and trouble that all of us, as well as the poor, must understand and allay. I'd even recommend the prayer they recommend - out of my conviction that the worst of the problems will respond best to spiritual solutions rather than to just a little more economic, social or political tinkering.

Atop these actions I have no hesitation in continuing to "sell" New Haven sincerely along its front streets, too. We need believers confident enough to put cash behind good opinion, to build taxable structures in an old city that still has much to offer. Civic conscience we want. Civic confidence we need. And both are essential to community vitality.

A week in Vancouver, British Columbia, has just given me

some comparative urban insights. Twelve times as large as New Haven, 237 years younger (1875), currently the greatest wheat port in the world, beautifully seated on a deep Pacific harbor ringed by high mountains, Vancouver is booming, flower-garlanded, with hundreds of downtown skyscrapers that look hardly 20 years old.

On an early morning walk there were men in boots and white coveralls power-hosing the downtown sidewalks (an answer to New Haven's midtown dishevelment?). The high-rise buildings are offset by broad stairways and many little parks and plazas, each dotted with innumerable flower-filled clay planters. A grown man could walk away with any of these pots (and in New Haven somebody would). In the heart of downtown, the Vancouver Public Library sits serene in a modern glass cube with computerized, supermarket-style checkout lines, a sign in the window offering job counseling inside and a placement service. Impression: dignified as a bank.

Mid-block jaywalkers and drivers who cut corners on the "walk" light are instantly ticketed. Graffiti-wise, the only inscription I could find, on the back of a bus stop bench, said primly and with punctuation: "Go home? Oh! No." Vancouver is full of young people, walking and biking, so its street spirit is informal. Its minorities are Asians - Vietnamese, Indians, Japanese and Chinese. It has the second largest Chinatown in North America - a bustling, fragrant Oriental village at sidewalk level, a neighborhood of seedy, grimy-windowed flats in its upper stories. The educational sensation of my week in town was hard-nosed study that said that the province had a 30 percent high school dropout rate. Its proposed solution: Cut off high school at the end of the 10th grade; make admission to the 11th and 12th grades dependent on scholastic achievement alone.

Such views of Vancouver are impressionistic, perhaps superficial. But comparisons with New Haven are implicit. They show why, even with fewer resources, we are challenged to improve just to stay "modern" like Vancouver. They show why investment energy and people service and unending attempts to keep the community interactive for rich and poor are as necessary for us as for our distant Canadian neighbors.

Saturday, July 6, 1985
Editor's note

Closing A Powerhouse

Just a footnote to the news, a dozen asterisked paragraphs in John Quinn's Elm City Clarion last Sunday marked the announcement of the closing of St. Francis Convent on Ferry Street in Fair Haven.

Like many other things that once were at or near the center of a very good life, the convent now has become an anomaly - a quiet retreat, nearly empty, that seems out of place and of doubtful purpose as our noisy, technology-driven society, beset by electronic amplifiers and images, heads toward the year 2000.

When I was a child, the St. Francis Convent stood serene on green lawns in a community that looked to it, and the school and the lofty church and the rectory beyond it on Ferry Street, as the core of a simple, devout and meaningful way of life.

Before the school bell rang in the morning, and at lunch, and in the afternoon when school was dismissed, as many as 20 nuns made their way between classroom and convent. We children knew them all, felt great affection for some and feared a few for their tough discipline. They were nuns out of religion's long past, women - who had pledged themselves to God, who vowed obedience, chastity and poverty as their way to service and salvation. They wore heavy black habits that reached to the ground. Starched white wimples framed their faces stiffly - but within that calculated disembodiment there were eyes that flashed and lips that smiled or turned severe. The humanity, the personality inside the roomy black envelope was never doubted. Around their waists were long beaded rosaries and wide black leather cinctures. They fingered the beads in quiet moments, and if heavy work was needed they cinched up their skirts inside the belt and pitched in.

Such intense commitment is today called activism and expressed in public statement. The nuns of St. Francis expressed it in communal prayer.

That was 60 years ago. The convent and the women in it were then a powerhouse for unity, diligence and devotion among the mostly immigrant working families of St. Francis Parish. Sister Basilia, who had a slight Irish brogue, could never have imagined a 1985 mix-and-match habit, with discreet cross on the lapel and Adidas running shoes for comfort. Sister Rosita, whose name bespoke a vague unorthodoxy, was lively but nothing like the "flying nun" of movie and television fame.

They and the other sisters performed the corporal acts of mercy. They visited the sick. They knelt beside families praying for the dead. But mostly they taught us, grade by grade and nun by nun. And their success over decades is hallowed by the memory of their students and affirmed in the city's educational records.

In mid-morning on days when it was too cold or wet for a recess in the firmly segregated boys schoolyard or girls schoolyard, they would throw open the doors of each classroom. An exercise record with metronome music and a clear voice calling out calisthenics was played loudly on the Victrola in the stairwell. And children and teachers on three floors moved their limbs dutifully.

When school was dismissed the pupils - 500 or 600 kids - marched to recorded band music out of the school, nuns monitoring all the way. Girls first, then boys, by grade, we walked single file for a block, up the street past the convent or down the street to the church, and a nun at the corner of Pine or Clay Street saw to safety at the intersection.

Uniformity was everywhere, but individuality was nurtured. The only identity a sister then had was the name of her saintly patron: Sister Alphonsus, Sister Denise, Sister Francis Xavier, Sister Assumpta, many others. Their teaching skills were probably unsophisticated in worldly terms, but they were dedicated to excellence and they had a sense of ever-present opportunity for those who would grasp it and "make the most" of themselves. Their sheltered lives were fulfilled in the way their pupils learned to live successfully - from books and from religious conviction.

There is irony in the fact that over time the most fragile of their accomplishments was the convent community itself.

The convent was never an accessible place. I recall once taking a note for some unremembered reason through the front gate and waiting for the large oak door to be opened - only wide enough to pass in the message. On Saturdays the bustle in the school was replaced by bustle in the convent. Nuns, old and young, in great Mother Goose aprons, could be seen on the porches or at the doors scrubbing floors or washing windows. Such a sharing of labor was undoubtedly as old as their order, the Sisters of Mercy.

That sense of community, of a shared effort in the larger world and of unshakable duty within a disciplined inner world, has been evaporating in our time of personality and ego gratification, of theological upheaval and churchly disarray amidst other waves of revolutionary change.

In 1928, when Alfred E. Smith of New York was the first Catholic to run for the presidency, the men of the St. Francis Holy Name Society gave the nuns in the convent their first radio so they could share the excitement. The pastor gave them permission to listen to the radio in their common room until 9 p.m. The lights in the convent began to burn longer - and though we did not know it then, we had a symbol of how old ways would be changed by the new urgencies and emotions that are the eventual fruit of all new technology.

As I think of St. Francis Convent in my childhood, I realize that next to my mother the Sisters of Mercy were the women most influential in everything I did then - and in many things I do now. The big brick house in which they lived, with its chapel, its long back porches, its sunny lawns and shaded yard may soon - and sadly - be empty. But the spirit sheltered there, and fostered widely, is more persistent even than the memory of those many good women in black.

Saturday June 8, 1985
Editor's Note

Reviewing the lively arts

Art is providing people today with a spiritual gratification which cannot be found to the same degree in any other part of their lives."

Panelist No.1: said that, and he added:

" ... Yet not just in small communities does this ghastly issue of boosterism raise its ugly head - where arts writers are under obligation to promote anything that calls itself artistic activity. What that really means, as everybody knows, is to lie about art, something that would be absolutely impermissible in almost any other area of journalistic activity. In coverage of the arts it seems to be permitted because it may be doing the community some good. The thing that would really do the community some good would be to hear somebody who knows something about art - and to let him tell the truth about it.

"These are finely spiritual values we're talking about (as art), matters of lasting importance. They're not just contrivances for killing time in the evening."

Panelist No.2: "If a performance is good, the public knows it, and they scream and stamp their feet when it's over. If a performance is bad, the people are not so dumb in the final analysis that, they sit there and listen approvingly to bad performers.... (If you're short of experts) you shouldn't send somebody from the copy desk to cover George Szell (in critical terms). You need somebody perhaps, to report about the concert, what was played and perhaps from a personal point of view what was seen or heard. But don't send such a person as a 'music critic' - two words that are rather dangerous side by side and imply quite a lot....

"I have in my own time as a singer been judged by a young woman who studied the flute for two years in a very small California college. It's unfair to me and it's unfair to the people who are reading what she writes.... I have walked into theaters where there was such electricity before, during and after a performance. And I've opened up the newspaper the next day and couldn't believe how boring the event was (to the critic). More investigation should be put into the hiring of critics. They sit and count the appoggiaturas at a Mozart concert - they're listening to that divine music and counting appoggiaturas!"

Panelist No.3: "One of the problems with arts coverage is that there's a sort of disease that overtakes a middle—sized American city and infects it (with hope) about being a major league city. There's a kind of checklist of what you need to do that. You need a major league ball team, if possible a domed stadium, an 'intercontinental' airport even if no flights happen to take off from there and land on foreign soil, a philharmonic, and an opera company if you really want to be big league.

"So art things are treated as part of that - and, of course, the chairman of the arts center, who's putting it all together, may turn put to be the publisher of the paper. And not out of corruption, or out of anything but good citizenship, when the first opera comes to that place, I think it's true that there's some 'understanding' given to the performance and maybe a willingness to give people the benefit of the doubt. The person who criticizes is considered 'nasty" or is accused of 'trying to tear things down' etc."

Some opinion from the lobby of the Shubert or The Palace? A seminar discussion at Long Wharf, the Yale Rep, or Woolsey Hall? It's the kind of comment we frequently hear from arts-concerned people in this area. But actually the sentiments reflect national views and attitudes.

The statements were made at the most recent convention of the American Society of Newspaper Editors in Washington. Panelist No.1 was Hilton Kramer, critic and author arid formerly arts and culture editor of the New York Times. Panelist No. 2 was the distinguished soprano Beverly Sills, now director of the New York City Opera. Panelist No. 3 was Calvin Trillin, writer for the New Yorker and the author of books on eating in America.

Taken together - even cut short as they are - these quotations give some idea how tough an issue the arts review can be for the local newspaper.

Here at the Register and Journal-Courier, arts events as news events have been taken seriously for decades. We try to cover everything that is produced professionally in the area. And except in the direst emergencies, our reviewers are experienced and knowledgeable in their fields.

I use the word reviewer, not "critic," because of my own experience and observation as a theater writer and as a newspaper editor. Daily journalism, always with short deadlines and often with tight space limitations, does not permit the aesthetic reflection or the background research with which a true critic can illuminate and penetrate, for the permanent record, an artist's creative urges and accomplishments.

The newspaper review is written swiftly for the potential audience, not the artist, respecting the integrity of both. The newspaper review should, in my opinion, aim at a clear and interesting - possibly amusing - statement of what the performance is about, what takes place on the platform, and how the audience responded, with an evaluation of the quality of the artistic offering and of the performers. The opportunity to criticize should be handled as a discipline. If, even in adverse judgment, the reviewer can encourage rather than discourage more of the hard work on which creativity is based, so much the better. Beauty and truth may eventually be the fruit of such encouragement. Discouragement is always barren.

Within that outline of a newspaper review, individual reviewers - challenged by their job to analysis and opinion - can run a wide gamut, from resigned acceptance to slashing rejection. So long as they focus on the public art and avoid private bias, they're probably on the right track. So long as the readers remember a review is one person's opinion, and not much more, things should stay in balance.

But it's not an easy role.

Saturday, April 12, 1986
Editor's note

Rituals And Readership

In spring, the fancies of journalists turn toward the annual meeting of the American Society of Newspaper Editors. This year it's in Washington. The president will be there for a luncheon talk. And the full range of current news room topics will be explored: from coping with drugs and reporter bias to good writing, libel, credibility and color as a news factor.

Dr. Ruth Westheimer will advise us on sex. Georgi Arkadievich Arbatov will outline all the ways in which we misunderstand the Russians. There will be a panel on the "Merger and Acquisition Frenzy in the News Business." Halley's comet and South Africa will be analyzed. Some of the smart young kids from Children's Express will interview some of the political celebrities on stage. There will be a reception at the National Gallery, a performance by Lee Iacocca, huge breakfasts, heavy lunches and unending concentration on how to make newspapers better. Back home again by Sunday. Tired, sure. Wiser? Well...

When George D. Vaill died last week the written word, everywhere, lost an intent and witty guardian, and Yale lost a vigorous sacristan who kept the altars of college tradition incensed and all the campus litanies remembered. Even when, as Yale's associate secretary, he was invoking, or imposing, rigid decorum at some university processional or convocation, George Vaill held his colleagues on the verge of laughter.

At the same time he cherished curmedgeonship. In his cataract-clouded later years, when he drew an outsize magnifying glass from his pocket it was often to focus an audience on some Old Blue historic fact that had been misstated or on some intolerable abuse of language in the official statements, the academic appendices, or the inside pages of newspapers that he read as avidly as literature.

George was newspaper-prone. He read them all, and he stumbled painfully over the misperceptions of fact or the misconstructions of language toward which his eye intuitively turned. We were fellow Bethany-ites, and his wife told me that an evening by the fireplace, with George reading newspapers or magazines, was an evening of groans and expostulations and hot penciled notes that later became letters to the editor. George's father and later his brother Ted were editors of the Winsted Citizen, and for three years in the '50s George embellished life in Bethany, Woodbridge and Orange with his weekly, the Amity Star. He never ceased his search for accuracy and grace in the news reports he followed.

This made him a constant reader of the Register. His objections and strictures became familiar on the news room bulletin board. On a bad Sunday in 1976, George wrote two letters, one taking apart in 10 explicit paragraphs a report on a testimonial dinner for Yale Chaplain Sid Lovett. "Woolsey Hall is the auditorium on College Street. The building on Grove Street is the University Dining Hall, popularly called 'Commons.' How has such an elementary point escaped you?" The second note criticized our use of a photo showing a weeping father outside the Boston home in which his family perished. " ... The epitome of execrable taste.... It is difficult to imagine what you think is accomplished in terms of public information."

"Dear George," I replied in part, "... I am purged, deterged and near submerged in the pure fire of your vitriol - and ready to try again. I'm sure you are, too."

And of course he was. A year later he wrote:

"Dear Bob: Although it has been reported that I am considered a laughing stock in your office and that nothing I write is taken seriously, I cannot refrain from expressing my horror at two bloopers which you permitted to sneak into your editorial column in the past week. On Sept. 18, 'Carter could care less'; and on Sept. 19, 'One standard for you and I.' Surely somebody in your shop knows better. Peace. G.D.V."

"Dear George: To answer your question - People in our shop

always know better, but the knowledge escapes them.

"Now, as to the canard about your not being taken seriously. We may indeed laugh - in the hope that you are also laughing as you take us to task. But the laughs are always edged in rue because, once again, you've caught an error that, for one good reason or another, we missed. Whoever used the phrase 'laughing stock' spoke crudely, unfairly and inaccurately. We appreciate being set straight, and we don't resent the right of any reader to call us on our misses. Keep complaining, curmudgeon! Keep writing, reader. We need to know that somebody out there cares. A common standard for you and I is the goal."

Less than three years ago, still undaunted despite retirement to Colebrook and grave reading problems, George wrote my successor, Don Sharpe:

"Dear Sir: The person who composes your headlines should be sent back to the sixth grade to learn how to spell," and then, still upholding Yale pre-eminence in all things, he declared that the three bells in St. Mary's new steeple could not be a carillon. "Until 1966, Harkness Tower at Yale contained a chime of 10 bells. In that year, 44 additional bells were installed to create a carillon. What St. Mary's will have is a chime. "

George D. Vaill's unending contributions to life and levity at Yale are widely appreciated. For an editor he was that special boon, a reader who cared about everything and one whose complaints always resulted in some improvement of fact or expression or understanding. George will excuse some sentiment in a comment like this - but if there is a word misspelled, I expect lightning in the sky.

Saturday, March 29, 1980
Editor's Note

Some Amendments, Some Abhorrences

The connecticut primary voting left a lot of good citizens frustrated. Many independents didn't realize that our primary was strictly a party-list affair, open only to officially registered Republicans or Democrats.

I had one telephone call from a reasonable reader in Hamden. He urged the newspapers to get about the business of educating the Connecticut electorate to this requirement. As, a voter of some 15 years standing he had not realized that, his none-party status would mean he was barred from the polls on primary day. He will make sure henceforth that he joins a party and makes himself eligible to share in the choice of a standard bearer and presidential possibility.

There are probably a lot of others in his situation.

On that account these Jackson Newspapers will continue to discuss primary voting requirements just as we attempt to inform the electorate of the Election Day rules and procedures.

But a cursory check of our clipping files indicates to me that we didn't neglect proper warnings about the primary. Away back on Nov.18, we had a news report with the headline: "Primaries Will Disenfranchise Many.'" It said quite emphatically: "Connecticut's new presidential preference primary law takes effect for the first time in 1980 and lets Democrats and Republicans do their own thing while disenfranchising for a day the nearly 550,000 other registered voters in the state who are not affiliated with any party. I found several subsequent news reports in February and March which explained that independents could not vote.

Now that the ineligibility has been proven in hard reality at many polling places, there's a chance that the state primary law will be changed to permit open access by all voters. If that happens we'll let you know. Meantime we'll remind you next time around that you'd better join a party early enough to vote in the primary. That kind of balloting is becoming more fashionable than a November vote.

"The second amendment" wrote a reader, "deserves as much support as you give the First Amendment." I do not dispute this. And I support the amendment's text: "A well regulated militia being

necessary to the security of a free state, the right of the people to keep and bear arms, shall not be infringed."

Like the other elements of the Bill of Rights the right to keep and bear arms is a concept fundamental to the freedom of this country when it was founded and since. For that reason I think that the currently-debated Connecticut gun control bill is too broad and too nearly confiscatory to be accepted or to be workable.

But handguns are a never-ending and constantly worsening problem in this country. The assassination of Allard Lowenstein a few days ago and the murder of a young man on Dixwell Avenue last Tuesday are but the latest, closest examples of the dangers and, the evils that accompany too-easily-gotten weapons.

Would the right of the people to bear arms really be infringed if an environmental impact statement was required, to go along with each handgun? We require that much public protection if' you're building a factory or leveling a country road.

Our town's newspaper problems and programs are the concern of this Saturday column which leads us to an occasional look at other mediums of communication. So last Tuesday night's television presentation of the Pulitzer Prize play "Our Town," by Hamden's Thornton Wilder, is reasonably within our purview.

The play was carefully mounted in the scenery-less mode conceived by Wilder. It was afforded its full running time of two and one-half hours and given a top-quality cast. Then the network shattered art with hucksterism. While CBS strove commendably to project the universal insight and the poetic power of Wilder's play, it cheapened his truth and it assaulted his haunting, deliberately simple message with commercial cacophony.

There were 45 commercials woven - or bellowed - into a dozen breaks in the play. And almost every one of them was a blaring, mechanistic negation of the gentle, enduring human values which Wilder sought to explain and uphold.

Wilder was a scholarly universalist, a man of the world who considered this his home community. He went to Yale - and came back often throughout his life. His father, Amos Wilder, was at one time the editor of the Journal-Courier. And the study of his Deepwood Drive home has been recreated, with its original furnishings, in the new Hamden Arts Center as a local memorial.

When "Our Town" won the Pulitzer in 1938 it looked back 40 years to the turn of the century in a small New England town. And now, 40 years after the drama was first presented, it has become the most-performed American play. Its simple, poignant pondering of life, love death, the truths of human existence, offer a favored and, familiar message in theaters countrywide. And though its Yankee spareness of view focuses on a New Hampshire hill town, it has been shaped as well by New Haven attitude and experience.

The core of "Our Town" is Wilder's effort to explore human destiny at the workaday level and to express philosophic thought in smalltown colloquialisms and routine situations. The play represents, he said, "an attempt to find a value above all price for the smallest events of our daily life."

On Tuesday "Our Town" was once again moving, tender, and generally uplifting, a credit to the artistry and care that CBS and director George Schaefer put into its production. But the advertising breaks that punctuated the performance were heartlessly inappropriate. They made a counter-comment on the endless noisy diversions that may prevent us and our children from ever again enjoying easily the beauties that Wilder pursued.

The first act closes with little Rebecca Gibbs, the doctor's daughter, describing to her big brother, George, the letter a playmate got from her minister when she was sick.

"On the envelope the address was like this. It said: Jane Crofut; the Crofut farm; Grover's Corners; Sutton County; New Hampshire; United States of America; Continent of North America; Western Hemisphere; the Earth; the Solar System; the Universe; the Mind of God - that's what it said on the envelope. And the postman brought it just the same."

The second act opens with the Stage Manager, who functions like a Greek chorus, telling the audience: "Three years have gone by...The First Act was called Daily Life. This act is called Love and Marriage. There's another act coming after this; I reckon you can guess what that's about."

Between Wilder's acts CBS started its commercial assault with a raucous, neon-yellow and glo-color green teen-ager on roller skates touting Faberge Babe fragrances, "the new babe in town." After that the progression in the wrong direction was unyielding - every message in some way a refutation of Wilder's plea that we reach beyond surfaces, to look and listen and touch one another through the heart.

The sequence capsulized and truncated:

The clean in your mouth is Colgate; a trend report on primary voting; the TR-7 convertible "sports car for the open-minded"; touchtone calling at the Telephone Center; a primary vote report; "a great gift", Black and Decker drill guide; Coca Cola classic glasses at MacDonald's with your Big Mac; a plug for "more to see, more to do" at the Hartford Civic Center; more about Babe anti-perspirant and spray cologne for the young and vigorous; a Bedding Barn superman special; this Budweiser's for you; Joe Namath with it's your Brut day; Cooking-Good Chick en, "you'd be yellow, too, if you ate this much golden corn;" Irish Spring soap, "to get a strong man fresh."

It went on in a score of other variations, each far wordier than the summary above, each matched by images more important than the words and more intrusive - crowded with loud, lusty, young, joyous, inter-acting, group-related, men and women and imitative children who had no links to the yearning, doubting, awkwardly affectionate people of Wilder's play.

Enterprising commercialism is important to television as it can be to newspapers, too. But this clangorous series of brightly colored, high-decibel messages was insistently at odds with Thornton Wilder's theme of continuity, accomplishment, and human satisfaction found in quiet days and quiet places. The result was discomfort and contradiction rather than comprehension for anybody who tried to follow "Our Town's" slow unfolding through the franticness in which it was embedded.

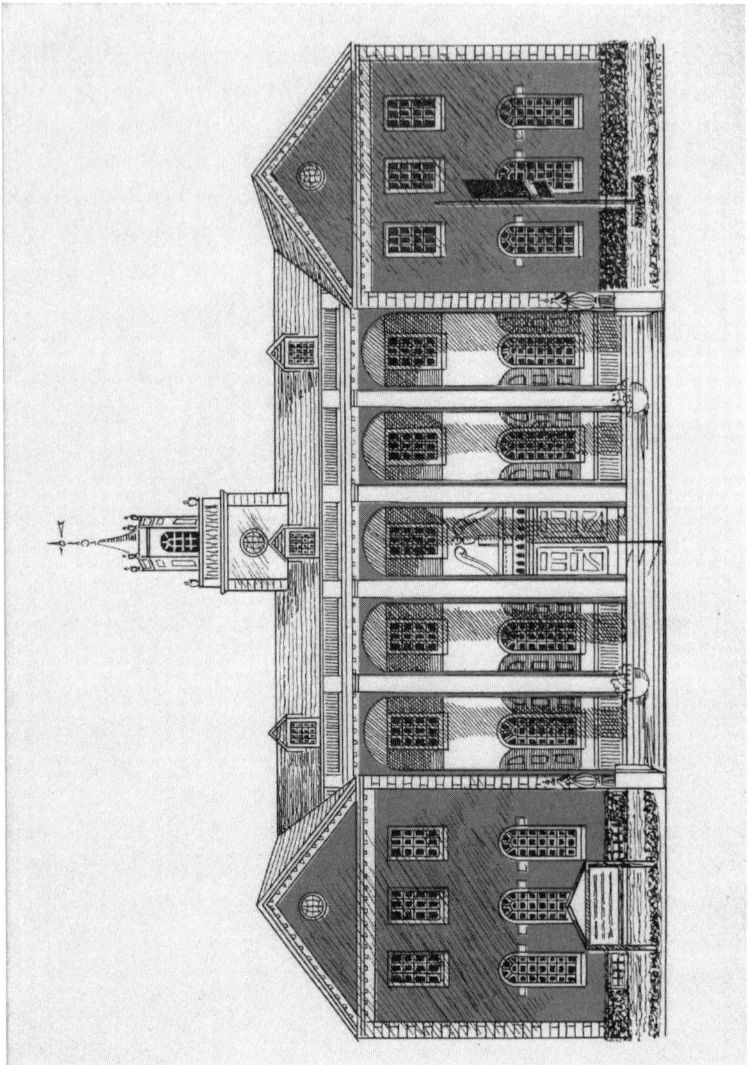

New Haven Colony Historical Society, *114 Whitney Avenue, 1929. History archives, antiques from the city's first year preserve here what we need to remember.* *Sketch: John O.C. McCrillis.*

Saturday, February 16, 1985
Editor's note

Some Dandy Occupations

"Connecticut is worth more than a feather in your hat," said the lady at the State Capitol the other day as she drew a bead on "Yankee Doodle" and tried to dismiss it as our state song. But the fact is, if you have to have a state song, "Yankee Doodle" is better than most. It's as recognizable and lively as "Dixie." It's short. It's authentically historic, not a mere football pep tune like "Io-way, Io-way" or "The Eyes of Texas Are Upon You." And it has a Connecticut ring to it as well as its Yankee reference.

The words, I agree, are a problem. A man with a feather in his hat, who calls it macaroni, doesn't say much to the Boy George generation or the rest of us, even though "macaroni" was the British term for "dude" back when the tune was first popularized during the Revolution. But the alternative state anthems, as they come up in General Assembly hearings, lack sparkle and any sense of fun.

I think somebody with skill should tackle the job of writing a brief modem chorus that could be sung to the tune of "Yankee Doodle" on ceremonial or festive occasions. This would not be my final choice, but to start the lyrics flowing I offer a verse found on a. crumpled shopping list beside the macaroni shelf at my supermarket:

Yankee Doodle is our song,
And freedom's our foundation.
Apply what's new, respect what's old
In service to the nation.
Land where Steady Habits hold,
And citizens are handy,
Our Connecticut we praise
With Yankee Doodle Dandy!

Saturday, March 17, 1984
Editor's note

Some Salutary Influences

St. Patrick's Day falling on a Saturday is a reminder of our Register associate Charles T. McQueeney. Charlie died in 1974. In the last Saturday Journal that he devoted to St. Patrick's Day (in 1973) he repeated his time-honored formula and specifically saluted at least 500 friends for whom he wished happiness in the wearin' of the Green.

The mid-March column was a tradition of Charlie's Saturday Journal. He did it each year with infinite care, working on it - as an old-school managing editor - in whatever time he could snatch from writing his own Page One headlines and running everything from photography to sports in the news room.

The new guard sometimes thought that all those names in closed-phalanx down the page were "too much." The old guard loved it. I had a chance to note the impact when my father's name was included in the year of his retirement. He bloomed in the warmth of Charlie's recognition and it was not only the personal accolade but the all-day stream of phone calls that followed which gave the column its extended influence.

For Charles McQueeney news gathering was action. On-the-spot coverage, not conference or questionnaire was his technique. Immediate fact from the mouths of news makers rather than research or file-hunting was his goal. His firm, fast, accurate, no fooling, nothing-fancy standards are still guides I use when gauging the news of this new decade.

In his last greeting to old friends Charlie - typically celebrating the O'Shures, the O'Markles, the O'Celentanos and O'Giamimos, and the O'Markiewiczs along with a half-thousand other neighbors - over-ran the page and had to be continued on the next. He wished the best "to all good Irishmen everywhere and to those who might boast they were Irish just for today at least."

Thus Charlie signed off, another Register St. Patrick's salute done. We didn't know then that the road would soon rise to meet him, the wind at his back and heaven's fair weather at his heels.

The memory and the cheery word stays green, though - and flourishes on Irish days like this one.

Saturday, February 21, 1987
Editor's note

State Air And Fresh Air

As winter's cutting edge softens a little, there comes a letter from New Haven reader Christopher J. Reynolds:

"I wonder if any residents of the Edwards Street School neighborhood remember the 'Open Air School'?

"Merely a shell-like frame, it held forth in the back yard of the conventional school and was completely exposed to the elements, save for canvas drop curtains. These were used only in the severest weather and at close of each daily session. Though (it was) quite vulnerable, we do not recall the premises ever being vandalized.

"The students were primarily of grammar school age and in attendance for periods of recuperation from temporary ailments. There was one teacher for all grades and all subjects -Miss Joslyn, who presumably has long since gone to her reward. She was an inspirational leader and made a lasting impression on her charges, the writer included.

"In the winter it was often necessary to brush snow from desk tops and walk the aisles in heavy boots. Writing with mittens on was no easy task - especially if the ink froze. Miss Joslyn was an authority on just about everything, and capable, in stormy weather, of playing the piano - with gloves on, no less!

"Despite the handicaps, our morale was unexcelled and many friendships were born here. In pleasant weather we had it made; every day was like one at the beach - warm, sunny, and with plenty of fresh air. There was never a school more aptly named.

"Even to this day, we always sleep with the window open." The link between fresh air and good health is attested by the fact that reader Reynolds has passed the biblical mark of threescore and 10 years. The outdoor classroom must have been operative some time about the mid-1920s. He said that some 40 children, from all parts of the city, attended - usually for a single school year when they were attempting to overcome the many problem illnesses of that time before antibiotics. Infantile paralysis (or polio) and tuberculosis were major childhood diseases then. Fresh air was considered both a therapy and a hygienic need in a day when indoor classrooms may have helped spread infections.

The old Edwards Street School is now the site of the Clifford W. Beers Guidance Clinic. An outdoor classroom today might be considered cruel and unusual education. But then, it worked.

Saturday, December 9, 1989
Editor's note:

Success On The Local Scene

The silver anniversary season at the Long Wharf Theatre is currently offering Arthur Miller's 1953 drama, "The Crucible." About witches, witch hunters and victims, it is a revival of the first play produced at Long Wharf and initially presented there on July 7, 1965. I went to the current production's opening night as nostalgia's chief advocate - since I wrote the very first review that went (thumbs up) into the official Long Wharf scrapbook.

Though there was no ceremony, this was still a ceremonial event because it rededicated the Long Wharf stage - by the ancient rituals of performance - at the end of a remarkable quarter century of community entertainment, instruction and accomplishment.

With a new generation of actors and playmakers on the arena platform, with artistic director Arvin Brown and executive director M. Edgar Rosenbloom replacing 1965's Jon Jory and Harlan Kleiman, a few audience oldsters and a sturdy quorum of the original Long Wharf directors viewed "The Crucible" through time's long tunnel - and were cheered by the light at both ends.

The Long Wharf story is one of the proud links between the '60s and the '90s in New Haven - local people making a bold leap of faith that has paid off. Between the first "Crucible" and this one, 203 other plays have been presented on the main stage at Long Wharf - a cornucopia of such creativity and excitement (with an occasional letdown) that the enrichments offered New Haven and Connecticut, and the American theater, can hardly be measured.

Since the theater's opening, 24 Long Wharf productions have been world premieres. There were 33 other American premieres, importations of significant theatrical efforts from abroad - so that cultural cross-fertilization has exposed us to drama from many lands. Some 20 Long Wharf plays have gone on to New York seeking "commercial" success. Four have been seen nationally on public television.

It wasn't all "Encore! Encore!" There have been bad nights and tough weeks at Long Wharf. There was a dark time in the opening years when the show of the moment was in deficit, the next show's budget couldn't be met, and serious talk of absorption and unified struggle was shared with Yale University and The Yale Repertory Theatre. But Long Wharf wooed and won larger audiences and firmer financing. Over time a risky community inspiration has become a community institution. Long Wharf today is one of this region's proud resources. After 25 years the confident goal is 25 more - in which, if the current serendipity rules, each night's audience, the Long Wharf company and the general community will continue to share "quality time" with each other.

As for the play, it was formally reviewed last week by the Register's Robert Viagas. "The Crucible" remains an intense and poetically effective look at the witchcraft trials in Puritan Salem, a continuing testimony to Arthur Miller's insight and craftsmanship as a playwright. Arvin Brown's aerobic pacing arouses in the cast a dark driven vibrance that stresses what's eerie and sensual in the action. It is gripping theater.

As a recognized fab1e-with-moral about McCarthyite political witch hunting, of course, the play carries its own unavoidable irony in this exciting winter when the people of central Europe are tearing apart the Communist Party and the Iron Curtain and any who might defend them.

For those who may still be looking for "The Crucible's" emotional freight from the '50s, I offer a program note of sorts in recalling that Eric Bentley, the distinguished drama critic of the unconservative New Republic in 1954, said: "'The Crucible' is a play for people who think that pleading the Fifth Amendment is not only a white badge of purity but also a red badge of courage." After the fall of Marx as well as McCarthy, those who at first endorsed the play, and later venerated it, may now be persuaded by shackle-breaking East Europeans to prefer it as 17th-century sociology rather than as mid-20th-century politics.

In my own search for topicality, alas, the stubborn uprightness of actor Frank Converse playing decent yeoman John Proctor - a citizen who might err in the flesh while remaining heroically unbending in the spirit - seemed oddly close to the public picture I've gotten of Lt. Col. Oliver North. And surely that's not an acceptable parallel.

Still, the theater's ultimate, human gift is to indulge us all in just such private perceptions, conjectures and emotions. And that's just what Long Wharf has been giving New Haven for 25 years, a shared experience that is first class, plus a chance at quiet personal judgments.

What does a theater like Long Wharf do for us? Much philosophic theorizing exists about "magic time." But I like something the late John Gassner, a New Havener and a Yale theater scholar, once wrote in a book for school students: "The theater, an enterprise at least 3,000 years old ... is the mirror that shows men to themselves. By making men and women share an experience publicly, the theater, moreover, gives them a sense of communion and welds them into a community for each performance, in this way making society recognize its emotional and intellectual and spiritual unity.

"The artists of the stage, in working together, themselves constitute a temporary community in which, like the larger community of the audience, city or state, involves mutual understanding and common endeavor. And, finally, the theater is the repository of all the arts developed by civilization. Writers, dancers, singers, musicians, painters, costume designers, architects and technicians of all sorts (with the actors) - they all come together and pool their talents and techniques to create one total art.... The theater is the school of life."

Second act! Please take your seats.

Saturday, December 17, 1988
Editor's note

Stocking Stuffers And Salutes

Looking at stocking stuffers suggested by our Register advertisers - dozens of ingenious suggestions ranging from perfumes and watches to videocassettes and flashlights - I was carried back to simpler times. In the years of my childhood there was never a Christmas stocking that did not contain two fixed items among the annual miscellany. My mother considered each stocking incomplete without one orange and one lump of coal. The orange was a throwback to her own childhood, when oranges were a rare Christmas treat in a working man's home; the coal was an old-fashioned reminder, in effect a warning, that boys and girls who'd been bad might get only a sock-full of coal from Santa. In any case, the orange was still eaten then as something "special." The coal went back into the cellar bin for burning in the stove. The major stocking stuffer - a hand pencil sharpener, a magnifying glass, a compass, a box of crayons, a spinning top - would be treasured long beyond the season.

The socks themselves were not today's red Yuletide ornaments. We thought that Santa would need each child's personal sock for identity, so an old but freshly washed sock was hung on the dining room sideboard (our substitute for a fireplace). The bulges in those knee-high cotton socks were as exciting on Christmas morn as the larger packages under the tree. And a sock in those times was probably filled for less than a dollar.

From socks and booty to the frugal living of the late Depression years is a natural digression. Across the Register's pages for this December week in 1938 spread a great grab bag of Christmas possibilities.

Those oranges my mother favored were selling at 19 cents

a dozen "fresh from Florida" in the Mohican market on State Street.

Dewar's Scotch whiskey went for $2.59 a fifth, and imported French cognac was $1.99 a fifth. All the popular cigarettes were selling for $1.39 a carton. Speaking of socks, Lowenthal's men's store was featuring "dated sox: 6 months of wear or 6 new pair." On the big-ticket side, Malley's advertised a Lionel electric train set, "with automatic watchman" who waved a lantern, for $6.95. An all-rubber Betsy Wetsy doll, with diaper, cost $1. Harvey & Lewis were offering pen-and-pencil sets for $1.75.Loft's had Christmas hard candy for 19 cents a pound.

The prices reflect the good side of bad times, the bright side of stocking stuffing. There were problems in the Depression. But there was also – marvelous to recollect – a general serendipity in which innocence and low prices were somehow intertwined and shared as elements of a life we all found good.

The name of Maurice Bailey, who shared those times with the rest of us, deserves remembrance in New Haven. He made the Shubert Theatre a successful, nationally known legitimate playhouse worth preserving and restoring - giving Connecticut playgoers more than 30 years of a busy stage bright with "hits." And he gave a quarter-century of unbroken service to the people of this city as a member of the New Haven Board of Finance when that board was the authority and the arbiter for all municipal spending. In his time no shrill, wasteful school board-vs.-mayor war over cash would have been conceivable, because Bailey spoke so firmly for the taxpayer.

If he were alive today Bailey would be halfway through another Shubert season, looking toward a 95th birthday on Jan, 8, 1989. That birthday deserves attention because it coincides with the Shubert's 75th anniversary and the beginning of the successfully restored theater's fifth "born-again" year. To date nothing has been done in the performing arts center to recognize Maurice Bailey's part in building the Shubert's reputation, and New Haven's, as a significant site for drama and entertainment.

Now there's word from Judith Lisi, the Shubert's executive

director, that a plaque in the name of Maurice Bailey is being considered. The appropriate comment, from my point of view, is, "At last."

Arriving in town as an infant immigrant at the turn of the century, Maurice Bailey grew up in New Haven's Jewish community, sold newspapers, went to Hillhouse High, earned his way through Yale. He got a management job with an old New Britain hardware company, learning there the hard lessons of meeting payrolls, dealing with creditors, fighting plant obsolescence.

Bailey understood entertainment and respected art, but he was also a certified public accountant, and his shrewd, energetic business methods, guaranteeing profits for traveling stage shows as well as the theater, made the Shubert and this city a major "tryout" stop just as the golden era of the American musical comedy was unfolding. His practical "show biz" attitude was demonstrated in the peak years. He mounted two bronze plaques in his narrow lobby. They were dedicated not to grand artists of the stage but to producers Cheryl Crawford and George Abbott, the legendary impresarios who pulled together .the money, the stars, the creative music and mountings for big shows.

In civic terms Maurice Bailey was also an "original." He was appointed to the city Board of Finance in 1952 by Mayor William C. Celentano. It was probably the last significant act by a Republican here before the continuing 35-year dominance of .Democrats set in at City Hall. Bailey's acumen worked as well municipally as at the Shubert. He held the job for 25 years, avoiding the limelight but endlessly analyzing Finance Board options and tirelessly asking people, from mayors to bookkeepers, if they could justify expenses to the taxpayers as well as to him.

A no-nonsense enterpriser, who believed in accountability, straight talk, and balanced books, he created a magical place at the old Shubert by putting such undramatic ideas in service to theatricality. The new Shubert, for all the difference in its "mission," could not invoke a sounder example or honor a more worthy patron of the drama.

Saturday, July 27, 1985
Editor's note

Taking Tapes, Taking Trains

The Beirut hostage tapes that have just been subpoenaed at the television networks by the Justice Department are a unique news record. But even if the pictures and the information broadcast are readily within the government's reach, the original and unedited tapes may be another matter.

News gatherers place no restraint upon the news as published or broadcast, but the added information that may be put in the file through private or personal investigations has - as journalists argue it - the protection of the First Amendment. It can be kept private.

The performance of all television broadcasters during the hostage crisis has been praised in some respects and questioned in others, because the events were conceived for the camera by the terrorists. There has been a clear expectation among Americans that the networks would launch a review of the things that seemed informative and the things that seemed manipulated in hijack coverage.

The federal subpoena injects a new note into this review. While declaring a willingness to cooperate fully, the television people are right, I think, in saying they want to consider the subpoena carefully before giving officials what constitute their unselected news notes and working materials. The precedent could be significant in domestic as well as foreign news coverage.

On the other hand, terrorists everywhere must find some new inhibition in this Justice Department action. Any assumption that they can blatantly exploit or extort news coverage, make deals with American television, or duck the reach of the law, is punctured by the federal indication that the United States will dig for all the facts it can get in pursuit of indictment. This, in itself, may be an anti-terrorist therapy.

The old railroad station made news the other day as it became our new railroad station. The glowing restoration of the terminal designed by Cass Gilbert - first opened in 1920 and abandoned and boarded up in 1973 - is a reminder of the beauty and value we can preserve in old things if we respect them.

For 12 years rail travelers to and from New Haven have been forced through a subway corridor of sleazy plastic chairs and stain-mottled synthetic carpeting. Bureaucrats and a succession of frustrated financiers, who apparently were numbed beyond reason by the financial problems of the railroads, designed that hovel as if to show the pain of a shoestring budget. They succeeded in penalizing every railroad user and discouraging every customer who passed through it.

But worth remembering now is the fact that politicians and bureaucrats, working as public servants, beside the Preservation Trust, also labored imaginatively and patiently for a decade to put together - in ways that made sense and justified hard-to-get public dollars - the multimodal rail, bus and taxi project that has now come to shining fruition.

New Haven's Railroad stations, even in their heyday, have had ups and downs. Register tradition says today's dignified station was more the dream of its designer than an eagerly funded showplace for the directors of the New York, New Haven & Hartford Railroad. Having rallied public opinion and interested a major architect, having debated various locations and new traffic connections, having eventually constructed South Orange Street as a special extension to the station from the city's center, Register Publisher John Day Jackson and other Chamber of Commerce leaders were forced, the story goes, to talk very tough turkey to the New Haven line's president before he finally agreed to go ahead with the depot then so badly needed.

In a letter to the Journal-Courier in 1917 George Dudley Seymour, historian and city booster, wrote:

"New Haven 60 years ago was as proud of its railroad station, erected at an expense of $40,000, as New Haven three or four years hence will be proud of its new railway station, which, it is reported, will by itself cost about a million dollars, to which 3 or 4 millions may be added for further improvements ... "Today's refurbishment (with the addition of a large parking garage) is costing 10 times the original investment, about $30 million in tax dollars.

Gracefully conceived by Cass Gilbert, who did the famous Woolworth Building in New York, our own Free Public Library building and (says Seymour) the Supreme Court building in Washington, the New Haven depot replaced one built in 1874 at the foot of Meadow Street, where the new depot garage will stand. That replaced an elaborate station, built in 1840, between State and Union streets. It straddled the rails that ran under Chapel Street and had a 140-foot bell tower and a gas-illuminated clock to keep travelers on time.

Of that old station George Dudley Seymour reminisced: "Below stairs at the level of the tracks was a cavernous place, dark, confused and filled with smoke. I remember very well the effect made upon my youthful imagination when, in that murky atmosphere, I encountered a large sign: 'Beware of pickpockets.' It seemed to me that ruffians were ready at any moment to spring upon me out of the smoke." Some things never change.

Seymour also told of the young country child, accustomed to the hellfire-and-damnation sermons of the time, who descended to those railroad tracks with his father. "Is this hell, father?" asked the boy. "No, my son," was the reply, "this is New Haven."
Ten days ago the 19th-century joke applied. But the bright and airy spaces put into use again this week do much better by New Haven. Rail travel, as the Amtrak budget makers in Washington complain, is still a dubious moneymaker - though our jammed highways hardly seem a practical long-term alternative. In this populous region, in which so much strain is put on airport, highway and in-city transportation, an attractive place where travelers can arrive and depart and make interchange with comfort and convenience seems essential to the kind of community New Haven wants to be clean, spacious, even inviting, today's railroad station is, in every sense, the way to go.

Saturday, February 25, 1984
Editor's note

Tapes, Cassettes, And Memories

The discount store was showing off its video cassettes to Saturday shoppers and a crowd of youngsters watched Michael Jackson cavorting slickly on the tube. He is electric, hypnotic. They were absorbed in his taped music and movement, admiring and perhaps envious as the young millionaire flashed his white socks, singing and dancing with the odd, high-voltage energy which is his genius and his generational trademark.

Lambent eyes brooded behind the plastic remodeled face. The shyness of the smile behind all that commerce and acclaim, the puzzle of the fine-boned right hand in its constant glove, the recent fiery danger during another elaborate production number, were all parts of the presence that moved from the cassette to the shopping floor.

The kids were customers and consumers first. But even in that setting they were also seekers, looking for sights and sounds that could move and enlighten them, give meaning to vague emotions, hint at answers or questions barely perceived in the rush and clamor of their daily lives. So they stared at the tube - a small, wistful tribe gathered amid the best-buy announcements and the color-coded counters of the store, within the popcorn turbulence of the shopping mall.

I envied them their impressionability but was thankful for how much simpler things used to be.

When I was 10 or 12 electronics was a concern for laboratory pioneers alone. We had a hand-cranked home Victrola and perhaps 40 records to play on it. Radio was still a hobby for fans who twiddled a half dozen dials and listened mostly by ear-phones

- and hooked up a squawky amplifier only when the "reception" was very good and the broadcast was very special.

Music was then something you made yourself. In St. Francis Church the choir alone sang the hymns, except perhaps for the Latin "Tantum Ergo" during the holy day processions. In a working class neighborhood the mother or father who sang a little over the dish washing or the ironing in the kitchen was considered musical.

Marketing - no gray flannel pursuit - was then only a task for vegetable growers. Mass culture was only an Ivy League theory (propounded with dismay). A dime for a Saturday cowboy matinee was the entertainment peak of the week for most kids.

One winter the family that lived next door on Lombard Street in Fair Haven acquired a player piano. It was second-hand and occasionally balky, and my playmates, Stanley and Isabel Gailunas were torn between protecting it against careless use and enjoying its lyric rhythms. Since it was fruit of the loving labors of an immigrant father and mother who worked long hours, the younger generation mixed custodianship with enthusiasm and played the piano, discreetly but often, before the grown-ups came home.

Though mechanical, it was the first music I ever made - an experience like that of pagan Pan blowing upon the reeds by the river. And melody aside there was unending fascination in pumping the pedals, in watching the words move past on the roller, and in seeing those 88 keys respond unerringly, with skill and syncopation the length of the board, to invisibly dancing fingers.

Talk about Michael Jackson!

Even more impressive musically was the way Bill Conway used to sing "Moonlight and Roses." Bill lived next door on the other side - a young father who was a toolmaker at the National Folding Box Co. In the summer of the Conways' moving-in, when everybody's windows were open one evening, there was a sudden revelation. From their second-floor parlor came the sound of a piano - and with it, Bill Conway singing "Moonlight and Roses."

He had a robust tenor voice and I found amazement, and satisfaction, in the fact that next door we had a neighbor, a regular guy who talked with me across the backyard fence, somebody's father, who could sing well - loudly enough to be heard out on the street by passersby and confidently enough to share his sentiments with the neighbors!

Bill played by ear and probably didn't have a great repertory. But after supper on a summer evening he liked to relax, to keep hand and voice flexible and renew a little of youth's romance with the old songs.

I have a memory like a dream - of warm, starry nights, darkness gathering under the trees of Lombard Street, children quieted by the dusk, painted rocking chairs on the porches, amiable and unhurried voices sharing the easy talk of that time before there were too many cars and too much unending entertainment from everywhere.

The memory shimmers. Sometimes there is ice cream. Sometimes there is laughter. Or fireworks. Sometimes there is the rumble of the rickety bus that shuttled Ferry Street "E" trolley riders around the back blocks of that part of Fair Haven.

Always in the background there is the ultimate distillation of that old contentment and the ultimate definition of the youthful stirrings that challenged it - the sound of Bill Conway singing "Moonlight and Roses" in his clear enthusiastic tenor.

As time and technology rush us toward the year 2000, and beyond, I hope Michael Jackson endures as well for the kids in the discount store.

Saturday, December 30, 1989
Editor's note:

The Beginning Of Another End

Here we go - again! The closing years of each century so far in America have been just what the calendar and common sense make them, years of transition. And here in New Haven in 1690, in 1790, in 1890, our predecessor townfolk may well have looked down the arching years of their last decade in a familiar century and wondered - like Mayor-elect John Daniels and the rest of us - about changes surely coming and problems tough to solve.

The historic process of closing out a century is not just a local challenge. It's a challenge the generations face everywhere under all kinds of conditions. Our fathers, when they did it last, immersed their Gay '90s in wine, women and song, with bustle--backed, wasp-waisted ladies and paunchy, moustachioed men - a model of little use to us in a decade when breathing aerobically inside Spandex tights is a universal goal.

But whether we're prepared or unprepared, a new batch of the '90s begins for us on Monday - and every indication from the past is that - as in the words of that ancient Oriental curse - we will "live in interesting times."

Old New Haven town was a mere 52 years old when the year 1690 arrived. By that time its first-generation adults - the original colonists who had arrived full of religious zeal were dead or of great age or had returned to England. Their successors in this small community on the watery edge of a vast unknown continent may have had good reason in 1690 to wonder if there would ever be prosperity and security enough to go around. The settlement here had lost out as an independent colony, forced by royal order to be part of the Connecticut Colony at Hartford. New Haven's first investors had a sense of what junk bonds were when that happened.

The community's only industry was the ironworks out near Lake Saltonstall. The settlement's only public communications system, the old ship's bell in the meetinghouse tower, had been taken down to be recast in England; when made bigger it would ring louder. The major construction project for New Haven, if not for all Connecticut at that point, was the laying out and grading of a road between this city and Waterbury. Anything comfortable or decorative in local life came down from Boston, paid for by the provisions New Haven sent north.

In the next 50 years New Haven would become the seat of Yale, a lively market center, a thriving seaport - but in 1690, even from the perspective of its own senior generation, it came close to being Dullsville.

All the surfaces were brighter when 1790 came into view. The Revolutionary War was done. The stiff old piety was in decline. Yale College now had three impressive brick buildings and a fine clapboard president's house. Packet boats carrying passengers and merchandise linked the city to New York and New London. There were 30 New Haven-owned ships busy between Long Wharf and the sugar, molasses, and rum ports of the West Indies. Nearly 60 shops in the Nine Squares met every general need. New Haven had become a city by charter, with Roger Sherman as its first mayor.

The constitutional convention of 1787 - in which Roger Sherman played an important role - produced a federal government. President George Washington came to town in his first year in office. There was a bank and a chamber of commerce, and the Green's elm trees were already a distinguishing mark of the place. The first years of the federal republic, which were the last years of the 18th century, were good here.

After those '90s the new 19th century was darker. There was the War of 1812, which destroyed shipping; an economic slump; the heat of the anti-slavery debates; the tragedy of the Civil War. But also there was the whir and hum of industrial energy spreading itself wide in town.

When 1890 rolled around New Haven was booming. Manufacturing of all kinds built community prosperity. The city was a railroad center linking New England to the West and South. Pioneer electrical, gas, water and telephone services gave the city metropolitan facilities. And over the century's course, wave after wave of European immigrants had brought a rich mix of cultures, talents and energies to town. The city's population in 1890 was just above 100,000 people, a quarter of them born in some other country. The prosperous had a lawn club for tennis and a country club for golf and Yale, nearing its 200th year, had a huge bicentennial building program in progress.

There were problems, but basically they involved ways to meet the call for added urban services, schools, housing, better health, easier transport. Great wars, depression and the threat of technologies that could destroy us all lay not far ahead. But these were the Gay '90s - closing the 19th century with great good cheer. And they provide us with our handiest but perhaps least applicable model for the 1990s.

In distant 1690 the dream of a New Jerusalem, moral and plenteous, was physically fading; the realities of a fragile settlement on the edge of the known world were there to be met. In 1790 new freedom in a new republic was both glorious and demanding, and the new Yankee virtue was hard work, self-sufficiency, and the ideal of opportunity born of equality. In 1890 there was noise, smoke, dirt and danger amid the excitement of a thousand new enterprises with 100,000 personal hopes and ambitions to be pursued.

As 1990 dawns, New Haven's good life is challenged by forces erupting - politically, socially, economically - all over the world. Within varied and liberated lifestyles we are challenged more than ever before by our own inner failures and public uncertainties. Leadership today is daunting. But history celebrates survival. And to launch the 1990s, which will point us toward a new millennium, the best immediate goal is to start with:

A HAPPY NEW YEAR!

Saturday, November 4, 1989
Editor's note:

The Season For Endorsements

Election day is Tuesday. So tomorrow and Monday the Register will be making recommendations, "editorial endorsements," about the people and parties seeking elective power in this immediate vicinity.

This year the Register's editorial board has met with the candidates for top jobs in New Haven, West Haven, East Haven, Hamden, North Haven, Orange and Milford. The latter two communities are new to our endorsement list - an indication that there are interesting political contests and strong readership communities developing to our west. We stick to the larger cities and towns because of their political impact, and also because we couldn't possibly conduct timely research and candidate interviews for each of the nearly three dozen towns the Register covers.

The choices we make are pretty generally the consensus of editorial board opinions after meeting with the candidates, discussing the issues with them, and analyzing the answers and impressions that emerge.

Who sits on our editorial board?

Tom Geyer, the Register's chief executive; Dave Butler, editor; Walter Nester Jr., general manager; Charles Kochakian, the editorial page editor; Cynthia Baran, an editorial writer; Bob Rich, editorial cartoonist; and, when on hand, ye olde editor emeritus, Robert J. Leeney.

The effort is to find the candidates and the proposals best suited to serve their communities well; to make the most effective choice we can, based on the facts at hand; to set up some guidelines and considerations for readers who will be making their own choices and casting their own votes. So read what we have to say. Ponder your own opinions. Then, vote.

A newspaper's endorsements may be - and are - looked at from many points of view:

(A) As a natural and necessary acceptance of responsibilities created in the Constitution. A free press must be eager to express its free opinion - or waste the privilege and perhaps encourage its decay. This is the classic view of American newspapering.

(B) As a journalistic presumption. Why should publishers and editors and their networks to the "establishment" instruct the voter in the street about the best ways to run a democracy? Let the people speak for themselves and vote without advice. That's the equally classic populist view.

(C) As an Election Week contradiction in newspaper sales efforts. Papers spend the rest of the year trying to convince everybody - young or old, rich or poor, the upwardly mobile or the "underclass," the artist or the athlete - that the paper is universally useful because it reflects our life and times without favoritism. So why Election Day favorites? Newspaper marketers, and a few papers, go for this argument.

(D) As an intrusion by a crew of urban excitement-seekers into the affairs of decently run, comfortably kept suburban communities. "Let them clean up the mess in the city (where they print and pay taxes) before they come out to tell us what's wrong in this town."

(E) As the "kiss of death." This is the claim, and the hope, of those whose political arguments we reject or whose political opponents win our nod. But newspaper editorials are rarely the only factors in an election victory. And sometimes a newspaper's admiration does nothing to stave off defeat for its chosen candidate if the voters feel differently.

Among such views I've always taken the "A" train of thought. The Register pokes steadily into public affairs in every town and city in the region. It is the major source of information on what's going on. Its 365 editorial pages each year comment seriously on news events and public issues. In that context we'd be derelict not to choose among candidates or take sides on voting questions when the election season rolls around. With press credentials we have more access than the average citizen can muster for gathering fact about public problems, and our day-to-day analysis fits us for timely expression of opinion. So we sound off.

Most editorial endorsements these days are offered as reasonable choices, logically made between or among candidates. They are not the lightning bolts of righteousness and truth that were in style a century ago. They are simply guideposts, statements of our own responsibility in looking at the questions every voter is asked to weigh and act on. The whole point is to tell you what we think, to make you think, and then - most importantly - to move you to the polls.

A little old-style thunder may make even disappointed candidates for endorsement see how much tougher political editorials used to be. Back in 1896 William Allen White won fame with an editorial jeremiad in The Emporia (Kan.) Gazette. And this is only an excerpt:

"What's the matter with Kansas?

"We all know; yet here we are at it again. We have an old mossback Jacksonian who snorts and howls because there is a bathtub in the statehouse; we are running that old jay for governor. We have another shabby, wild-eyed, rattle-brained fanatic who has said openly in a dozen speeches that the rights of the user are paramount to the rights of the owner; we are running him for chief justice, so that capital will come tumbling over itself to get into the state. We have raked the ash heap of failure in the state and found an old human hoop skirt who has failed as a businessman, who has failed as an editor, who has failed as a preacher, and we are going to run him for congressman-at-large. Then we have discovered a kid without a law practice and have decided to run him for attorney-general.

"Oh, this is a state to be proud or. We are a people who can hold up our heads! ... "

There's lots more. But that kind of lashing is no longer the way that editors talk to their readers about office-seekers. We've discovered civility. Political criticism and political endorsement remain, however, an important part of a community newspaper's function. And this is the season for endorsements.

Saturday, February 11, 1989
Editor's Note

Things Literate And Lactic

Literacy and newspapers, like love and marriage, "go together like a horse and carriage." A paper's primary asset is the people who can read it. So it's only natural on this last day of National Literacy Awareness Week to remind each other that there are some 30,000 people in the New Haven area alone who can't read the newspaper well enough to make sense of it.

The problem is, if they can't make sense of the newspaper they can't make sense of the other written words in their lives - highway signs, instructions on medicine containers, the bewildering and word-crammed arrays of boxes, bags and wrappings that confront us all in supermarkets, the selections on a restaurant menu.

Statistically, one in five American adults is functionally illiterate. Here in affluent Connecticut the figures indicate that 400,000 adults, or one in four, can't read. Though few have learning disabilities, most illiterates - for varying reasons - have been frustrated in the educational system. The social cost of illiteracy is reflected in the fact that 60 percent of the country's prison inmates can't read; 85 percent of all juvenile offenders couldn't handle the news in this newspaper; 75 percent of all unemployed adults find reading or writing a major problem.

The answer to this emergency situation obviously must go beyond normal educational channels. If we are to convince the generation in our schools that reading is important, we must do it by bringing the generations now outside up to par. The Literacy Volunteers of America have pulled together more than 400 people in the New Haven area who are mustering individually and as a group - the patience, the creativity and the compassion to deal, one on one, with men and women who can't read. Last year more than 300 illiterate adults completed local studies and emerged able to read and write. Thousands more need - and want - such help.

If you can back the effort, just drop a note to Literacy Volunteers of Greater New Haven, Stetson Library, 200 Dixwell Ave., New Haven 06511. Or phone part-time staffer Chris Santella, when he's in, at 772-4346. There are satellite programs operating in Branford, Milford and the Naugatuck Valley. Instructors attend a 20-hour workshop before being assigned. The personal satisfactions, they say, are immense, the contributions to society immeasurable.

The old milk bottle box, galvanized against rain and snow and insulated against the extremes of winter or summer, was removed from the back porch last week. For the first time in more than six decades of memory, the milkman has recommended that we pick up our cow juice at the supermarket or perhaps the "superette." The delivery customers are too few in Bethany to support his route.

As changes go, this one is minor. Still, it is the end of something with which I started life. The milkman was once a neighborhood fixture, as precise as the mailman in his door-to-door rounds daily, as persistent in his collections as the fellow who removed quarters from the family gas meter. It's not a surprise, but it's a sadness, to find him obsolete.

Sometime when I was between 8 and 10 years old perhaps - on a Lenten morning when altar boys went early to Mass in Irish Fair Haven, perhaps in some precocious display of insomniac brooding - I became aware of the milkman's pre-breakfast arrival on our block. In the winter there was a stealthy, small clinking from the dozen quart bottles in his metal basket. That was all.

But in the spring and summer when the bedroom window was always open for healthy, hygienic sleeping, there was an extended medley of milkman noises. Alerted first by a parent's kitchen rustlings, a listener could catch the gentle clop of the horse's hoofs, the crunch of the wagon wheels as our milkman turned the corner. He would run - hardly ever walk - from street to alley to rear porch, serving the neighbors, sometimes with the city's grudging bird sounds his herald as starlings and sparrows stirred in the trees. Then, beside our house on the tar walk that led to the latticed backyard gate, came the hurried scuff of his rubber-soled shoes. There would be a pause, the soft rattle of his empty bottles, the rhythm of his retreat. On the other side of home, at the house next door, running feet would again move quietly, the bottles strike their random sunrise chime. The milkman would pass down the block, a modest Mercury in overalls, his muted sound, even in its living moment, the stuff of memory.

His horse was trained to follow him, but sometimes old faithful might snooze. Then through open windows came a single modulated whistle, or a hushed but urgent call of "Rusty!" Hoofs would clop, the harness leathers strain, the wagon lurch as Rusty and his load moved forward.

This bucolic memory, of course, gave way decades ago to the clank and squeak and rattling shift of the milk truck, the stain of its exhaust on the air, and the almost-any-hour arrival of the milk at the suburban back door. And that ended, we must now brace ourselves for the supermarket with its high-rise coolers of half-gallon cartons, their dates turned carefully to the wall to maximize shelf life, their degrees of fat or calcium or lactose or (Oh, horror!) cream each scientifically delineated.

But it's the muffled, careful, sleep-respecting regularity of that long-gone milkman's tread that I'd like to hear again - a halcyon sound from my mornings of childhood dreaming, but also a remembrance of service given with a smile hardly ever seen. Through that early jogger's faithfulness my truck-borne milkman earned a quarter century of automatic respect and got credit for the indispensability of milk down the long years.

After all this running and rolling milk delivery I wonder: Can we now switch allegiance to the carton stacker at the Stop & Shop? And what will we do with the milk box?

Saturday, August 16, 1980
Editor's Note,

Using A Platform -- And A Stage

Locally, the Shubert emerged again in the week's news, moving toward aldermanic discussion - and reminding us of the theater as public event in the same period when the Democratic convention was demonstrating the public event as theater.

For a city with New Haven's many problems, the plan to restore the Shubert has got to create concern and controversy. A $5.6 million investment of public dollars is a tremendous challenge. The prospect of annual subsidy is something that every taxpayer should weigh cautiously.

But we subsidize the Coliseum. We subsidize the construction of parking garages. We have found that carefully monitored commitment of city tax dollars can provide measurable returns, and concrete public benefits, for New Haven and its general prosperity. And in the Shubert's case, it seems to me that what's important, as we think subsidy, is the uniqueness of the College Street theater as an asset very special to New Haven - something no other city has. It is a theatrical resource with a national identity among theater professionals, with national recognition among informed theater-goers, with a history, a tradition, and even a myth, which keeps it a living theater even amidst the disuse, the dust, and the disarray of the present.

An entertainment institution and' a theater edifice with so treasured a reputation, with so persistent a glamor, with such continuing potential is the envy of countless other American cities as they go about the business of building or restoring theater centers. But only New Haven has the Shubert -- "the birthplace of the nation's hits" for 50 years. And only New Haven has the particular opportunity our College Street theater provides.

The Shubert situation was strongly outlined in the articles written earlier this week by Register reporter Arthur Horwitz.

There is some feeling particularly among local people with professional theater connections, that the Shubert's palmiest days are past, that a "house" seating between 1,600 and 1,700 can't provide the guarantees, produce the money, needed by modern road shows geared to play new civic centers and other large halls seating 2,500 to 3,500 people. The economy of the American theater today, they seem to say, has out-run the remembered glories of the Shubert. The musicals are fewer, the comedy and the dramatic productions are down, the cast of a theater "tryout" outside of New York has been fiercely inflated. The days when the Shubert booked 25 to 30 productions a season may be no more - and this means that the golden success of the box-office in the past isn't guaranteed for the future.

There is also some feeling, particularly among people with an interest in local performing groups, that the Shubert's future should not be too strongly linked to Broadway, or the Theater Guild's road shows, or other "commercial" theater schedules. Their argument lifts the Shubert beyond its profitable past and suggests that it help to stage art for New Haven performers and use its stage – at least part of the time – for dance, for opera, for theater which emerges from the community's own talents. The prospect of programs generated in this region need not be a negative one in terms of art, or in terms of self-support and profitability, so long as the community's stake in both aspects of a Shubert operation is the measuring stick when schedules are booked.

The aldermen who have discussed the program to date are not knocking art, local or on the road - but they do stress minimum subsidy and maximum profitability as the key to the Shubert project if it is to take off. Their concern, like that of Mayor DiLieto and his development administrator, John Sawyer, is with the restored theater as a downtown, business generator and as a symbol of fun, excitement, culture, and the good life of New Haven for people who come into the city and enjoy it. The cost of the renovation and operating the Shubert and its possible payoffs for the downtown merchants and restaurateurs - and the taxpayers - is what will be weighed politically. And interestingly, most of the neighborhood spokesmen agree that a going Shubert and a prosperous shopping district can produce advantages along our backstreets, too.

As a Shubert partisan, shaped by 30 years of first nights, I personally endorse the effort. The Shubert, as noted, is an asset unique to New Haven.

Other towns have coliseums, exhibition halls, civic centers - Hartford, Springfield, Providence to name the nearest. Most outclass us with a better investment in facilities. In an era when the promotion and the subsidy of such centers are accepted civic endeavors linked to the general prosperity, the Shubert could be a special and effective augmentation. It comes - already marketable - with a ready made function, tradition, reputation, and following. It offers opportunity in a field – even a field of risk - where New Haven would be unchallenged.

It stands there now on College Street, rubble - surrounded but strong in its basic design and location. You couldn't replace it for three – maybe four - times the city's $5.6 million working figure.

We may have to be careful in the way we develop such calculations and apply them to our tax rate.

But not to have a try at saving the Shubert, and re-ornamenting downtown too, would be- at least -shortsighted.

Saturday, February 14, 1987
Editor's note

Using Heads, Using Hearts

The most romantic place in town for a Valentine's Day tryst? That was a question posed by food writer Bonnie Tandy Leblang and answered by her readers in last Wednesday's food section. It made an interesting feature. I had an answer but considered myself ineligible for the contest.

The most romantic place for a valentine meeting is always in your lover's eyes. No other place counts.

A long time ago, when such things concerned us, too, my girl and I shared two or three rapturous pre-World War II valentine suppers at Hyland's bar and grille on State Street. In retrospect that sounds like a joke. The address is most unglamorous. But the memory remains pure romance.

Hyland's then stood on State Street between East and James, across from Blake Field and close to one bank of the Mill River - which ran so dark and turgid there that tide gates were used to keep its murky currents out of East Rock Park. Hyland's and the dubious river and the haphazard landfill on the other bank have all been buried in the vaulting concrete and steel that now carry I-91, with its rumbling ramps and barriers, across that part of State Street.

Then it was a neighborhood bar with a stucco front and a disheveled parking lot. Next to the original barroom they had added a small dining room with booths along a windowed outside wall. At night there were white tablecloths, an amiable waiter in a black tie, and small candles on the tables by the windows. And those were the outer boundaries of "ambiance" at Hyland's. Through a side door at the front came the lively sounds of good cheer at the stand-up bar. And through a swinging side door toward the rear came the clatter and hiss of work in a too-small kitchen.

If, planning to see a downtown movie, you called ahead,

Hyland's would hold handy a bottle of white wine to chill (Barton & Guestier sauterne), or, if red was the choice, a strawbound chianti. Wine was not routine there. The regulars ordered from the bar. The bill of fare was equally sound and simple. And in memory the dessert was always pie. But those were merely creature comforts.

The valentine magic was in the February moon you both could watch through the window, riding high above the James Street trolley barns - its reflection, in the kindly night, a silver shimmer on the surface of the hard-used river. The romance was in the word half-spoken, the hand half-touched in the booth's deep shadow - while the candle flickered on the table and all earth's mystery and beauty seemed reflected, unfolded, renewed and multiplied in those eyes beyond it.

Old Khayyam, the Persian poet, knew and sang 800 years sooner about the boon of a loving relationship:

"Here with a loaf of bread beneath the bough. / A flask of wine, a book of verse - and thou / Beside me singing in the wilderness - / Ah, wilderness is paradise enow."

We can laugh now, especially the girl who didn't even drink. And probably old tapster Hyland himself could laugh then at the thought of valentine hearts entwined forever in the spell of his modest alehouse.

But the memory lingers. The romance remains. The tryst is in the people, not the place. So, wherever you are today or tonight, don't fret about location. Celebrate your valentine.

Saturday, September 28, 1985
Editor's note

What A Free Press Means

What a free press means to America" is the title of a 75th anniversary volume produced by the Society of Professional Journalists, Sigma Delta Chi. It consists of 254 personal statements by practicing newspaper, radio, and television news gatherers, editors, and commentators. Though the statements taken all together may seem a bit declamatory, they are - when examined one by one - sincere and careful efforts to define the way in which all American citizens, not just reporters and editors, draw personal freedom and civic strength from the First Amendment and from the vigorous and vocal activities of a free press. Consider these observations.

First by Donald W. Sharpe, editor of The Jackson Newspapers:

"From the libel trial of John Peter Zenger in 1735, through numerous civil and foreign wars and up to Grenada, Central America and the issues of the moment, the press in the United States has been at least partly responsible for that very special openness of attitude and public spirit that identifies our society and all it represents.

"The press, for all its diversity and all its imperfections, has been vital simply because it serves as a conduit for news, information and views from all segments of the political spectrum. We function best when we transmit that information to the American public without fuss or furor, without color or bias, without slant or cant.

"The public trusts us most, it seems to me, when it is certain that we present all the facts, without regard to our own editorial views.

"Two lengthy conferences with editors from the Soviet Union have only reinforced my belief that the very nature of American democracy, its exuberance and its freedom, are rooted in the concepts of a free press. We must continue to be the guardians of that tradition."

The Miami Herald's editor emeritus, Don Shoemaker, asks: "What of the editor's right, under a free society, to express himself as freely as is fitting for the good of society? ...

"Good editorial judgment is like any other judgment, business, professional or political.

"It calls the shots one by one.

"It does not adhere to party or ideology.

"It responds neither to fear nor to favor (and if this seems trite, look around U.S. journalism today).

"It neither comforts nor afflicts for the sake of either sentiment.

"It does not seek to promote the institution for its own ends or the individual for his ends, which are usually a sense of power.

"It seeks to inform and to guide, but in neither role must it be too far ahead of or too far behind its readers.

"It is not necessarily to be feared and it is unlikely to be loved, but it should strive to be respected for its fairness.

"It should be 'different' in the sense that it can establish an identity in the midst of sameness.

"And it requires a sense of humor."

"All other things being equal (though they never are) the newspaper may then claim to decorate its civilization.

"In many countries an editor would not be free to express such a creed - much less act upon it. That is one of the many things a free press means to America."

Says Thomas Winship, editor of the Boston Globe, in a statement made just before he retired:

"However benevolent a government may be, its people are not exercising essential self-government unless they are able to reach decisions about the performance of those in public office from freely obtained and freely published information. The free press is to American democracy what yeast is to bread. Without it, this system of government we prize falls flat."

Speaklng seriously about the way he makes fun, Art Buchwald declared: "Since I write a humor column, I have a vested interest in a free press. I don't seem to have any problem making fun of the president of the United States, the Cabinet, Congress, the CIA and the FBI. I don't know if our leaders read the column or not, but since I've been writing it I have had no visits from anyone in a raincoat telling me I better knock it off.

"The people who attempt to do the same thing I am doing in 95 percent of the world are either in gulags, under house arrest or are jobless. For some reason not too many governments can handle satire. My heroes in the world are the men and women in these countries who, knowing the consequences, persist in holding up their leaders to ridicule.

"The problem, if there is a problem in this country, is that because we have a free press people have no idea what it's like to live in a country that doesn't."

Wrote John E. Leard (once a Register staffer) from the Richmond (Va.) Times-Dispatch and the News Leader: "This principle of a free press is prominent in the Constitution ('Congress shall make no law ... abridging ... the freedom ... of the press') but it is buried in the pages of history and too often in the minds of officials and the public.

"It is not something to be brought out occasionally and polished like the family silver. It is not something to wave on the Fourth of July, like the flag.

"It is something that we of the press must keep alive daily, nurture with diligence, encourage with fairness, not mistreat or abuse.

"Those who cherish and honor it must work to gain for it the understanding and respect it deserves as a basic tenet of our national philosophy."

The essential thing for you as a citizen-reader and me as a citizen-writer is that the constitutional right protected by the founding fathers is "freedom of speech (yours), or of the press (mine)." They are interlocked in the First Amendment. So, when the press is pinched, or imperiled, your right is as much under challenge as mine - because they are both the same.

Saturday, February 27, 1982
Editor's note

Who Clobbered The Connector?

"We have met the enemy," says Walt Kelly's Pogo, "and they is us."

When the State Transportation Commissioner announced in mid-month that the extension of New Haven's Oak Street Connector has been put on the back burner for lack of funding, there was general dismay. After nearly 20 years of waiting must we wait some more? Are Hartford agencies toying, once again, with New Haven's needs?

There's a serious case to be made for the final construction, of a modern inter-connecting highway link with the Naugatuck Valley communities northwest of New Haven.

But, as recorded in the The Register's files, the news clippings are a case-study in poor politics, poor planning, and misplaced piety. We got little help from the state in the effort to make this project "fly." But we also laid endless confusions and contradictions on the state's doorstep. Consider this chronology.

The Oak Street Connector opened as far as Howe Street in 1959. It was designated the Richard C. Lee Connector in 1978, but Dick himself had created the Oak Street reference which still prevails. In 1963 engineers estimated the road could be extended to Route 34 at the Maltby Lakes for about $63 million.

February, 1965. Gov. John N. Dempsey recommended that the state appropriate $20 million to push the road through to the Boulevard. His message said that the Route 34 connection would be completed by 1970.

July, 1965. "State Capitol - The State Bond Commission today gave final step approval for the first allotment of funds on the

Route 34 extension project in New Haven."

Mayor Lee: "The completion of construction of Route 34 is going to provide New Haven with a great highway network, one of the finest in America. I recognize that a recommended appropriation is yet a long way from the concrete and steel construction but all of New Haven now rallies its support to the recommendation of the governor.

March, 1966. "At Long Last, A Hearing On Route 34."

April, 1966. "The city's chief executive is currently locked in veritable hand-to-hand combat with the state (Highway Department) and it appears he will not be the one to back down. Major issue is the design for the construction of an interchange that would, under the state plan, take some 25 acres of the West River Memorial Park at the Boulevard. The city has come up with a plan that, it is claimed, will only take 17 acres." State engineers wanted to use land fill in the park; the city wanted a bridge or viaduct. The state said this would cost $5 million more; the city said it might cost $500,000 more.

June, 1966. "Parley Takes Bumps Out of Rt. 34 Plans."

November, 1966. The state started acquiring property along the connector's path beyond Howe Street.

March, 1967. "Money For Rt. 34 Extension Won't Be Available Until '71."

October, 1968. "Route 34 Foes to Offer State Alternate Plan." The Hill Neighborhood which had rioted in the "hot summer" of 1967 wanted housing not highways in the area. Others challenged the 480-foot-wide right-of-way needed for the highway, two frontage roads, and two collector-discharge roads.

December, 1968. "City, State Reject Rt. 34 Alternatives."

January, 1969. "Four New Haven legislators Wednesday filed bills which would halt - if only temporarily - the building of controversial Route 34 through the city." State Senator John DiRienzo, also a New Haven alderman, said:

"Let's face it. We're not going to stop the highway permanently ... But if we can stop it right now, and bring it out into the open, we can see who's going to be the governing body in this city."

March, 1969. The ambivalence of public feeling about the

connector was displayed when a Chamber of Commerce spokesman went to support the road before the General Assembly. "Ralph Ernst, legal affairs director for the Chamber, told the Legislative Committee he was 'torn by conscience' after hearing a constant chorus of voices citing human misery, the possibility of social disruption, and general 'disaster' because of the highway."

July, 1970. "Expressing concern (in a letter to Gov. Dempsey) that the proposed Route 34 highway project 'may not meet the current needs of the community,' U.S. Rep. Robert N. Giaimo has called for a thorough re-examination of the project by the state to 'determine the feasibility of using the land ... for housing purposes instead.'"

"Opponents again dominate Hearing On Rt. 34." July, 1971.

Again July, 1971. "(Vincent J.) Sirabella, along with (another) Democratic mayoral contender, Henry E. Parker and GOP mayoral contender Paul C. Capra supports a bill now before the Board of Aldermen which would prevent construction of a relocated Rt. 34. The bill is opposed by Mayor Bartholomew F. Guida."

October, 1971. "Department of Transportation Commissioner Earl Wood informed the city Friday that his department has decided to build the first half of a relocated Rt. 34 basically along the line shown at a public hearing last winter and estimated that construction could begin by the spring of 1974." Wood had also told State Rep. Robert G. Oliver, who swung pro-and-con on the project, that the road from the Boulevard into West Haven was "penciled-in" for a start in 1976 and completion in 1979.

January, 1975. "Route 34 Stalled Again." February, 1975. The Regional Plan Association for the New York-Connecticut-New Jersey region, in a report on Connecticut Transportation Issues, supported extension of the Oak Street Connector to the Boulevard but not to Rt. 34 in Orange. It said the existing route beyond the Boulevard "has sufficient capacity for suburban access to downtown New Haven."

Later in February, 1975. Gov. Ella Grasso spent a day inspecting the right of way from Legion Avenue to the Boulevard.

July, 1975. "The planned extension of Route 34 in New Haven became a larger campaign issue Wednesday as Mayor Bartholomew

Guida dismissed as 'total distortion' Alderman Frank Logue's alternate plan for the highway, and a labor group joined in Guida's criticism."

August, 1975. "Early Start Vowed on Route 34."

State Transportation Comsr. Samuel Kanell, who grew up in the Legion Avenue area, said: "Every possible effort will be made to make dirt fly before the end of the year."

December, 1975. "Review Will Delay Start on Route 34."

The Transportation Commissioner said he would review and respond to a report in which the State Commission on Human Rights and Opportunities claimed construction of Rt. 34 would "perpetuate and reinforce a ...pattern of racial segregation and isolation" in New Haven.

December, 1976. "William Keish, director of communications for the State Dept. of Transportation Monday affirmed that the state no longer has the money to build a depressed highway from York Street to the Boulevard."

January, 1977. " ... Immediate construction of a three-block long extension of the Oak Street Connector to Howe Street will be proposed to Gov. Ella T. Grasso by a broad-based Route 34 Action Committee, Mayor Frank Logue's office reported today."

July, 1977. "A federal environmental impact study of the path of the Route 34 Connector could forestall full construction for a year."

January, 1981. "State Transportation Com sr. Arthur B. Powers has backed a plan to extend Route 34 all the way to the Orange-West Haven line."

February, 1982. "Rt. 34 Halt Angers Officials." "'It would take between $80 million to $100 million to complete construction ... The project is not going anywhere because of a lack of money,' said J. William Burns, commissioner of transportation."

What this demonstrates is the challenge Mayor DiLieto faces in Hartford next week as he makes one more pitch to extend the Connector past the center of town.

The need is greater than ever - downtown and in the Hill neighborhood devastated by 20 years of destructive inaction. The

Boulevard is now a direct link to 1-95. Route 34 itself is becoming obsolete between Ansonia and New Haven. Few projects have been so genuinely needed, or so inexcusably delayed. And really, we did it all ourselves.

Saturday, September 30, 1989
Editor's note:

Working With Our State's Officials

Last week's newspapers, let's face it, can be a problem in a world increasingly concerned about anything left over. So a steady review of ways to recycle - or otherwise use - old newsprint is something the newspaper industry must embrace. That's why the amended Connecticut law on the use of recycled newsprint offers promise from the public's point of view and from the publisher's.

Originally the legislature was offered a bill that would have taxed newspapers on every pound of virgin newsprint put through their presses. It also set mandatory levels for the use of recycled paper starting in 1993. The idea was to increase the level every year until 90 percent of the paper on which we published would be recycled paper. The concept is attractive. But it ignored the fact that Connecticut newspapers could not buy, beg or steal that much acceptable paper. Recycling plants are just not producing that much volume - and if they eventually do produce it, recycled paper is not efficient at all times on today's high-speed presses.

The compromise bill retains mandatory levels as a recycling goal. But a newspaper that can certify unavailability or excessive cost can ask for an exemption. A task force with one representative from the Connecticut Daily Newspaper Association has also been set up to report to the General Assembly on longer-range controls by next February. This cooperative effort is one that newspaper people endorse. The American Newspaper Publishers Association recently approved a recycling policy statement that says in part:

"Newspapers will be asking for more recycled newsprint and are working with newsprint manufacturers to help municipalities and recyclers to increase recycling .... Newspapers are doing their part and will do more."

Journalists and politicians gathered the other night in Cromwell to salute Jim Mutrie, the Register's longtime State Capitol bureau chief, as he heads for retirement. He even received a letter of personal reminiscence from President Bush.

Jim is an exceptional newspaperman. We hired him back in the autumn of 1955 to expand our coverage of state government. He stuck with that assignment for 34 years, taking over the leadership of the Hartford bureau in 1961, reporting the administrations of Govs. Abraham Ribicoff, John Dempsey, Thomas Meskill, Ella Grasso and William O'Neill. In that time the population of Connecticut has gone from 2,007,000 to more than 3,160,000 and - as a simplistic measure of change - the fine-print index to state agencies and services in the Connecticut Register and Manual, or "blue book," has gone from 38 pages to 55 pages.

Jim Mutrie reported all that growth and coped with its demands in terms of constantly increasing bureaus and agencies to be tracked; constantly mounting hours, days and weeks of government effort at taxpayer expense that had to be analyzed and evaluated. When I asked him what were the most intense news coverage recollections of his long time on the job, Jim's reply was typical: "The times when we were short-handed."

When Mutrie started work in 1955 only two or three Connecticut daily papers had a regular presence in the Capitol press room. Now there are dozens of reporters, including television and radio journalists, constantly in and out of the government center. The Register took a giant step forward by installing a teletype machine to link Hartford and New Haven at a time when Hartford and Bridgeport reporters went back to their offices to write. Because the Hartford-New Haven link-up was then so tentative, there was traditionally more Hartford reporting and analysis in the Sunday editions of the Register - when the staff could come to New Haven on Saturdays and deliver copy directly to the editors.

Today the Register copy is fed instantaneously from keyboard and screen in the Capitol into our New Haven computer and onto the screens of the paper's editors.

In presenting Jim with his traditional retirement watch at the Cromwell party, I summed up his service this way:

"From the time when he succeeded Carl Clyma in 1961 as what we later called legislative bureau chief, Jim Mutrie has been a master reporter. He never misinformed New Haven area readers about the increasingly complex, steadily more expensive, constantly growing services rooted in state government. He never abused a state employee in his news writing. He never embarrassed a news source. And he always played it so carefully, so fairly in journalistic discussions at the Register that to this day, after 34 years, I could not say the name of a single major politician or public administrator whom I know that Jim Mutrie especially liked or especially disliked. He has been the soul of objectivity and discretion, even among his working associates.

"There came a time when Jim turned down a managing editorship in New Haven because in his own quiet, unflappable way he loved the lure of a news story. He found a sort of secret zest in watching and personally recording the way party politics and public needs interact in Connecticut. The ultimate reporter, he respected the next day's breaking news more than he craved peer recognition or management authority.

His special claim to authority has always been the reliability, the fairness and the honesty of his reporting. His special claim to recognition has always been the personal decency, the steadily perceptive and carefully 'unflashy' nature of the record he has created on official Connecticut's day-to-day activities over 34 years. We are all here tonight as a sign of our recognition of Jim Mutrie's authority, the quality he put into every news story."

Jim's successors in Hartford will have a firm foundation on which to build. But in the State Capitol and at the Register, he will be missed.

Saturday, September 17, 1988
Editor's note

101 Years On East Rock

The East Rock monument was rededicated one year ago this weekend. It's nice to be able to report that the Soldiers and Sailors Memorial has added 52 weeks to its previous century without appreciable new wear and tear. East Rock Park itself bears up, a natural treasure amid mounting urban pressures. And if municipal plans can be maintained, the park and its priceless summit looking closely down on the city will grow steadily more attractive, and more publicly accessible, than in its neglected past.

I drove to the top the other day, just as Tuesday's rain clouds were clearing away. The Sound was still shrouded in mist. A hawk rode the rising breeze above the face of the rock. In the monument mound's ankle-high grass I flushed three mourning doves, the whoosh and sudden drumming of their wings a reminder of wildlife unseen all around me. Below the overlook, and beyond the path to the Giant Stairs, the rain-cleansed city was emerging in dappled light beside the pewter harbor.

It's a heartening view, one I've known for 60 years, but always different in its details and always rewarding in its revelations. We'd be fools not to reclaim it and preserve it securely from the graffiti grinches and the beer-can bullies who had begun to claim it as their own until last year.

There are still problems at East Rock - mostly because there is such intense use of the place with its many natural attractions. Improvements can be made only piecemeal on a limited budget. But the gains far exceed the losses.

The monument and its lights are pristine at the moment - clean and bright and strongly fenced. Some lamebrain has inscribed "Espo" on the new white granite curb at the foot of the memorial, a degradation that the four columns of Espositos in our phone book don't deserve. On the way up, the usual dozen or so cars with their single male drivers are clustered on out-of-the-way curves, "cruising" without moving - a pastime that can't be ignored, whatever the rights of parkers, if we're to restore East Rock to its best uses.

At the automobile overlook itself, the summit's prime feature, there are continuing deficiencies. There's much worn graffiti on the broad red granite curbing where the cars line up for the view. And below the edge, the path to the "steps" and the steep margin of greenery is a mess - a dumping ground for thoughtless parkers who trash it despite the regular efforts of park department workers. A telephone caller complained to me that one youth surrounded by pals had recently gestured at her with a drug syringe as she tried to show two grandchildren the view. An old New Havener told me that on every visit he made in the past three years there were beer drinkers at the brink. And sure enough, before I got back to my car a fellow in a pickup truck, bare-chested and looking as if he'd done a good day's work, stepped out into the breeze and uncapped a bottle of ale as he relaxed. That's no great crime, perhaps, but three or four more people with three or four more bottles would be a clear affront to others who prefer their panorama without partying.

Now for the good news that overrides the negative. Parks director Bob Sheeley says that by next year at this time there will be a security guard on horseback and a security guard in a four-wheel-drive vehicle on duty at almost all times in East Rock Park - and there will be similarly equipped security people in other parks.

At East Rock a new road and parking layout will be put in place at the summit, commencing in the spring of 1989. Traffic to the very edge of the cliff overlook - something that has been permitted since the first carriage road was laid - will cease this year. Next year cars at the top of the rock will be parked in the large parking lot on the Hamden side of the monument. That space will be repaved and groomed. And carefully graded walks, providing for wheelchair access, will lead from the automobile area past the monument to an overlook redesigned for pedestrian use only. The car culture, with its carry-along drinks, drugs and noisy radios, will be challenged to see the summit as a special place requiring a little special effort for its enjoyment.

For old-timers like me and my wife, there's an element of loss in this. In more innocent times, on a summer night in a Model A Ford, bright moon and stars in a velvet sky you could almost touch, a sleepy city below and a shimmering sea on the horizon were romantically routine atop East Rock. The cars lined up discreetly, quiet in their comings and goings, and about every 90 minutes a police patrol drove by, tolerant until midnight, inclined to move the stragglers down after that.

Such harmless dalliance lacks defenders in this era when the million-dollar teen-age rock hit is "I Want Your Sex." And anyway, the summit's moonlight spell is only a memory now that the steel gates on the park's lower road are locked at sunset.

The significant East Rock fact, at this point, is that the community's regard for the park and its summit has at last been harnessed. The depredations and degradations of careless users are being met and matched by the endeavors of people who care, by an increasing civic sense of the importance of the park's natural beauties - and of its safety as a place for young and old m every season.

Beneath the summit, in the Cold Spring entrance area at Orange Street, the park ranger's headquarters is being significantly improved and expanded so that nature appreciation programs on the flora and fauna of East Rock can be enjoyed along with the prideful viewing.

As autumn comes our way, with the idea of encouraging more people to return to the top of the rock, the park ranger is scheduling Wednesday noon, from 12 to 1:30, as a time when a look at the view and at the summit itself can be formalized. Sometime between now and the middle of October, grab an early lunch - or better yet, brown-bag it with a carry-along sandwich - and head for the top to hear about the park, the monument, and the great New Haven view. See you there!

Saturday, February 4, 1984
Editor's note

Wrapping-Up The Recollections

Basic newspapering is the normal concern of this column. I've strayed into other fields on occasions when there was some knowledge on my part or a special interest on the readers' part. A couple of times recently the refurbished Shubert Performing Arts Center has cropped up as a subject, mostly because its restoration and reopening has been a matter of major advocacy with me since they lowered the curtain and locked the doors in 1976.

Keeping it going will probably present some challenges to New Haven in the period ahead. Live theater on a community-supported stage is a pretty complex, sometimes risky, undertaking in days when so much entertainment is accessible electronically and when so much big business is focused on taped, recorded, and otherwise "canned" art and amusement.

At the same time, keeping the Shubert closed would have signaled a bankruptcy of spirit in New Haven, a failure of vision, beyond any recent setback we've faced - and fought. The Shubert was an obvious asset for some 60 years. It was ours. Its renewal, and the public's delight at its reopening, is a reminder of the many other neglected assets this region has to share and to bring to productive new life.

The wave of nostalgia that accompanied the opening of the Shubert has left me with a couple of loose ends. One is the story of Rex Harrison's nervous balk within hours of "My Fair Lady's" opening. The other is the claim that in the community wide remembrance, the old theater's house manager, Ben Witkin, went unmentioned.

If you'll indulge me in these, I promise not to say Shubert in this column for a whole month.

Ben Witkin may have been slighted in reference - but not in memory. Quiet and self-effacing, able to take without complaint the endless griping of showgoers who always wanted better seats than they were buying, Ben had few fancy notions about serving "art" or celebrating the Shubert as an institution. His job was filling seats.

He almost managed to conceal a kindly, considerate personality behind his intent regard for the ducats in his ticket racks.

Ben was a man who would have appreciated today's mini-theaters. He once said: "If I could build a theater it would have 10 rows. Everybody asks for a seat 'in the first 10 rows.'"

At the peak of its post-WWII success, management redecorated the Shubert. On the day the work was finished, with all his associates admiring the job and congratulating each other, Ben looked around. He didn't disapprove, he simply said: "It won't sell tickets."

That was his attitude about unchanneled theater enthusiasm, too. In those days I did a Sunday column with the inherited title of "72.3 Miles From Broadway." (Some early Register vaudeville buff had devised that label and the editor liked it.) What Ben Witkin didn't like was the fact that I often printed word of incoming shows before he was ready to sell tickets at the window.

"If I have three February shows that aren't yet sellouts," complained Ben, "I don't like customers to be saving their money for a show that you tell them is coming in March."

That difference aside, Ben Witkin was always knowledgeably obliging and informative about the Shubert and its shows. When Tom Bosley was married in Mayor Lee's office and Maurice Bailey stood for a champagne toast all around, it was Ben Witkin who made the arrangements. When Rex Harrison got cold feet Ben must have been stunned to see so great a ticket sale at risk, but he phoned his boss and manned the barricades until the situation eased. When mercurial Broadway press agents and the newspaper got into a tangle, as they might, Ben was always a gentle moderator.

Glamor gilds the old Shubert theater's memory these days - but the cautious reasonableness, the down-to-earth practicality, and the day-to-day integrity which had so much to do with its success were all part of the way Ben Witkin did his job.

As to the Rex Harrison story. One of the ironies of Shubert history is the uncertainty and confusion that - just before curtain time - beset one of the greatest artistic and financial successes the College Street theater ever launched. The incident is still shrouded in some mystery. Long-circulated versions around town become apocryphal, or dubious, when analyzed.

Talking separately to four sources who should know, I've come up with this as the likeliest story:

"My Fair Lady" was scheduled to open (1956) for "preview" on a Saturday night; it would be reviewed on Monday and then run through the following Saturday. Lots of New York, and even London, hoopla and fanfare had preceded its coming. Its authors and designers, its cast, its production company were crusted with "big" show biz names. It was already a hot ticket on Broadway, a sell-out in New Haven.

Suddenly on the opening Saturday the biggest name of all, Rex Harrison, said "not ready." The reasons are unspecific. But it had a richly melodic score which would be sung by "a collection of fine voices, from Julie Andrews' lyric soprano to comedian Stanley Holloway's impeccably-timed music hall baritone. Harrison was no singer and was slated to "elocute" his lyrics - to speak the lines to the music's rhythms, even in duets with other singing stars. Though he eventually triumphed with this trick, Harrison may well have worried about carrying it off.

At any rate, on a snowy February afternoon Maurice Bailey was summoned from standard Saturday relaxation at the Woodbridge Club. The British star wanted to cancel the performance. The Shubert's operator had some 13,000 sold seats on the line.

When Bailey reached the Shubert the house was deep in gloom. The company's manager - a Broadway power in his own field, Bailey, Ben Witkin, a representative of the other actors, sat in orchestra seats down front and debated disaster. Harrison was self-exiled in his room at the Taft.

Intermittently the company manager would phone Harrison to plead for a change of mind. All his future contracts would, the warnings went, be endangered. The "word-of-mouth" would be fatal. His fellow players were outraged. All the forces that could converge in the final hours before show-time were converging. Celebrity admirers of Harrison were climbing into New York limousines. The musicians would soon be assembling.

Harrison proposed canceling Saturday, rehearsing day and night Sunday, opening Monday. Maurice Bailey ruled: If we're not ready now, we're not ready next week. As the impasse held, the musicians were informed, as a contract requirement, that they might NOT be playing.

One version has it that Bailey's last card was a personal call on Harrison in his hotel room. Eating with friends in the Taft dining room, Bailey excused himself to go upstairs. When Harrison let him in he said: "The British were never quitters. You're letting your country as well as your company down if you don't go on tonight."

Another version is that Bailey's last card was his typical trump card - basic business. "We can't cancel a night. We must cancel the whole week. If I take back one ticket I should take back every ticket. The show will collapse."

What reason will you give the papers? was the question from the Taft. "The only reason there is. Mr. Harrison isn't ready to go on."

Which ever pressure worked - and the solution may have combined them - Rex Harrison pulled himself together and prepared to take the plunge. But uncertainty persisted.

An early diner at Kaysey's showed two buyable extra tickets, the result of a friend's non-appearance. "There'll be no show, anyway," he was told. "The orchestra went home."

At curtain time the overture was delayed. Finally Moss Hart, who'd been working as "doctor" or consultant on the script, stepped between curtains into a downstage spotlight. He told a hushed house there might be problems. A revolving platform or turntable essential to the scene changes wasn't working properly.

The production depended on it. But - with a little bit of luck...

Everybody clapped. The house lights dimmed. The orchestra swung into its introductory pastiche of all these wonderful "Fair Lady" tunes - and Rex Harrison came on to savor a night of wild applause and encores and the greatest popular success of his long career.

Maurice Bailey checked to make sure he had another cigar for the first intermission. And Ben Witkin, listening to the show from his distant box-office, moved the Standing Room Only sign into the window.

Saturday, December 24, 1988
Editor's note

The Unchanging Christmas Message

Christmas is most of all a memory of love that we carry through our lives. It begins with the child in the manger whom so many generations of the Western world have worshiped as the son of God. That expression at birth of humbleness, hope and transcendent family harmony, with its biblical end in mortal pain and disgrace before resurrection, is the model that rules the Christmas season, bringing out in all of us the best impulses of generosity, mercy and peace.

Time and tradition augment this spirit. Each year we turn again to the old carols, the ancient traditions of evergreen trees and candles, the sweet characters of Dickens and O. Henry and countless other writers - even the worst of such creations ennobled by the season and the warm communal memory we've built around them. The catalog grows constantly as we add Bing Crosby singing "White Christmas," or the Salvation Army with coin kettle and bells, or the rhythms of "Jingle Bell Rock." Using such strands of mood and atmosphere, we weave for today and tomorrow our personal recollections of Christmases past and our hope of those to come.

I remember a Christmas long ago when my father and mother brought me and my infant sister into the living room. Then, candle by candle, my father lighted our Christmas tree until it was a shining delight, the candles mirrored by bright ornaments as we oohed and aahed, the room all light and shadow and flickering celebration. The show didn't last long. My father was too careful a man to risk a falling candle - but that is the first Christmas memory I have, and it outshines all the electrical decorations since.

• From some vague experience of that same formative period, the scent of drying pine always takes me back to the "crib" and the Christ child that marked Christmas week on the side altar of St. Francis Church in Fair Haven. There the familiar manger scene - the sheep and oxen amidst straw bedding, the kneeling mother and father, the newborn babe who didn't appear until Christmas Day - had a massed backing of evergreens. These were cut and mounted early in the church and their fragrance, for a city child unused to the forest reality, has become the link between moment and memory whenever pine's special scent is in the air.

• There was a wonderfully confused Christmas in my youth when I gave one pretty girl the first Christmas present I'd ever chosen for a woman other than my mother, a pair of matching black and white stuffed Scotties. A day or so later I sat by another pretty girl's Christmas tree, vibrant with the sudden hope that we would spend all our future Christmases together. And we have.

• There came a wartime Christmas Eve under palm trees in the Philippines, homesick boys feeling sorry for themselves as they sang the old carols beneath unfamiliar constellations. Stars were the only light in the blacked-out camp until the warning siren wailed three times. Then two or three Japanese planes passed over, heading for the airstrip on the point. The ack-ack batteries sent up three lingering flares to illuminate miles of sky, followed by fountains of tracer shells, a Christmas display that blunted the attack - if it was one.

At midnight there was a Catholic Mass in an abandoned country church where a red supply parachute was hung to lighten the gloom. A dozen candles on a makeshift altar provided illumination. Soldiers of every faith came, joined by barefoot, holiday-decked Filipinos who knelt to greet the Christmas babe in a poor, humble setting that was part of their own lives. Next day there was turkey, a two-bottle beer ration and, when the bottles were empty, a brilliant glow on the China Sea as the setting sun moved beyond the Pacific rim on its way across Asia and Europe to rise in the Atlantic for New Haveners.

• There were golden Christmases thereafter with our three children, when other family members arrived from far and wide.

The 8-millimeter home movies, converted now to videocassette, authenticate the year the parakeet came, the year the piano was a family gift, the rocker-bottomed endurance of Puncho the plastic clown, a long sequence of dolls and junior lab sets and magic kits and things for skiing or other outdoor activities.

• The elusiveness of Christmas lies in such swings from the inanely material to the spiritual. There came a Christmas 12 years ago when there was no holiday feeling in the house until suddenly the doctors at the Gaylord Hospital suggested Christmas Day at home for Anne. Struggling back after a grave stroke, my wife had been away for two months, reaching for new living patterns in that unsurpassed rehab center on a Wallingford hill. How we rushed, after grim weeks, to get the tree up and the rooms refreshed. Lifting the wheelchair through the door that Christmas Day, lighting the tree, renewed the wonder that started so long ago with candles and the sense of a life still unfolding.

There was a day in Bethlehem before that. Not at Christmas, but a few short weeks after it one year, I made a journalist's journey to Israel. The cold in Jerusalem penetrated the bone. Nightly, stars shone diamond clear and icy against velvet skies. Some mornings snow dusted the ancient streets where Christ carried his cross. How cold it must have been to make that census journey from Nazareth nearly 2,000 years ago, the young wife and the aging husband moving across treeless hills in the winter wind.

Then in Bethlehem - in the old town where Arabs and Jews and Christians today remain at odds - the air was harsh on Manger Square. We crouched to go singly through the low stone doorway, meant to bar infidel assaults, at the Crusader-built church above the crypt of the Nativity. Generations of worship have left it worn and without majesty, ill-served by so many centuries of varied decoration by so many pilgrims in so many styles. The thoughtful eye rejects what it sees. Then the feeling heart, sensing the living reverence in those who kneel as their predecessors knelt, remembers the manger birth and the message of love that it has unendingly inspired.

Each Christmas is for all of us a memory of that love as we have personally fostered it, and abused it, down the years.

Saturday, November 10, 1990
Editor's note:

Some New Beginnings

The first election in New Haven this week was the election for the Free Public Library. It took place last Sunday, and it was a landslide. In three afternoon hours thousands upon thousands of New Haven area adults - and kids - poured up the stairways, through the doors and between the aisles of shelved books. The People glowed, they gushed, and on every level they sat on the floor or at the tables to read - bookworming their way among the library's 300,000 volumes. After outlasting 25 years of poor-mouthing and neglect, they pulled all the affirmative levers, emphatically endorsing the $17 million in public funds that have renewed the library.

Politically the celebration demonstrated a constituency for the library that many local leaders have seemed to doubt. Administratively it raised more questions than it answered mostly about reasonable and practical ways in which the mayor, the aldermen, and hard-pressed municipal managers can support this excellent teaching and learning facility in such tough times.

There are only 40 full-time staff members at the downtown library. That restricts hours and limits services. No part-timers are budgeted because laid-off full-timers get first work priority. But with this week's surge in popular enthusiasm for the library, can't the part-time possibility be re-explored? Is there a fair and acceptable way to organize unpaid volunteers? After all, there are school volunteers. How can the library and its staff, and the library's users, get the most productivity from this bright public resource?

The library "election" last Sunday left no doubts about citizen endorsement of the facility. Now the follow-up is what challenges library lovers as well as New Haven officials.

Some enchanted evenings were Mary Martin's repeated gift to New Haven. She was an entertainer of such skill that she made performance seem like an exchange between old friends, of such energy and effervescence that she seemed never to age; of such warmth that she dominated the Shubert stage each time she walked it, even in the best of company.

The local memory of Mary Martin is special. In this week of memorial tributes there has been a lot of visual emphasis on "Peter Pan," which she did for television in 1955, and on her first hit song, "My Heart Belongs To Daddy," as she sang it in a 1946 movie. But New Haven's love affair with Mary started with that song in 1938 when she first presented it - and herself - on College Street as the not-so-ingenuous ingénue in Cole Porter's saucy "Leave It I To Me."

My best girl and I went "rush" in $2 top balcony seats to that show - a great way to start a relationship with a wife-to-be and with Mary Martin, too.

Mary Martin had agreed to sing "Daddy" again at the Shubert 75th anniversary party last year but, 51 years after she introduced it here, she fell ill and couldn't come. The memory of her first performance suffices. So does the mind's eye as it lingers with Mary and operatic basso Ezio Pinza near Bali Hai, with Mary and Theodore Bikel in the Bavarian Alps, with her and Tinker Bell and the Darling children in Never, Never Land. That's entertainment!

Saturday, January 20, 1990
Editor's note:

Flu Bugs And Cherry Blossoms

The 1990 census of the United States is getting under way in Washington. By late spring and summer, say the Commerce Department news releases, it will become a blizzard of facts and figures pouring into federal computers. It's big government doing its ultimate thing, putting us into pigeonholes. But the census once provided me, briefly, with a living.

At this season 50 years ago I had taken up residence in Washington in the red brick G Street YMCA to lend a hand in the census of 1940. Earlier I had taken a civil service clerical test. Along with the word that I had passed, however, came a note saying that the FBI job I wanted was not then open, but the Bureau of the Census considered me eligible for instant assignment to the legions it was massing for the national head count. I took the job at $1,440 a year - about $27 a week in take-home pay - boarded the train here in early January, and found that almost everyone in the cubicle-crowded corridor on my floor at the "Y" was also a census worker.

The job was a paper-shuffler's delight as hundreds upon hundreds of us sharpened lead pencils and coded returns already submitted for the national census of business, which had been taken in late 1939. But the half-year I spent in Washington introduced me to the nation's capital just as it was about to become the world's capital in World War II. The experience left me, ever since, with a sure sense - my wife calls it a delusion - about knowing the ins and outs of the federal city in peace and in war.

(I'm telling you all this because I've been housebound with the flu, unable to pick up my Register mail or consort with the Register associates who keep me timely in my media comment.)

Washington in 1940 was not the metropolis it wants to be today. It was a beautiful Southern city, complacent, its avenues broad and clean, most federal buildings graceful and proud but not yet grandiose, its populace almost all comfortably middle class, with the instinctive neatness of good bureaucrats. There were bad slums within sight of the Capitol's dome in the northeast and southeast quadrants - where Civil War shacks in the back alleys of Maj. L'Enfant's original plan had become jammed and festering. But mostly the grand avenues swept up from Foggy Bottom to higher ground, or out to Arlington and Alexandria, through circles and squares and cul-de-sacs where ordinary people lived amid flower boxes and fragrant Southern foliage. There was a sense of order: C Street was followed by Church Street in the one-syllable streets of the alphabet, by Chapin in the two-syllable sequence.

Our incoming census crews checked in at the eight-acre Commerce Department building, basked in its monumentality and were then put to work at second-hand desks in a remodeled garage far out on North Capitol Avenue near some railroad tracks. After a week or two I found a room on Connecticut Avenue near Chevy Chase Circle. My host was a quiet husband, addressed as Mister, who had a heavy gold watch chain, a law degree and an undefined job in the Library of Congress. His gray-haired wife was effervescent. In introducing me with great formality in a Southern accent to her shy daughter Sabina ("I know you'll be friends") she was a precursor of the genteel, manipulative mothers I was to meet later in the plays of Tennessee Williams. Plenty to do downtown became my goal.

I took a weekend-plus-Monday off, came back to New Haven to see my girl and to pick up my Model A Ford. There were no interstates, just two-lane roads through every small town in New Jersey. After riding from mid-morning to 9 p.m. through the Garden State and through ferry slips, posted "speed traps" and miles of after-dark Baltimore I reached the District. With a car parked safely on side streets, the town was mine to explore through Washington's long, flowering spring.

In cherry blossom time my best girl came from New Haven for a long weekend - bewitching, newly shod and newly coiffed, imperviously wrapped in her mother's warnings. She stayed in a "Y"-approved home off Kalorama Road. Each time I drove up a prim matron stood at parade rest in the hall - impassable. She would call up the stairs "Your visitor, dear!" while tiered hydrangeas, begonias and I all blushed.

I showed Anne the drive through bridgeless Rock Creek Park where the cars, like old-time carriages, splashed through hub deep fords wherever road and creek came together. We took the 16-mile spin out to George Washington's gracious Mount Vernon. We heard a famous torch singer (Hildegarde) in the swank Blue Room of the Shoreham Hotel and pretended not to notice when the maitre d' palmed a tip and then seated us by the back wall. We checked out Constitution Hall where Marion Anderson had recently been refused a platform, then saw the Lincoln Memorial, where 50,000 had heard her alternative concert. We rode through Arlington's gates to the old Lee-Custis mansion on its high hill with its magnificent view of Washington - where 23 years later they would light the eternal flame on John F. Kennedy's grave. We saw the White House, the Capitol's House and Senate wings, the remodeled garage in which I coded census papers, and the Great Falls of the Potomac near the Chesapeake canal. We had a dandy time.

The decennial federal census has, since then, been an institution I support. But in that spring I received a Western Union telegram from the imperious managing editor of the Register to whom I had submitted free-lance articles. He had a job at $15 a week - if I reported promptly. I told him sadly I was earning almost twice that. He countered with the offer of a summer reporting job at $25 and a chance the arrangement might become permanent. I took the job that June - and his hint of permanence still holds.

Now, the flu and its cures raise old ghosts around me, and I watch the census armies muster for 1990. I hope there will be young head-counters this year who, statistics aside, will get as much basic poetry, "emotion recollected in tranquility," as I got from the census of 1940.

Saturday, March 16, 1991
Editors Note

Gulf Homecomings Stir Memories

Watching the boys and girls come home from the Persian Gulf has put me in mind of my own soldier homecoming at the end of World War II.

So joyous an end to separation could never quite be disastrous - but for me and my wife it was a lifetime synonym, a worst-case scenario, for things planned.

It was December 1945. By then I had spent two years and 11 months in service, had moved north in the Pacific from Guadalcanal and Manila to Tokyo. I started home from Japan not with my Air Forces unit but on the basis of individual points - time in service, battles, dependents which was the way most troops were discharged then.

The great victory parades of September 1945 were over. Public acclaim was ours. But the miles were long and time was short. Soldiers and civilians were all rushing to put war behind and take up the interrupted patterns of their lives.

There were 16 million veterans to get home by ship and train and bus (no commercial planes). Mail was slow. There were lines at every public phone. And often, when the phone was won, circuits were jammed.

The homeward journey started for me in five feet of Hokkaido snow. After five days in a flu-ridden Yokohama airplane hangar it led to a dinky U.S. freighter, the Sea Devil. By the northern route, from Japan past the Aleutians and Alaska to Seattle, we tossed on gale and rain-swept seas above decks and through 10 days of battened-down seasickness below.

After an impatient Thanksgiving at Seattle I rode a soldier-filled train over the Rockies into the stark winter of the northern plains, past Laramie and a dust storm in Cheyenne, past North Platte and Des Moines, on to Chicago nights and days merging on the worn velour seats.

I had phoned from Seattle, so by my standard I was present and accounted for. In Chicago, amid swarming troops, the Army transport desk told me that if I ran I might catch the overnight to New York. I ran. And in the lurching darkness came Cleveland and Erie and then dawn already breaking on the still-magic streets of New York.

In Grand Central every phone had a line of waiting callers. The familiar train home was on the lower level. In a gray December morning it rambled past the factories and back yards, the tin cans and old mattresses, and the contradictorily neat gardens and garages that tie New Haven to New York on the rail line.

The next day would be the fourth anniversary of Pearl Harbor's destruction, and I was awash in old memory, new hope and the joy of a family coming closer. In New Haven, where I charged up the long ramp with the killer barracks bag, the phone alcove was again jammed - and at the curb the Orange Street bus was idling. It took me, swift as a magic carpet, to Edwards Street. The driver thumped my big bag down beside me on the curb.

On the doorstep, pressing the bell like a stranger, I realized it was still morning. I had been by the Pacific when I last took time to phone. I heard the startled gasp of my mother-in-law as she opened the front door to me and called at the same time into the living room: It's Bob! It's Bob! Bob's home!"

The moment of joy and crisis in the kitchen vibrated through the house. It vibrates wordlessly today. There was a baby crying - diaper newly wet, I later learned. There was a sobbing wife in my arms. We wept and laughed, and the baby boy I had not seen before kept up his steady obbligato. Through tears my best girl, turned mother and home-holder while I was away, said: "You didn't call. I wanted to be beautiful for you."

All I could say then, as I would now, was: "Stay this beautiful." And she did.

And I was home.

Saturday, June 12, 1993
Editor's note

Symphony Starting Second Century

One of this community's real reasons for pride, the New Haven Symphony Orchestra, is launching its 100th anniversary celebration these summer nights. Every time its instruments are tuned, every time the conductor's baton is raised, there should be supportive audiences alongside. Tonight at 7:30 on the New Haven Green the orchestra and the community will have a chance to share their pride harmoniously. Try to be there - on the orchestra's home ground.

There are only four cities in America that have 100-year-old symphony orchestras - New York, Chicago, Boston and this old town. Consider the great metropolitan centers that support the other three orchestras with their millions in population, their wealth, their history and their international cultural status.

Then consider New Haven with its time-worn grace, with the many adornments and advantages that warm our hearts but also with its endless struggles and challenges and limited resources. From such comparison you draw some sense of the wondrous inspiration and the constant work - creative rhapsody and sharp money management - required to make 100 years of music in a small city like this with so few merchant princes to smile upon art.

There are grand formal celebrations of the orchestra's centennial year to come. Tonight in summer mood on the Green the NHSO will perform al fresco, free, for all comers. There will be added music June 18 in West Haven, June 20 in Branford, June 26 in North Haven, and then Aug. 22 back on the city's Green. So put your blankets and beach chairs into the car and join the orchestra in its summer rounds.

The New Haven Symphony Orchestra has its roots in town-gown cooperation - in Morris Steinert, a German immigrant who loved music as much as Horatio William Parker, the first chairman of the music department at Yale. Steinert pulled the musicians together and provided Steinert Hall in 1894. Parker, then a leading American composer, became conductor of the new group. The Yale factor has since been a key in the orchestra's growth and development.

Concert notes in 100 years of old programs, and the dry minutes of thousands of board and committee meetings, probably can't capture the experience of beauty and emotion shared time and again by New Haveners in the concert hall. Nor is there a measurable record of the lasting human insights and excitements brought home from Woolsey Hall by generations of concert goers through crunching winter snow or under springtime stars.

The symphony's civilizing spell has been its gift to New Haven, and that musical art, intangible but unforgettable, is what the coming centennial season celebrates.

In 1903 Woolsey Hall became the permanent home of the NHSO - and 90 years later there is still dispute about its design and its acoustics. After Parker the conductors reflected the times - Edward Stillman Kelley, David Stanley Smith, Hugo Kortschak, Richard F. Donovan, Harry Berman for the pops concerts, Frank Brieff, Keith Wilson, Erich Kunel, Murray Sidlin, and today Michael Palmer with Peter Sacco as assistant conductor.

Young People's Concerts were initiated in 1932. In 1945 a pops concert series was started in the old New Haven Arena and moved that summer to the Yale Bowl, where it lasted almost a decade. In 1953 free concerts were offered for the first time in New Haven schools. In 1965 free summer concerts began on the Green. In 1983 the orchestra performed to critical acclaim at New York's Lincoln Center. In 1988 it first made music with the Shubert Opera Company.

Come October the orchestra will be awhirl. There are 19 concerts with distinguished guest performers scheduled in a bit more than six months. Program highlights will include Yale dean

Ezra Laderman's Eighth Symphony, generously commissioned as a musical centerpiece marking the NHSO centennial. Gustav Mahler's monumental Eighth Symphony will salute the 100th anniversary of the founding of the Yale Music School. The Laderman symphony will also be performed when the New Haven orchestra provides a guest concert on Jan. 21 in New York's Carnegie Hall.

In the months ahead the NHSO will be doing what it has been doing for a century - bringing composers, musicians, its conductor and its listeners together to reach for a shared experience of musical beauty and human understanding. As the outdoor concerts get under way tonight, and through other summer nights nearby - with fun more than formality the goal, who'd dare miss one?

Saturday, March 26, 1994
Editor's note

State FOI Laws Still Need Defenders

Freedom of information is hardly the "in" phrase in Hartford these days.

Jobs, sensible taxes and ways to refinance and reorganize disintegrating public services are at the top of Connecticut's needs for the '90s. But what about keeping such public choices and costs open to public scrutiny?

In tough times, Connecticut citizens should be urged to keep a steady eye on their freedom of information defenses.

That was the theme of the 1994 Freedom of Information Conference held in Farmington the other day. It was sponsored by the state Commission on Freedom of Information, the new fund-raising Foundation for Open Government, the Society of Professional Journalists in this state, and the long-established newspaper and broadcasting Council on Freedom of Information.

The watchword: Be vigilant. The warning: Times are changing.

Freedom of information laws have guaranteed the state's citizens access to their government and supported their right to know about the doings of public officials since Gov. Ella Grasso made them a basic tool of her administration 20 years ago. The assumptions of 1974, however, are not always those of 1994.

Smart lawyers have worked constantly to find a courtroom logic for "privacy" that helps to cut the original FOI pressure for public disclosure.

Crime-swamped officials in judicial and police agencies find judges are often skittish when free press vs. fair trial issues arise

- so they try to minimize arrest news and instruct the police in secrecy.

Finally, the computerization of all records - even in small towns - means that the printed word on the printed page, stored handily on shelves and in file cabinets, is giving way to electronic data storage. Transferring such official facts to tapes and disks for study and disclosure may be a lot more costly and complicated than a search of the old paper records.

The conference talked a lot about such realities as 150 participants, mostly town administrative personnel, checked ways to do the right thing by observing FOI law.

Today's fast-moving information technology challenges all record-keepers. Dick Conrad, the Register's own reporter-turned computer-specialist, offered a utopian view of the way any citizen might some day use the public library to hook into the state government's computers and extract direct, personal answers about any area of state operations or expenditures.

That won't happen tomorrow. But the presence beside Conrad of the director of the state Office of Information and Technology and an official of the state Department of Administrative Services signals changes in the future.

On the "up" side for FOI there was crisp lawyerly discussion about a recent Supreme Court decision relaxing the traditional privacy around compensation agreements with public employees. The court ruled that sick leave records of a schoolteacher – the number of days for which she was paid, not the details of the illness – were OK for publication. Such disclosure would not be "highly offensive to a reasonable person."

On the "down" side for FOI is on-going controversy over Chief State's Attorney Bailey's view that parts of a prosecutorial probe and details need not be outlined nor explained until the case is in court. This could reduce police news to names and charges - but more facts than those may be needed to enlighten the community.

Conference conclusion: The coming "information superhighway" will need a whole new set of FOI on-ramps and exits - soon - to link Connecticut agencies and the citizens they serve.

The program's oddest bypath was labeled "Guns and Gangs." It featured a Hartford Courant columnist, a Channel 30 TV reporter, Beatrice Codianni Robles, a Latin Kings spokesperson from New Haven and moderator Ken Venit, a media maven.

Chief State's Attorney Bailey, listed as a panelist, sent word he wouldn't debate with a gang member.

The journalists basically testified that bad things happen to urban youngsters - through street - gang pressure and police mishandling. Once in trouble, kids don't get adequate guidance.

Beatrice Codianni, a soft-spoken 40-ish mother, insisted the Latin Kings are more a Hispanic family than a gang. "There are thousands of members. They want jobs. They work with churches." She said she was more afraid of the Hartford police anti-gang task of force than of the gangs.

Of New Haven's Police Chief she said: "He will call me. I will call him (about street troubles)." Asked if she reported illegal guns to the police, she said: "We take care of our own. Come and get us if we do anything dirty or wrong."

The discussion didn't do much to advance the FOI laws democracy-based goals. But it may have illustrated why such patient, courteous legal procedures are eroding – and need vigilant protection – in a society full of adversarial violence and confusion about what's right or wrong.

Saturday, December 10, 1994
Editor's note

Shubert At 80 Years Is Still A "Belle"

On College Street 80 years ago this weekend there was a sense of holiday excitement. The Shubert Theater was opening.

Financed by the New Haven Hotel Company which had launched the imposing Hotel Taft in 1911, the theater was named for Sam S. Shubert, one of the three brothers who were the most famed entertainment investors of the day. The Shubert name meant big-time theater had come to New Haven.

The first night of first nights was Friday, Dec. 11, 1914. The opening show was a frivolous revue, "The Belle of Bond Street," starring the brash Broadway comedian Sam Bernard, "direct" from successful engagements at the Adelphi in London and the Shubert in New York.

Sam Bernard brought down the house with his suggestive rendition of "Who Paid the Rent for Mrs. Rip Van Winkle?" Miss Mollie King naughtily offered "When I'm With the Boys (I Can't Help Loving Them All)" and London's Miss Minerva Coverdale sang "Prunella." Dancer Sammy Lee, backed by the chorus, introduced "The Tango Dip."

The Register called the evening "a society event of the first magnitude."

That night was the beginning of a now-familiar but still unfolding story for New Haven. The city's other theaters were then, in pre-movie days, cramped upstairs halls or, like the Hyperion just across College Street, converted churches. The Shubert, designed by architect Albert Swazey of New York, seated 1,500 in orchestra, mezzanine and upper balcony, facing a stage and scenery loft that compared with the best in the world.

As a first-class facility the Shubert instantly became one of New Haven's boasted advantages, but it was a fun place, user-friendly and relaxed. Its everyday ties to the town are reflected in the way the Register has always followed newspaper style in references to the Shubert Theater - even after management went upscale, with the French spelling - "theatre" - on its playbills.

Walter Mulconry, the New Havener with the most detailed files on Shubert shows, can provide a cornucopia of great names in entertainment from those first Shubert bookings.

Mrs. Patrick Campbell (1915), "Buffalo Bill" Cody (1916), Yvette Guilbert, friend of Toulouse-Lautrec (1917); opera stars Nellie Melba (1915), Maggie Teyte (1917), Geraldine Farrar (1923), Madame Ernestine Schumann- Heinck (1915, 1924), Jan Peerce (1939), Dorothy Kersten (1944), Ezio Pinza (1949); Sergei Rachmaninoff at the piano (1918, 1923), violinist Efrem Zimbalist (1924), dancer Anna Pavlova (1915) a month after the theater opened, Vaslav Nijinsky and the Sergei Diaghilev Ballet Russe (1916), matinee idol John Barrymore (March 1916), his sister Ethel Barrymore (May 1916).

They were personalities from the great old road tours. Then from the 1930s to the 1960s the Shubert was a Broadway satellite. Major talents trod the stage, popular ballads shook the rafters, famed playwrights and directors labored over the laughs, Tallulah Bankhead - overheated - dragged her full-length mink coat behind her down the aisle.

As Maurice H. Bailey, who owned New Haven movie houses, took over from the Shuberts in 1941 the fabulous, dramatic years - so cherished in local memory - took shape.

The American musical, evolving over decades, burst into artistic splendor at the Shubert after World War II. The house became the "tryout" site for 20 to 30 Broadway-bound shows a season - dramas, comedies, extravagantly mounted musicals. Maurice Bailey's canny management over 35 years, his "show biz" reputation nationally, his cigar-chewing zest for good theater, helped mold the Shubert as legend and profit center.

In 1976, with Bailey aging and the Shubert, like Broadway,

weakened in the new era of electronic entertainment, the house of dreams went dark. Then, in 1984, restored through public subsidy, it emerged as the elegant Shubert Performing Arts Center.

Today's Shubert is the new heart of New Haven's downtown entertainment district - which is, in itself, the most dynamic element in a depressed city center struggling to find new functions.

On stage, old echoes from 1920s vaudeville, classical drama, the dance and Broadway "hits" still liven a 1990s cultural institution with varied subscription choices (not just tickets) and all the new socio-theatrical obligations imposed by grants and tax breaks.

The smash shows are fewer, the essential box-office "nut" harder to harvest. The directors currently seek tax dollars to mend a roof only 10 years old.

Still, the "Belle of Bond Street" spirit generates continued hope. As belle of College Street the glowing Shubert draws faithful crowds of the affluent and the artistic. Coming soon, in celebration, there will be an 80th season gala for the Shubert in 1995.

But after that the challenge looms: How do we best find the money to renew the art and extend the memory of what began on this pre-holiday weekend in 1914?

Saturday, March 27, 1993
Editor's note

Savin Rock Etched In Fond Memories

Just saying "Savin Rock" prompts smiles and good thoughts among old-timers in this region. For a half century the Rock was a childhood wonderland full of fantasy, fun and a lot of freakish sideshow, too.

"Savin Rock Memories" are currently a project of retired Register pressman, Gil Johnson, and some other West Haveners. They're planning a summer book about the old amusement park and want as much recollection as they can get.

My Fair Haven family rarely got to Savin Rock more than once a year. It was a long trip by trolley car, and Sunday at the Rock, even with 10-cent hot dogs, took lots of prior scrimping and planning. But the place stuck with me.

My first memory is offbeat. There was a mazelike House of Mirrors that kept you bumping into your own reflection along twisting, polished alleys. In memory I'm a preschooler.

There is comedy mixed with true confusion when my father suddenly moves me in front of a distorting mirror. I see the little boy I know transformed - with a pin head and stubby legs and a great round middle. I still laugh at that memory, but there lingers a side-sense of shock and unwanted change in the mirror's curved surface.

In later trips to the Hall of Mirrors, laughing kids and grownups pointed at each other, and me, in shapes that were silly - but also tinged with the surreal and the mysterious.

The rest of the recollection is kaleidoscopic. My mother in a white dress and white shoes, my father coatless and wearing a straw hat. My sister and I eating frozen custard, Jake's hot dogs, crumbling cubes of chocolate, vanilla and strawberry popcorn, salt water taffy. My sister, mounted and strapped, and my mother standing beside her at one flying horse. Behind them, buckled-in, I was a bold, lone rider at full gallop as the automatic drum and the cymbals and the hurdy-gurdy waltzes swept us past a blur of summer celebrants.

There were other, noisier contraptions. Did we ride them? Or did we watch and share the screamers' thrills? The Whip, the Tilt-a-Whirl, the Lightning Bug.

There were roaring, clattering, boastfully boarded roller coasters, the Thunderbolt over the water, the Sky Blazer in the White City. There were benches in the grove, and Sunday band music, and people of all ages, sizes, conditions.

If, for any reason there were momentary blues - a hot dog dropped, a kewpie doll chipped - there was always the contagious hilarity of the life-size Laughing Lady as she chortled and chuckled and wheezed for the throngs that laughed back around her glass case on Beach Street.

Twice I remember the great treat of taking the cross-harbor excursion boat from Lighthouse Point to Savin Rock - a sea voyage plus two beaches in one sunburned afternoon. There was a "shore dinner" one special day at breeze-swept Wilcox's Pier on pilings above the beach.

By the time I had a job and a car and a best girl, Jimmie's hot dog stand (counter only), and, Chick's and Turk's were drawing 1,000 cars a summer night to the 10 o'clock Rock. By the time my best girl and I had a family, the old amusement park was tacky in some spots but still pluckily magical in others.

There was no better way to lighten a day for the kids - when the Kentucky cousins left for home or the dentist fumbled - than an hour or two at Savin Rock driving the race cars, riding the horses, revisiting the Fun House. Late in the 1950s, there even were some great toy discounts at Christmas in the old take-a-chance booths along the shore - a last commercial hurrah for people who once had handled warehouses full of the Rock's summer prizes.

The trolley car stitched greater New Haven together and gave

Savin Rock its heyday. Distant, designer-shaped, cutely marketed theme parks replaced it in the age of the automobile and the family airlines package. The Rock's amiable ways ("25 cents, please") and casual machinery ("So sue me"), and its exhilarating combination of thrills and neighborliness would be hard to keep going in the age of Ninja and Nintendo.

But, if you knew it once, take a spring stroll along today's West Haven waterfront promenade and check the Savin Rock site markers. You'll remember frosted root beer and - ghostly on the breeze you may hear the crowd of riders' single shriek as the Thunderbolt tips in its first lo-o-ong plunge toward the ground.

If you hear it, tell Gil Johnson, 884 Campbell Ave.

Saturday, January 30, 1993
Editor's Note

Are Mashantuckets Blazing A Trail?

One of history's ironies is at work in Connecticut today, and it suggests that we all take at least a cursory look at the Indians among us.

The Mashantucket Pequot Indians - once impoverished, isolated and ignored like all native tribes - have developed with Gov. Weicker a plan to produce $100 million a year in state revenues if given, in return, a state monopoly on slot machines at their Foxwoods casinos. The Indians, in a sense, are peddling financial "firewater."

The politics of gaming and casino operations in Connecticut will be in flux for months to come. But the changing civic power of the people who were here ages before the English settlements is probably more interesting anyway. At the New Haven Colony Historical Society from now until June there's an exhibit of local Indian facts and artifacts, "The Quinnipiacs: First Settlers of New Haven." And last Saturday the exhibit was augmented when 100 or so Indian scholars and admirers- held a daylong discussion of the native peoples and the land of South Central Connecticut.

The exhibit is not about Indian empowerment, but - in sparse detail and with a hint of lost values - about the Indian encounter here with people from a more technologically advanced world.

The Indians of Connecticut first made a mark on the land more than 10,000 years ago. They have been better documented by archaeologists over the past 3,000 years but only fragments survive. They lived in scattered settlements in small tribal groups, supported in their homelands by crops the women raised, by game the men hunted and by fish from the rivers plus the rich shellfish beds - oysters, clams, mussels - of Long Is land Sound.

By the time New Haven was settled, studies hint, the Indians of New England had already been decimated by European diseases caught in casual trade for furs with English, French, Dutch, Norse and other adventurers.

The Quinnipiacs were peaceful when the New Haven colonists arrived in 1638. Already harassed and paying tribute to warlike Pequot neighbors, they may even have seen the English, briefly, as protectors. By the end of 1638 they had formally deeded much land to Theophilus Eaton and John Davenport and the "planters." By 1686 there was a 1,000-acre reservation on the east shore or New Haven harbor - solely for Indian use but implying, also, that they had no access to other lands except on the colony's far edges.

The exhibit at the historical society building, 114 Whitney Ave., records all this and gives it human dimension. There are old contracts and maps, the signs of the sachems - Momaugin, Montowese, Quosoquonch (near Totoket), and of the Menunkatuch female sachem, Shaumpishuh.

There are pictures of round bark wigwams, sheltering about seven, and of the long houses which might bring together seven or eight related families in winter. There is a picture of the local ceremonial rock, still in thin woods off Woodward Avenue, where sacred powwows were held until about 1850.

There are locally made Indian awls of deer bone, hammer stones, ax heads, wampum shell beads, wood splint baskets from North Haven, other artifacts found in Hamden, Branford, and other nearby sites.

There is a reproduction of a dugout canoe - made from a felled tree trunk, chopped and carefully burned and scraped to hollowness. There is an example of the planting - corn, beans, and squash in a single hill, the cornstalk supporting the runner beans, the broad squash leaves shading out weeds, fish used as planting-time fertilizer.

The Quinnipiac Indians lost their ancient homelands swiftly, in a couple of generations. They retreated into poverty and proud individuality outside the Yankee culture. Some moved as a group to Farmington about 1750, to merge with the Tunxis tribe. A few holdouts lived for decades in the Guilford woods. Others moved on to Oneida lands in New York. About 1830 a group trekked to a new Indian heartland set up in Wisconsin. In recent decades Quinnipiacs, like other Indian groups, have begun to pull together and to reclaim the identity so long submerged and so long withheld from the communities around them.

The flashy rise of the Mashantucket Pequots, exciting not envy but comparable effort, is probably no model for statewide revival among indigenous people today. But the compact historical exhibit on Whitney Avenue is a reminder of the Indians who were here first - and who finally find some hope in tomorrow.

Crawford Manor, *Elderly Housing, George Street, 1965, balconies with a modern urban prospect on the edge of the Oak Street Connector near Park Street.* *Redevelopment Agency Collection.*

Saturday, January 28, 1989
Editor's note:

Stepping Out At The Inauguration

One of Yale's bright hostesses 40 years ago was Margaret Bush Clement. Her husband, Stuart, a Yale administrative officer, headed the university's placement bureau. She was a community volunteer with a special interest in the Red Cross - and her annual party educating local press people in that good work was how I got to know her years ago. Occasionally, she had around the house her nephew George, a Yale undergraduate and first baseman on the Yale baseball team.

Last week it was her turn to share in a party she didn't have to plan - as guest at the extended Washington bash that inaugurated George Herbert Walker Bush as 41st president of the United States. It was a festive romp for a party-loving lady - despite the fact that she is 89.

Best fun? "The family, more than a hundred of us, talking endlessly and taking over 90 rooms of the 100-room Jefferson Hotel." Biggest problem? "Stairs. Washington is full of mountainous stone steps and carpeted staircases with hardly a rail to hold. I never climbed so many stairs I couldn't see but had to feel - or lose my dignity."

This week Marge Clement is breathing easier at her apartment in the Whitney Center, Hamden, sorting out her impressions of the 96-hour family kaffeeklatsch and reunion that ushered nephew George into the White House. She is also answering a few notes - like the one she got from her old housekeeper, now retired in Scotland. "You always told me, Mrs. Clement, that George would be president some day." Marge disremembers: "I don't recall that prophecy at all, but I do know we thought George was one of several nephews who could do well if they applied themselves."

The first family is a nuclear family in its most extended form. There were 17 already aboard the Amtrak club car when Marge clambered on in New Haven to don her red, white and blue corsage. Others joined them down the line. It was a crowded, dressy carnival for the young people, a collection of precious cameos for those older.

"I didn't buy a thing to wear. I knew the family wouldn't be concerned, and nobody in Washington would recognize my New Haven wardrobe... My three children, their spouses and I had one dinner with the Bush cousins....On Thursday night the galas and banquets were too much. Dottie Bush (the president's mother and wife of Marge's brother, the late Connecticut Sen. Prescott Bush) and I had dinner in her suite. It was restful.... The schedules were frantic. Wake-up at 5:45 a.m. Breakfast, 6: 15. Buses, 7:20. Take only the bus that has your number. Then wait, wait, wait. ...

"One of the best times for fun was the Salute to the First Lady at the Kennedy Center on Thursday morning at 11. There were three nearly identical programs in the concert hall, the opera house and the Eisenhower Theater. Barbara and Marilyn Quayle appeared at each, and Barbara displayed her designer clothes. That's where she made such a hit. ...

"The family lunch at the White House on Saturday was a delight. Marine Corps musicians played at the front door. As George came down the stairs to 'Hail to the Chief' everybody clapped and cheered .... His mother in white gloves received us all from her wheelchair at the door of the state dining room.... Wine, and champagne, and a grand buffet.

"In the East Room we sat at round tables with George at our table .... My three Clement children and their cousins, the Houses, sang one of the in-joke ditties that we usually do at parties.... I was called upon as the oldest one there who was born a Bush. I said I thought my father and mother were the best married team of their time; I always thought my brother Pres and his wife were a top team; and now it's obvious who make the best team in America today, Barbara and George. In recognition of that I'm making a bequest to the Prescott Bush Scholarship Fund at Yale - and I hope that those students who benefit, women or men, will not be so engrossed in studies and so unwilling to make a commitment that they will fail to understand that it is a great thing to be part of a husband-and-wife team. Such a team can have public as well as private meaning.... The White House is a beautiful place for a party. It has great elegance, but everything is in such balanced scale that the formality isn't heavy or stilted."

Looking back on it all - including conversations with Secretary of State James Baker and Sen. Chris Dodd - Marge Clement thanks her stars. "I wouldn't have missed it. I called Dottie (the president's mother) in Hobe Sound (Fla.) and she asked me what I thought was the best part. I said the swearing-in and the family party. She chose George's speech. I'm going to go over that again. Sitting behind him, I didn't hear it well." She is saving her engraved invitation for the New Haven Colony Historical Society. It may be an addition to the Margaret Bush Clement Room there.

The celebration was labeled the Bicentennial Inaugural, 1789-1989, or "George to George," because it brought the country over 200 years of peaceful political change from George Washington to George Bush. How does she feel about such an achievement?

"My grandfather was a minister. My father was the volunteer, in my childhood, who always directed relief when the deep Ohio River floods arrived. We were taught that good citizenship is service, that good fortune should be shared. That idea pervades our big family, young and old. I know it will be at the base of the things George Bush wants to do. I count on him to get them done."

Marge Clement got home a week ago tonight. Up at 5:45 a.m., involved in a dozen forays including the climactic Saturday family lunch at the White House, she finally reached New Haven at 10:45 p.m. on the Amtrak train. "We came back by coach, no club car. I was exhausted. I thought the walk from the tracks to the car was the longest one I'd ever taken." But she's here. And George Bush is in the Oval Office. And both are, more or less, fulfilled.

Saturday, December 31 1988
Editor's note

The City Needs Good Partners

This is the last day of New Haven's 350th year. Our celebrations were inspiring and enthusiastically shared by almost everybody in the community. But New Haven's leaders had a tough time in 1988 trying to make financial ends meet and trying to keep political discourse civil. As we put history behind, we must seek new ways to solve New Haven's problems and to make the most of its potential.

Early this month A. Bartlett Giamatti, the incoming commissioner of major-league baseball and immediate past president of Yale, spoke to the 20th annual meeting of the Hill Health Corp. His remarkable summons to "the spirit of partnership that makes a city" has New Year's application to the problems that afflict all cities, including our old town. Excerpts follow:

"The basic fact to recall about cities - from the first, wherever it was, to today - is that they are artifacts. They are not natural; cities are made, not born. Forest, jungle, desert, plain - the organic environment - is born, and dies, and is reborn, endlessly and beautifully and completely without moral or ethic constraint. But ... nature has never made a city. Only human beings have ever made cities. And only human beings kill them - by the same means they made them - acts of choice.

"When people chose to stop wandering and to settle, they create cities as a site and symbol of their choice to combine, not separate. A city is not an extended family - that is a tribe or a clan. A city is a collection of disparate families who agree to live as if they were an extended family, who agree to live as if they were as close in blood as they are in physical proximity....

"Politics is the art of making choices in public - or the art of making public choices - and it is the constant activity of a city, as thousands of individual, private, personal decisions and choices all give way finally before one general choice. I choose not to live alone but among others. From that flow all the public choices about how we will live together publicly, while seeking to preserve our right to private choices, but private choices hedged in by the decision not to live alone....

"Cities are seen as the most difficult environments to make work, because so many competing and unique needs must constantly be accommodated. Yet...when those disparate energies are harnessed, extraordinary achievement flourishes. Think of specific cities great and small, and much more than commerce and law and trade will come to mind, though they will. But so will the names of great hospitals and libraries and newspapers and universities; so also will theaters and museums and opera houses and restaurants and galleries and cathedrals. So will stadia and arenas. In short, not simply commerce but culture, not simply work but leisure ... not simply that which ennobles us but also that which perfects us has forever been the purpose of a city....

"When we choose to give up on ourselves, we become suburban. A sub-urb is an under-city; it is a non-city. It is not rural. It is not urban. It is a choice, at its heart, to give up on the stress and pace and difficulty of city choices. A sub-urbanite is not urban, and no civilization or civilizing force comes from the suburbs. It is not meant to....

"In the suburbs, people choose to give up on the political existence of the city and to live not as if in a family but rather to live as if alone, near similar - that is, like-minded, like-colored, like-employed - families .... While anyone may choose to live in a city, because cities are inclusive, absorptive, open, not everyone can choose to become suburban. Suburbs are by definition economically or geographically exclusive or resistant or closed - hence their allure....

"Americans loved Ronald Reagan and his imagery of the woodchopper, the man on horseback, in large part because Americans are sick of cities. They are moving out of them; they are voting against them; they are isolating them; they are choosing to choose among political candidates who - this last time - ran suburban campaigns in every sense of the word....

"Thus, now is the time we more than ever need the spirit of partnership that 20 years ago formed the Hill Health Corp. It is a spirit of partnership ... that begins at the local level and does not trickle down but trickles across the community.... Like government and universities, business has a role.... There are dozens of ways to bring about practical, effective partnerships at the local level with state encouragement, where businesses, cultural institutions, educational institutions, local governments find the local pattern that begins to bring community attention and resources to bear on (local) needs.... The federal government also has a role; it should at the least be encouraging such partnerships nationally....

"(But) the lesson of a city is in mutual succor, not in individual petitioning. It is the reintegration of those local instincts for mutuality that saves cities, not successful grant writing to distant bureaucracies.

"So we posit a dream that is a model of partnership, but we are back where we began - with 20 years of Hill Health Corp .... (This) corporation is not a sentimental hope, not an urbanologist's abstraction, not a community activist's dream. It is a reality that has history, achievement, pride and a strong future ... (and) in fiscal 1986 only some 20 percent was federal.

"Our model works ... a model for our city and for cities like ours; a model for the spirit of partnership that makes a city."

More of the flavor than the substance of Bart Giamatti's city-boosting message comes through in this tight digest. But insight and implicit action are there as we reach for those central choices that will improve local living for all. And the pattern, if picked up by some of the leaders now at cross purposes, could help all New Haven's friends and backers - even those in the suburbs - to share reasonably and responsibly in what we all must wish for each other and the heavily burdened city:

A HAPPY NEW YEAR!

Saturday, May 22, 1993
Editor's note

Change Grips Newspapers Of 90's

Not too long ago, in the tough-guy tradition of Ben Hecht's novel "The Front Page," news could be defined as what happens when "man bites dog." The novelty of an event did much to make it headline-worthy.

Today the standard of novelty, of news as something more than the usual, still applies. But the adversarial attitudes of some '90s reporters when "man bites dog" require new degrees of documentation. (Ask anyone who has been through a presidential primary).

Was the dog a Rottweiler or a pit bull? Does the man wear dentures? Did the dog bite back? Was it the dog's bark that prompted the man's bite? Is this just a joke: could the dog, as some sources claim, have simply been stuffed, baked and served with a savory sauce - inviting biting? Was the dog, as the law demands, leashed or in a proper enclosure? Was either tested for rabies?

Exaggerated sure, but whatever the embellishments, the basic facts remain "man bites dog."The rest is just part of the information overload that dogs our days.

In an era of information overload, newspapers and their newsroom staffs keep searching for ways to better news reporting. Recently the editor of the Los Angeles Times, C. Shelby Coffey III, gave a talk at the University of California on "Newspapers in the '90s." He defined seven aspects of "editorial strength" essential to a '90s newspaper:

• News ... "We owe the reader a clear look at the naked facts ... What's most important, most fascinating, (or) changed both sudden and long-term, will continue to be the basics for papers."

• "Analysis and context are keys to our future: context in terms of better rounded explanations, analysis which marshals the past, and anticipates the future (to answer the question) ... What does this event or trend mean to me, my family, my city, my nation?"

• Literary journalism ... "The power of a great story well told ... Make sure our stories, long and short, have the appropriate style and pace."

• Investigative journalism ... "In-depth stories that look at institutions and officials ... We should be tribunes of the people with all the intensity and fairness that role implies."

• "Graphic journalism (in new design skills and new press capabilities) can convey and accentuate information in ways that complement our in-depth press coverage."

• Practical journalism that takes "account of the lives and needs of readers, showing them how to cope and deal with the blooming, buzzing confusion of daily life - whether with articles, or listings, or how-to explanations."

• Innovation ... "Learning to do (newspapering) better and differently is part of the drive for progress. The battle for people's attention (competition with fax machines, telephones, audio-cassettes, cable television, computers and not-yet-dreamed technologies) is forced on newspapers as the generators of information." That, and the current hard times, mean innovation must be a goal of newspapers in the '90s.

This message has been used as a recent discussion piece among Register news staffers. Editor Dave Butler says that its square-peg generalities can be shaved to fit the round-hole news objectives here in New Haven and Connecticut as news room rosters and daily news space allocations are expanded.

Coffey says, "Business coverage in the 1980s came to have the intensity of sports coverage." Dave Butler notes that the constantly changing economic picture in Connecticut - the shifts in bank ownership, in industrial mergers and shutdowns, in retail acquisitions and withdrawals, to cite just a few - have made the Register's daily business pages dynamic backups for the front page government and economic reports. What's been done with business, he adds, "will be done as well in meeting the needs of the "new woman" the under-30 reader, and other demographic groups of readers that shift as Connecticut itself shifts in so many ways.

"Change is the news coverage mode of the '90s."

Shelby Coffey closed his lecture by recalling newspaper mottoes from the past - the Chicago Tribune's "World's greatest newspaper;" the Denver Post's "Paper with a heart and soul;" the San Francisco Chronicle's "Independent in all things, neutral in nothing."

Here in New Haven the tradition is self-effacing. The Register never claimed to be more than, sturdily, "An Independent Newspaper." But I've been taken with the wide reach and practicality of what New York Newsday has recently been proclaiming as its values: "Truth, justice, and the comics."

Saturday, December 18, 1993
Editor's Note

135 Years At Hillhouse Portrayed

In the midst of our December doubts about guns in schools, and violence in classrooms and everywhere else, the New Haven Free Public Library is offering an exhibit about 135 years of high school education in this city.

It's called "Hillhouse High School 1859-1994: Reactions to Change in New Haven."

While it has no answers to the drugs, violence and economic depletion all around us, it is a pointed - and poignant - reminder of the ways our schools have striven to bring civility, respect for learning, and a personal sense of direction to young people in New Haven's changing generations.

The exhibit isn't exhaustive - only three wall cases are involved. But it is penetrating in its selection of materials. It uses yearbook and other photographs, memorabilia, the written reflections of students and teachers and documentary film interviews with graduates and students, old and young.

And it creates a sort of afterlife for itself by asking viewers with Hillhouse memorabilia to keep contributing materials that will enrich the archives of the school or the educational record at the New Haven Colony Historical Society.

The project took shape when Benjamin Filene, a Yale doctoral candidate who teaches a course in American studies, fired up three Yale undergraduates for a look at "public history" as people make it in their daily routines.

Liz Sevcenko, Nike Akinyemi, and Wendy Roth got out tape recorders and video cameras, set to work with the kids in a history honors class at Hillhouse, researched old records and recollections, and got the support of the library's staff in mounting an informative, community-linked display.

The show is "interactive," connecting with its viewers through personal memory and attitude. Seeing it is more effective than reading about it. But even a few of the highlights, as I saw them, may invite other investigations.

• There's a historical surprise, for openers. The Hillhouse High School was proudly established in 1859 - and after five years the Board of Education voted to close it! The board accepted the argument that children of immigrants needed job-training and jobs and that a high school was only helpful to children of the affluent heading for college.

That thinking produced an uproar and a referendum held June 6, 1866, in the Statehouse on the Green. New Haveners insisted on a high school by their vote. William Kinne, who was the threatened school's principal, wrote:

"It must be said that it was the votes of the foreign population ... that saved the high school that day - that is - the votes of the Irish and the Germans. The men who wore broadcloth (then the quality fabric) voted no."

• A century ago in 1894 the arithmetic unit of the Hillhouse entrance examination used these problems. "Reduce to decimals and find their sum 3/4, 3/63, and 1-3/40. Reduce to common fractions .0125, .06."

• In 1934, on York Square off Broadway, there were 5,621 students enrolled at Hillhouse, 2,636 across Tower Parkway in Commercial High School. Students came to Hillhouse, with its reputation as "one of the five best high schools in the country," from families of 43 different nationalities, starting with "American, Armenian. Assyrian" and ending with Welsh, West Indian, Yugoslavian."

• In 1967, after Hillhouse had moved to Sherman Avenue in Beaver Pond Park, anti-war tumult in the colleges and countrywide racial unrest was reflected in chair throwing and window breaking at Hillhouse. Student Sally Lee joined her classmates in a grievance march upon City Hall and upon the mayor, her father Dick Lee.

• In the 45 minutes of current video commentary that is linked to the exhibit, Principal Lonnie Garns talks about the challenges at Hillhouse in 1994, the way the burden of meeting social needs dilutes educational mission in the schools, the need for "a purer academic focus."

The sign above teacher Robert Gibson's classroom door tells all comers: "Enter only to learn." He and his pupils, among other students and faculty members like Emma Ruff, talk earnestly about study challenges, safety, the community of purpose inside Hillhouse walls, and the misperceptions that often seem to negate the goals of Hillhouse and its real accomplishments in a troubled city setting.

This is only a tight summary of some of the content of the show. It combines, overall, pleasant nostalgia with solid information on Hillhouse traditions from yesterday - and the school's needs today and tomorrow.

It pulls together 13 decades of remarkable change in the city itself and of even more dramatic change in the population of the school and the purposes shared by its pupils and teachers.

The Hillhouse exhibition continues through Jan. 14 at the public library on Elm Street, facing the Green. There's elevator access to the three display areas - and the library in its own right is cause for pleasure. Treat yourself.

Saturday, January 1, 1994
Editor's note

Can Suburbs Become Sister Cities?

This is the season for talk about, "the state of the city." When John DeStefano is inaugurated today, he'll make some remarks on that subject, and later in the month he and others will probably make formal speeches on the state of the city to the Board of Aldermen.

Since there's so much that's negative about the New Haven scene, we can only hope that actions, not words, will begin to spark a local comeback in 1994.

Cities, generically, are places where people gather to live and form a government. The city's goal is to secure public safety, protect health, maintain a market climate in which crafts and commerce and human interchange will flourish, provide education for the young, organize other reasonable comforts and administer all these things for the community in a context of law and order with tax levies that are fair and moderate.

New Haven is not achieving those goals today. Major department stores have left. Downtown parking fees are up as parking volume drops. The biggest employers are downsizing. Yale's gates are locked. Drug criminals average a murder on the streets every three weeks; the wounded are daily emergency room drop-offs.

While pupils and teachers struggle in the schools, city and state administrators and the courts squabble year after year over the shuffling of multimillion dollar educational funds. Parks, pavements and other public facilities are crumbling.

The library - which should be an all-hours dream machine - is only open half-time for dreamers. The rising tax burden on ordinary homeowners and small business people threatens their ability to stay in town.

Despite such challenges the city's Board of Aldermen spent crucial December debate time on improving the world, not the city.

It voted on whether it should make the U.S.-embargoed Vietnam city of Hue a sister city and on providing gay city employees with domestic partnership rights the same as married spouses. The aldermen voted "yes" on Hue and "no" on the domestic partnership benefits.

Both issues are interesting and clearly on somebody's agenda. But they hardly reflect the daily worries of the people most concerned with New Haven, its residents.

Two converging Connecticut issues for 1994, in fact, suggest that Hamden, West Haven or other suburban places could mean more than Hue as sister cities for New Haven.

The city's future may well depend upon rebuilding ties with nearby communities that began as spin-offs from old New Haven and that now want no part of its problems.

Quality shopping, arts and recreation, health services, and banking counsel are key parts of any regionally integrated economic plan and the central city alone generates such amenities.

Here in geographically tight, colonially structured Connecticut, regional renewal is the alternative to the kind of hundred-square-mile annexation that keeps newer American cities viable.

While campaigning, John DeStefano said he'd pursue some legal way of sharing taxes regionally. And the state's new law on diversified regional education assumes that city-suburb partnerships are the way to equalize school operations and opportunities, for the future.

The troubled state of the city today supports such new approaches. But the trouble also justifies the suburban concern that says: Clean up your act and get serious, New Haven, before you ask us to share the cost of any of your mishandled problems.

And that's the narrow ledge on which city and suburban officials, aldermen and council members, must look for common ground.

Is the situation beyond solving? History says we'll change and survive.

There was a time when any place five blocks from the Green was the suburbs. In 1694, having put behind their losses when the "Great Shippe" sank on its way to London, New Haveners were planting the sapling elms that made us the Elm City.

In 1794, after the Revolution, the Chamber of Commerce was founded as the key to centuries of trade and manufacturing.

In 1894, confident New Haveners concerned about the quality of life organized the New Haven Symphony Orchestra.

Those undertakings, each a century apart, continue today.

So in 1994 the state of the city is in no way the fate of the city.

Looking at regional possibilities, and learning to get along as self-governing parts of a beneficial whole, may be the answer. Today, for sure, it's the challenge.

Saturday, April 23, 1994
Editor's note

The Man Who Made A Nature Center

Anyone who grew up, or who raised children, between the 1950s and the 1980s in this region has probably heard of New Haven's West Rock Nature Recreation Center.

It started as a remarkable pioneer project in the community environmentalism that emerged across this country after World War II. In its heyday it attracted national attention as a model project, combining nature, recreation and education.

The center thrived as a field-and-school experience, an urban asset for a quarter-century - as long as its first ranger, Anthony Cosenza, rallied the volunteers who made it work and grow and infused it with creative concepts that merged outdoor pleasures and educational insights for children and adults.

The West Rock Nature Recreation Center eventually lost a lot of budget support in a changing, tax-deprived city. It continues to function, exhibiting small wild creatures, at its 40-acre site beside West Rock and Wintergreen Falls, though the hope for additional barnyard and seaside nature centers has long faded.

Tony Cosenza, whose book on his boyhood in old Hamden's Highwood village made good reading a few years ago, has produced a biographical second volume of "Backyard Nature Man." It's all about the West Rock center and ranger Cosenza's hands-on shaping of its physical features and programs from 1946 until 1979 when he retired.

It's an-impressive record. It's made more appealing by the way Cosenza has provided documentation and blueprint for the way ponds and paths were constructed, along with wildlife exhibits, shelters and cages, a totem pole he personally carved, and anything else such a facility might need to serve newer generations - if the will to serve them can ever again be publicly funded.

The book is a labor of love for Cosenza, who's 80, and his wife, Virginia. It includes 137 full-color illustrations - so expensive to print that they cost him almost $1 each in the first edition copies that are being presented to a score of public libraries regionally. The printer is John Henry Graef - the Nature Center's third child volunteer in 1948 and a constant supporter since then. He will be selling copies at $20, including postage, from John Henry's Copy and Printing Center, Washington Avenue, North Haven.

Cosenza sees a park's purpose this way: "In many communities the park is the only outdoors area remaining for free public use and it is extremely important that this crowded area with its perishable natural and man-made resources be most widely used.

"A healthy and wholesome group-living environment must be maintained in which each visitor finds a desired physical, mental or emotional outlet in the park, and at the same time respects the rights and privileges of others."

When Tony and Virginia Cosenza took up residence in the Nature Center in 1947, it was a sequestered nook in West Rock Park. This was before the West Rock tunnel made the Wilbur Cross Parkway one of the center's boundaries.

Later, as New Haven tried to be a "slumless city," displaced inner-city families were moved to city-owned land for the Brookside housing project, then the Rockview project and Katherine Brenan Elementary School, and finally the Oriental Masonic Gardens public housing project.

The center became a last leafy enclave in an increasingly populated neighborhood where urban problems were often intensified by the distance from in-town social or police services.

But amid new challenges there are also new opportunities. Southern Connecticut State University had established a Recreation and Leisure Studies Department in 1969 - only one mile from the Nature Center. Building on informal past relationships a new formal program was set up. There were 35 students in the first graduate course, 150 in the first undergraduate course. All had field classes and most also joined Cosenza's volunteer work crews. Such ongoing classes help stabilize the Nature Center even today.

By the time Cosenza retired in 1979, he was willing to go - disillusioned by city budget policies that wiped out hopes for program expansion, fed up with arguments that outdoorsy environmental experiences were less useful locally than a system-wide concentration on team sports for urban youth. But his convictions still burn rightly.

With his wife, he has produced two books since then, the first about a Highwood childhood, this second one focused on the West Rock Nature Recreation Center. Still to come is the third book about "backyard art/biology" as a hobby in retirement. There's not a lot of deep philosophizing in his message - but there's a powerful, always specific square-yard and cubic-foot exposition by a man dealing energetically, imaginatively, exuberantly and every day, with he world around him.

In this book he tells us what he as done and how he did it, and he shows why the West Rock Nature Center stays alive for those who shared with him its fun and facts about this place where we live.

Saturday April 30, 1994
Editor's note

Chamber Commences Another Lap

The Greater New Haven Chamber of Commerce marked its 200th year last night with a gala get-together in the Yale Commons and Woolsey Hall.

Its history makes it one of the first business-building organizations in the country. It started 13 years after the end of the Revolutionary War and 10 years after Colonial New Haven became a city and elected Roger Sherman its mayor for life.

The gala mood was appropriate to the chamber's substantial past achievements- and probably the best way to confront its many current challenges.

When it was launched in 1794 the Chamber of Commerce conveyed to city fathers, state lawmakers, and a newly organized federal Congress the concerns of this city's shipowners. They had free-trade interests that stretched from the West Indies to China.

Later, as deeper, bigger seaports were developing and shipping here declined, New Haven thrived as a market hub for lower New England, as a center of inventive craftsmanship in the early industrial age, and always as a Yale nurtured, intellectual center.

After the Civil War, New Haven prospered. Factories, railroads, banks and related business services, wholesale and retail commerce, and a steady flow of immigrants from Europe mixed entrepreneurial energy and profitable hard work with the cultural advantages of the community.

By the end of the chamber's first 100 years in 1894 the city had pretty much expanded to its boundaries. There were more than 200 factories producing useful things, steady jobs – and tax revenues. A booming central business district and a web of streetcar lines, successful schools and well kept parks, linked the city's diverse but unified neighborhoods.

The Chamber of Commerce led in planning for harbor channels and breakwaters, for sewers and gas, water and electric services, for elm trees and street lights, for playgrounds and parking spaces, for the Community Chest (United Way) and the airport.

Now at the end of its second 100 years the Greater New Haven Chamber of Commerce is no longer able to validate itself as a voice for business alone. It is challenged to join with New Haven's other institutions in reinventing the city, renewing its connections to the harbor and to its "gateway" functions by rail and road for this end of New England, and defining new ways to keep city residents working and new ways to do customer-attracting, profit-making, taxpaying business inside today's urban shell.

Because of its wide membership the chamber may have a chance, somehow to help the 200,000 or more suburban families with roots in New Haven turn around to look at what has been abandoned and to consider – from their outer residential ring – how some of the generational memories of New Haven's good past can be channeled toward a good-neighborly future, too.

Crime and drugs and random violence, family demoralization, inadequate schools, vanished jobs, lost public civility and lost private purpose all make it hard to find a shared vision in city-suburban relationships. But the problems are increasingly mutual.

The ocean shipping ventures of the chamber's first years and the prosperity-building manufacturing and retailing energies that followed were probably far less complex than the people-binding, region-unifying policies needed for the 21st century. But, with last night's gala chamber celebration completed, the region that was created by the New Haven investment needs to wooed back toward regard and some support for its beginnings.

April's end reminds me that I've written this column every Saturday for 20 years.

The column began in 1974. The "Editor's Note" was then a weekly consideration of the way we were covering news in New Haven, or of the way national and world news issues looked from local editorial desks. After my retirement in 1981, with the pulse of the paper and the daily problems of news coverage in other hands, I had a chance to widen the community focus and to personalize the opinions expressed. Even in changes of ownership I've been generously permitted to continue in a familiar Saturday corner on a major page of the Register.

I'm not inclined to break the habit. But the anniversary justifies a thank-you to the readers who have stuck with me through so many weekends. I'll be back next Saturday.

Note 'n' quote: The Long Wharf Theatre's production of "The Faith Healer" by Irish playwright Brian Friel won cheers this week in The New York Times. The play, said critic Ben Brantley, won't be seen in New York, So: "Any connoisseur of theater should take the next train to New Haven."

Saturday, December 30, 1995
Editor's note

Change Comes, Even In An Old City

At the New Year in Depression-time Fair Haven, the holiday 60 years ago was marked for most folks by nothing more than a new kitchen calendar from the grocer and perhaps by a moment of sleepy privilege if the kids in a family were awakened to a strange medley of factory whistles and church bells joining briefly to "ring out the old, ring in the new."

For youngsters spared the din and distraction of today's always beckoning media, it was an easy, innocent, almost dreamy transition - resolutions for self-improvement and a vague moment in time when a digit changed on the calendar while grownups smiled.

My father and mother, with a neighbor couple for company, might have allowed themselves a quiet congratulatory sip of the homemade elderberry wine - a permitted Prohibition-era pursuit - that we pressed from the hand-gathered fruit of some field-edge in Foxon or Montowese. But high acidity, old barrels and the next day's work in hard times discouraged any idea of excess.

And, for the adults I knew, today's far-flung celebrations and diverse group festivities - the Register's current listing of 180 places-to-go from Ansonia to Westbrook - were totally unimaginable for people who had only the trolley car for transportation.

All this comes to mind today as 1995 slides toward 1996, and we face the fact that in a few short years, the calendar will take us not only into a new year but a new millennium.

What the people of New Haven will be doing a few decades into the 21st century is, let's face it, unpredictable.

By then, the so-called Information Age may have led us toward new sources of knowledge and new ways to select what's significant from the unmanageable flood of nearly useless data, in indiscriminate detail, that threatens the literate and dismisses the illiterate in today's society.

By then, perhaps, today's thriving globalized economy will have found ways to rebuild the personal security and the local relationships that it sucks away from small places like New Haven in the name of unlimited profitability without focused responsibility.

Perhaps then Americans will have found the way to link democracy to humane public policy - the stuff of stubborn deadlock this in Washington - so that the poor and the insecure aren't suspended by bad law between the destructive disrespect of bureaucrats and the harsh denial of politicians.

Perhaps by then we'll find new sources of morality, or revive old ones, to strengthen the shared experience and the common ideals that uplift a culture and define a civilization.

Searching for such solutions isn't new. Old New Haveners knew all about such transitions.

Back at the end of the 17th century the first settlers were still trying to make their frontier colony workable and livable – planting elms beside the 40-year-old Green after King Charles II had made them subordinate to the Connecticut Colony at Hartford, after they'd built a palisade as defense against raiding Indians in King Philip's War, and after loyal, local militia had been drafted for British forays into French Canada. The thousand people here were still transplanted subjects of the king of England as their century turned.

A hundred years later, after the Revolution had produced a free-spirited citizenry and a remarkable Constitution, New Haven became a city with patriot Roger Sherman as its first mayor. It had, as cosmopolitan credentials, a bank, a Chamber of Commerce boosting sea trade, Eli Whitney's new gun factory and the scholars at Yale. At that century's closing, New Haven moved, with Yankee alacrity, toward a new role in the industrial revolution sweeping out of Europe.

Then, after the dreadful ordeal of the Civil War with its still unsolved issues of slavery, new waves of European immigrants created here a crowded, prosperous industrial center offering freedom, personal opportunity, public education and civic idealism. In New Haven just before and after 1900 there really was a "gay Nineties'.' mood based on industrial achievement in hundreds of city factories, on cultural achievement at Yale with its collateral arts and scientific activities and its world renown and in the metropolitan rail facilities and the recreational resources that all could enjoy.

Today these past achievements and assumptions seem no longer valid as premises for a new year. There is small need to list what New Haven has lost: its taxpaying industrials base, the vanished merchandising that once served a broad region of Connecticut, the locally rooted banking and investment traditions, the respect of ordinary citizens for their own and their neighbors property, and - most recently the merger-created drain-off to larger cities, or other countries, of local decision-makers and their personally constant, knowledgeable and native consideration of the city's problems as their problems.

Clearly there must be reversal of such deficits.

The message and the meaning of the new year is always about transformation and the hope of something better. The whistles blew their message of hope and the bells rang out for a new year in the 1930s in a city way down on its luck. The message today is pretty much the same.

Transformation is overdue. The hope for change is alive - and all those parties in the suburbs here hereabouts celebrate what's to come – in the new millennium if not right now. So Happy New Year!

Saturday, February 25, 1995
Editor's note

City Search For Solutions Is Unending

The more things change, says the old French proverb, the less they change. This applies, today, to New Haven as a seaport.

New Haven harbor cropped up in the news a couple of times last week, once as the setting for a "tall ships" gathering during the Special Olympics World Games in July, and once as another question mark in the budget plans of Gov. John Rowland.

The Special Olympics gala presents the harbor once again as an ornament to city pride, a scenic and historical background in sunshine and fair breezes, but not a dynamic part' of city life.

The governor's budget plans, on the other hand, could importantly affect the commercial future of the harbor as a community asset if there was a worthwhile official vision to justify public investment. But there's little there to ignite a sense of profitable or popular enterprise in these pinch-penny times.

When the first colonists came ashore in the late spring of 1638 they considered the broad, shallow harbor a key to their local future and a vital link to London and the other colonies. But the port had only a few years of maritime success in the early 19th century.

Then, 60 years ago, as the city's 300th anniversary celebrations neared, native scholar Arnold Guyot Dana wrote and privately published a careful study of "New Havens Problems." About the harbor he said:

"At the present time the city's foreign shipments are on a low scale. The imports for the year 1935 aggregated only 22,154 tons while the exports were nil. The last foreign exports from New Haven were shipped in 1933 - 5,311 tons ... The experience of other (states') coastal ports proves that by intensive and persistent effort concentrated on the development of port and harbor traffic, this business could be made to grow and benefit the community."

In the six decades since then, New Haven has come to handle more than half of the waterborne commerce of all Connecticut. But the totals are not great, approximating 9,500 tons in most recent years, about 10 percent of that outgoing.

Incoming shipments of petroleum products - 90 percent of what we receive - make this city the source of most of the fuel consumed from Hartford north through western Massachusetts and Vermont. Apart from pipeline connections, New Haven has the state's best-equipped port for loading and unloading cargo. It receives shipments of iron, steel, other metals and cement. Its primary outgoing cargo is scrap metal.

But none of these activities guarantees seaborne prosperity. The largest of 13 harbor-using firms, the New Haven Terminal, Inc., which also has a stake in Bridgeport, last year filed for bankruptcy protection while it weighs the details of an employee buyout.

Meanwhile Bridgeport refrigerates banana shipments from Costa Rico and Colombia, and in New London - the port closest to ocean shipping lanes - the publicly owned State Pier is inoperative after disastrous storm damage a couple of years ago. The Connecticut Coastline Port Authority, an arm of the Department of Transportation, seems an unlikely agent of change in the face of Rowland budget restrictions.

So, "tall ships" aside, New Haven's harbor in 1995 remains what it has been for most of 350 years - promising.

As for Arnold G. Dana's other views about New Haven problems in the 1930s, they still seem apt:

Regionalism: "As New Haven exists largely for the benefit of its satellite towns, (we should) press the plan for a Metropolitan District to finance some modest portion of our common services ..."

Yale exemptions: "It is open to debate whether all rights granted by the town in 1792 to a feeble college with two professors and two acres of land ... apply (to today's university) richly housed and endowed and owning more than 800 acres of a little city's best area."

Bridges: "The Tomlinson Bridge, over which passes the traffic of the New York to Boston Post Road ... was hardly designed for present day traffic ... (It) was opened 8,164 times in 1936. A trans-bay bridge and viaduct, crossing due east from City Point, built and maintained by state and federal authorities would seem the only adequate and reasonable remedy."

Property taxes: "When real estate is sick or overburdened the general property tax limps ... Foreclosures, tax delinquencies, and vacancies proclaim the breakdown, and it behooves New Haven to recognize the fact ... The area of the city left to carry the bulk of the city's taxes includes less than 4,000 acres or 6 ¼ square miles. On this small area, embracing the equivalent of a mere 2 ½ miles square of local real estate (after eliminating all city and other tax-exempt holdings) devolves the duty of paying operating expenses, upkeep, unemployment relief, debt service, and necessary improvements."

Sound familiar?

Saturday, June 10, 1995
Editor's note

Can We Draw Olympics Dividends?

New Haven as a backdrop for the Special Olympics World Games has been on many minds lately.

We all want the old town to do well - to provide an enjoyable and effective setting for the competitive events, for the athletes from so many far places and for the accompanying visitors. Thousands of volunteers are working hard for such goals.

But the other day, there was also enthusiastic discussion of the Special Olympics as a background for New Haven - for reminding this country and the world of the rich, varied and often unique amusements and cultural pleasures that can be found throughout southern Connecticut.

The idea is to tell people everywhere about this timelessly attractive place as well as about this summer's particular Olympics programs.

About 100 of the region's professional publicists and marketing specialists gathered Tuesday at the New Haven Colony Historical Society on downtown Whitney Avenue. Amid its fascinating treasures from greater New Haven's past - the colony was a "region" before it was a city - they shared a first look at a new press kit that will be distributed on a national basis. It is full of facts and figures about the "City Lights - New England Sights" that make the city and even its far suburbs a great single area for multiple-choice good times.

Those attending came from all parts of the community: the Chamber of Commerce and Vision for Greater New Haven, Yale and the other colleges, manufacturing companies and law firms, the Knights of Columbus and the Symphony Orchestra, the police department and Easter Seals Rehab, banks and hospitals and neighborhood groups, town officials and social agencies, and other groups public and private.

The afternoon's theme was "Back to the Future" as a way of linking the prosperous past and tomorrow's hopes to the current need for penny-wise planning and careful improvisation in a community down on its luck.

The new package of New Haven-based promotional materials is chock-full of organized information: on the region as the Special Olympics host, on Greater New Haven statistics from climate to taxes, health care and transportation, on what national media are saying about us, ob history and inventive "firsts," on our past and present sports activities, our colleges, medical achievements, the arts, city neighborhoods, architectural distinctions, regional and Yale tour maps, plus the Chamber's brochure on "Greater New Haven: A Slice of Life."

Many of the publicists present have already signed up to make an individual "pitch" by letter and telephone to newspaper and magazine editors, columnists, television commentators and other broadcast bigwigs. By linking a personal message to the press kit materials, the local participants hope to get some stronger focus, country-wide, on what New Haven is, and can be.

The Greater New Haven Visitors Guide for May-August '95, part of the kit, is a 66-page pocketsize calendar of events and alphabetical guide, reaching from art and attractions through beaches, bowling, farms, fishing, golf, music (live), nature and walks. It's a product of the Greater New Haven Convention and Visitors Bureau, 777-8550.

Also part of the Olympics-related flow of facts are two books: The New Haven Colony Historical Society's new 1995 edition of its solidly researched, "Illustrated History of New Haven" by historians Floyd Shumway and Richard Hegel - a fund-raiser for the society.

Henry S. Harrison's "Harrison's Illustrated Guide to Greater New Haven," a compendious, up-to-the-minute visitors' directory. All profits from the guide will go to a charitable affiliate of the Greater New Haven Association of Realtors.

Coming in the week when Mayor John DeStefano Jr. and Park Plaza owner David Cordish have announced agreements which may finally guarantee a good downtown hotel by 1997, this energetic regional image-building project is well-timed. It offers a solid way to move from the euphoria-with-anxiety of the crowded Olympics schedule to a post-Olympics emphasis on the good things we have here, and the good things we can provide for all comers.

It's an impressive volunteer effort - worth encouraging and expanding in every possible way.

Would you like to churn some butter? Mix ice and salt in the old ice cream freezer? Show the kids great-grandma's kitchen chores and great-great-grandpa's rifle drills? The New Haven Colony Historical Society is having its annual country romp on Sunday.

Tomorrow is family day at the old Pardee-Morris House at the end of Lighthouse Road in Morris Cove. There will be tours of the rambling farm home, 19th century games on the lawn, lemon squeezing for the beverage bowl, a magic man and flag and weapons demonstrations by the Sons of the American Revolution ceremonial color guard in Colonial garb.

The festivities will run from 11 a.m. to 4 p.m., rain or shine. There is no charge but donations will be welcomed. Have some family fun the old-fashioned way.

Saturday, February 14, 1998
Editor's Note

Black History and the "Amistad"

In Black History Month in New Haven the big local topic this year is the Amistad anti-slavery trial, just as it was in 1997. The absorbing story of black resistance to enslavement, and of white support for that resistance in this city 150 years ago, has been given new meaning for our time by Steven Spielberg's movie "Amistad."

Released in December and still on multiplex screens in this region, the movie sometimes gets its historical facts needlessly wrong - for instance giving ex-president John Quincy Adams credits far greater than those on the record. But "Amistad's" basic message about the human will to be free and its dramatic portrayal of black suffering, white sympathy, and this community's faith in liberty under law is uplifting.

There could be no better personal way to celebrate Black History Month, in my opinion, than a trip to the movie "Amistad" followed by a visit to the exhibit, "Cinque lived here," now at the New Haven Colony Historical Society.

The film captures the high drama of a remarkable anti-slavery incident in New Haven 22 years before the Civil War began. The historical society's show documents the real people, the identifiable Connecticut places, and the complex human interactions -- building confidence among strangers, learning the languages, shaping legal arguments -- that provided the decent, day-to-day moral base for Spielberg's Hollywood embroideries.

Weigh one with the other and you'll have a powerful experience for Black History Month.

Wrapping up the history-by-Hollywood appraisal of "Amistad," historian Howard Jones of the University of Alabama recently gave the annual Pitkin Lecture at the historical society.

Jones is author of the definitive study, "Mutiny on the Amistad - the Saga of a Slave Revolt and its Impact on American Abolition, Law and Diplomacy" (Oxford University Press, 1987). He has done research in New Haven, and he was frequently present at Spielberg's film sites.

Though he criticizes Hollywood's casual way with historical fact, Jones considers the Spielberg movie a powerful narrative. Stressing a black perspective that is too often minimized, says Jones, the film "Amistad" pushes the familiar local tale "into the mainstream of our American heritage."

He concedes that much complex local effort has been compressed. The Yale faculty role, the work of local church and abolitionist groups, individual sacrifices and services have been subordinated to creative cinematography and contrived but emotional visual images.

On the other hand, he notes, Hollywood's $40 million investment does make historical fact entertaining. It does provide unforgettable pictures of the slave trade's murderous cruelty, of the outrages that result when one person's life becomes another person's property. Jones said that lawmakers and educators in the old slave state of Alabama, where he lives, plan to make "Amistad" a part of the state's official school curriculum.

In that sense, the film's use as a national and global tool for widened education and understanding may be more lastingly important than an Academy Award would have been for Steven Spielberg.

In his talk Jones emphatically rejected the notion that Cinque, leader of the struggle and hero of the movie, later became a slave trader himself.

In comments on the movie a few journalists have repeated this idea because it was carelessly spread by historians of repute. In my personal copy of Samuel Eliot Morison's 1,100-page "History of American People" (1965), there it is as the last sentence on Amistad case. "The ironic epilogue is that Cinque, once home, set himself up as a slave trader."

Eminent Yale historian C. Vann ward and others made the

same mistake. Seeking a source, they traced it back to a 1953 novel, "Black Mutiny," by William Owens who taught literature at Columbia University.

Howard Jones told New Haveners that William Owens had never been able to produce authentication of his novel's claim. Owens first thought it might be among papers he gave to the New Haven Colony Historical Society, but no such papers were received here. Later he suggested it came from papers of the American Missionary Society. But these papers, now at Tulane University's Amistad Research Center, are unresearched and most are still bound in 19th century twine and wrappings.

In the late 1960s there were disputes among historians about the defamation of Cinque. Jones concludes that the idea first appeared as fiction in the Owens novel and was subsequently accepted as fact by professional historians.

Today Cinque stands unblemished as the noble leader always known in New Haven. With his "mutineers" he returned to Sierra Leone in 1842, dropped from the missionary records there in 1846, and - by African folk tale – may have found his family or may have searched in vain. In 1879 an old, feeble man returned to the mission, said he was Cinque and died within a few days. He was buried there - where he first found haven after heartbreaking, turbulent years as a freedom fighter in the United States.

Saturday, May 6, 1995
Editor's note

Maytime Mobilization Was No Picnic

On this date 25 years ago New Haveners were heading back downtown after the trauma of a nationally publicized "Free the Panthers" May Day weekend.

Nobody who lived through those day and night anxieties in 1970 would dismiss the event as "the riot that wasn't." By the standards of such subsequent domestic outbreaks as the uprising that followed the beating of Rodney King in Los Angeles, or even some of the boisterous and violent endings to recent baseball or football seasons, the physical damage that resulted here was not great. But for two intense days, Friday, May 1 and Saturday, this city was under siege.

All New Haveners were hostages to radical political groups demanding that Bobby Seale and other Black Panthers - charged with executing a man on Orchard Street - be released from jail. The country's most celebrated revolutionaries were on hand, including the endlessly theatrical and incendiary Chicago Seven. Legions of young people, alienated by the Vietnam War, streamed in from all over, some for the hell of it, some to make War on government.

Connecticut's National Guard was mobilized in the Goffe Street Armory. There were 2,000 Carolina-based Marines flown into Quonset Point, R.I. There were 2,000 paratroops of the82nd Airborne Division on standby at Westover Air Force Base in Chicopee, Mass.

The windows of every store on Broadway, plus Malley's and Macy's, and many buildings surrounding the Green were covered by plywood. The Register's ground-floor pressroom windows were sealed. The Connecticut Company's 30,000 morning bus riders dropped to 12,000 on Friday, fewer on Saturday. Gasoline station pumps were locked.

At corners of the city's nine-square central district Guardsmen in armored vehicles, with bayonets on rifles, stood 24-hour watch. When the crisis was over on Monday, the Chamber of Commerce estimated that the city had lost between $3 million and $5 million in business, not counting police or fire costs.

The daytime demonstrations on the Green were full of noise and threats. "Kill your mother and father," cried Abbie Hoffman. But there was also a lot of laid-back laughter among youths, smokewreathed, who believed "pot does more than Milton can to justify God's ways to man."

With classes spurned, Yale made itself the eye of the swirling storm. Under student pressure Yale offered its interior lawns, quadrangles, and dorm rooms as police-free sanctuaries, ladling out oatmeal and granola, warding-off damage to college property with official soft talk and protest advice from anti-establishment faculty members.

In the city's African-American neighborhoods there was great tension. Clergymen and other black leaders worked constantly to insulate children and youths from the excitement. Some youngsters were bused to suburban churches for the weekend. There were about 500 volunteers on street patrol to keep strangers away and residents in safe places.

During "the riot that wasn't" a building at the comer of Church and Elm, facing the thousands on the Green, sustained major damage in a two-alarm fire. Guardsmen held back crowds as firefighters battled the flames. After a rock concert, the glass front of Yale's Ingalls Rink was blown to smithereens by a midnight explosion. It did structural damage that took months to repair. Nobody was injured seriously.

There were touchy moments. A wall of Guardsmen and vehicles stopped one marching phalanx near the new Park Plaza Hotel on Temple Street. Another shouting group pushed up Chapel Street and rounded York toward Elm and Broadway. But it, too, was funneled back to the campus. The most serious foray came when protesters burst in darkness from the Old Campus onto the upper Green and long lines of charging police used tear gas to turn them back.

There is little point now in detailed analysis of May Day 1970. New Haven has 1995 issues to solve.

Police Chief James F. Ahern said there were 15,000 people on the Green on May 1, 6,000 to 8,000 on Saturday. The demonstration organizers said there were 20,000 to 30,000 present both days. Nobody, anywhere, found civil discourse improved.

The event was not a dud for the policemen or firefighters who were hurt and briefly hospitalized, for those who reported it in a couple of nights of high-adrenalin news gathering and photography, or for the thousands of worried citizens who watched a public fever here rise ominously and then subside. Those who prayed with the Council of Churches between 9 a.m. and 8p.m. on Friday and Saturday in the First Methodist Church at College and Elm clearly felt we had a city at risk.

The Black Panthers eventually got a mistrial - and the idea of justice for a murdered man, Alex Rackley, slipped through the courtroom cracks. The May 4 shooting of students at Kent State in Ohio - four dead, 13 wounded - showed what deep tragedy we had avoided.

For anyone in New Haven on May Day 1970, a "riot" calculation simply mismeasures 50 hours of intense foreboding and anxiety, imminent but unpredictable danger, and good police work that expressed New Haven's "No!" to a threat of radical force. It was far from a non-event.

Saturday, May 13, 1995
Editor's note

Old Hopkins Keeps Eye On The Future

There are not many New Haven institutions older than Yale. But the Hopkins School had been instructing youths in this city for a half-century when Yale, founded in 1701, finally came to town in 1716.

In fact, the first president of Yale, Abraham Pierson, had received his early education at Hopkins before matriculating at Harvard.

This afternoon the "grammar" school which began in a one-room building on the Green is observing a 335th anniversary at its spacious campus on the ridge above the junction of Chapel Street and Forest Road.

As part of today's reunion celebration Anne Tyler Calabresi and Judge Guido Calabresi are receiving the school's 1995 Distinguished Alumnae/Alumni Award for their exceptional public service. The 2nd Company, Governor's Foot Guard, and its band will add Colonial color to the afternoon award

The Hopkins School has played a key role in the education of New Haven leaders from the beginning. For the past 70 years, the school's local visibility has been somewhat reduced by its location on a wooded Westville hilltop.

But until that "country" move in 1925 it was a downtown ornament - starting with sites on the Green near Elm Street and then adjacent to the colony's jail and graveyard on the upper Green. Today's headmaster, Thomas Rodd Jr., explains that the original name, Hopkins Grammar School, indicated it was, then as now, a college preparatory school. He says "the 'grammar' referred to was chiefly Latin, but also Greek and sometimes Hebrew."

The Hopkins School was given its start by Edward Hopkins. He was a prosperous London merchant who came to Boston in 1637 with Theophilus Eaton and John Davenport. The latter two founded

New Haven the next year.

Hopkins settled instead in Hartford and served for a long time as governor of the Connecticut Colony. Hartford's Hopkins was married to Anne Yale, the stepdaughter of New Haven's Theophilus Eaton. She was incidentally, the aunt of Elihu Yale whose gift of books helped later to establish Yale College here.

Within this merchant-scholar context, John Davenport asked his old friend for help with school money. And when Edward Hopkins died in London in 1657, he bequeathed properties in New England to provide funds for "the breeding up of hopeful youths both at the grammar school and college for the public service of the country in future times."

When the Hopkins Fund was dispensed here and in Hartford, Hadley, Mass., and at Harvard, New Haven's share was enough to launch a grammar school in 1660.

Since then Hopkins has had 107 headmasters. Two famed scholars, the elder Timothy Dwight and Noah Porter, were headmasters of Hopkins before they became presidents of Yale.

Along with the first Yale president, Pierson, Hopkins has prepared four other Yale presidents: the younger Timothy Dwight, Theodore Dwight Woolsey, Arthur Twining Hadley, and Hanna Holborn Gray, a graduate of Prospect Hill who was Yale's interim president before she became the president of the University of Chicago.

In evaluating "genius" among Hopkins graduates, headmaster Rodd has cited Josiah Willard

Gibbs, pioneering Yale physicist (Hopkins 1854); Walter Camp, industrialist, "father" of football and advocate of physical fitness 1876); Charles Ives, innovative American composer (1894); and Paul MacCready, physicist and the designer of successful muscle-powered aircraft and "ecobenign" motor vehicles (1943).

In 1972, during the national move from all-male or all-female education, the Hopkins Grammar School and the Day Prospect

Hill School were merged. The combination has produced a student body of constantly increasing diversity and a new, simplified name, the Hopkins School. Since then the school's average enrollment has been about 550.

Hopkins in 1995 is remarkable both for its age and for its multiple responses to the challenges of education today. Some samples of its variety:

• This year 10 Hopkins seniors were named national merit scholarship semifinalists and 14 were commended students.

• Since 1993 the school has sponsored "Summerbridge/New Haven" on its vacation campus, using Hopkins students and faculty in a national program to provide supplementary school experiences for fifth- and sixth-grade inner-city students.

• A recently established Challenge Course, or "experiential learning center," using Outward Bound-type woodland rope webs, trapeze jumps, a climbing wall and other teamwork tests has been developed for the students and also made available to invited New Haven groups.

In announcing the purchase of the 52 acre woodland tract where the Challenge Course was installed, headmaster Thomas Rodd, Jr., said: "We have been citizens of New Haven for more than 300 years ... This additional land will allow us to meet the challenges in educating this community's young men and women for centuries to come."

Such students for a new millennium still share in Edward Hopkins' gift to "hopeful youths."

Saturday, March 25, 1995
Editor's note

State FOI Fights On New Frontiers

The Freedom' of Information Act in Connecticut has its 20th anniversary this year. The law has successfully opened public records and public meetings and made the state a national leader in establishing citizen access and official accountability at all levels of government.

But in the current era of unfolding communications technology, Freedom of Information advocates have to keep reminding themselves - and public officials - that all the gains of the past 20 years must be extended and vigilantly preserved in the way state agencies adapt to the new "information age."

Just when we've become accustomed, statewide, to the idea that the old bound folios and file cabinets of government are automatically open to inquiring citizens, the records are being computerized and it may require much more than a pencil and notebook to gather the information.

Just when elected and appointed officials have become accustomed to the basic duty of telling people how the public's business is conducted, the "privatization" of some public services - like running schools or collecting taxes creates new arguments about who discloses public information, or how.

At the annual, and now traditional, Freedom of Information Conference sponsored by open government advocates at the Farmington Marriott last week, such new problem's drew more attention than the standard discussion of FOI procedures in state offices or FOI decisions in the courts.

A morning session entitled "Who's Connected?" pointed to the new directions in dispensing information. State Librarian

Richard D. Akeroyd Jr. said cooperation between the library, the University of Connecticut and regional state colleges would soon create a "Connecticut archive" on the Internet, the global computer network.

To start, it will offer data on state laws, on elections and elected officials, on school facilities in the cities and towns. A steady expansion of such catalogs is foreseen.

The state Department of Administrative Services is preparing to offer direct-dial access plus Internet connections, to a system that will allow citizens with computers and modems to sift through records at many state agencies.

Still unresolved, however, are questions about how - or whether - citizens will be charged for such access, what commercial uses may be allowed, or whether some data will simply be withheld.

The Register's Dick Conrad, an experienced reporter who is now a computer systems administrator for this paper as well as a member of the state task force on electronic information, reminded the conference that linking up with town libraries and community schools is crucial so ordinary citizens can use the data.

"The information is important," he said, "and not just to people who own computers. We must make sure the data is not only available but accessible to everyone who wants it."

An afternoon panel on "Privatization and Accountability" had panelists from the Hartford Board of Education, the state teacher's federation, the Hartford Courant, and New England Business Services – which is collecting taxes for some Connecticut towns.

What they demonstrated, with out a lot of precise answers, is that in Hartford's privately managed school system, and in town tax offices, the familiar FOI assumptions may now be challenged by business people who have cost-cutting contracts.

Such executives claim a proprietary interest in programs they don't want to explain "for a competitor's benefit." They make no bones about their right to control, or conceal, computer programs on which a company's work plan is based, its contracts written, or its profitability estimated. Some personnel decisions are also put under wraps.

Clearly, there's a lot of uncharted ground between this vendor's view and the established right of a citizen or a newspaper to explore the ways in which tax dollars are spent.

There was talk, also, about "Private Lives of Politicians: Are They Fair Game?"

Then is national controversy on this topic because tabloid journalism is so intrusive. In the Farmington context it was inspired, to some degree, by the head-to-head election-time clash between Gov. Rowland and the news media over a police report - still unreleased - about a domestic complaint filed from his ex-wife's home. The fact that the issue continues to promote discussion~ without conclusion may say something about the need for public officials to air uncomfortable facts - or to live indefinitely with questions or implications they don't like.

For 20 years in Connecticut, Freedom of Information has been proven a workable ideal. Easy access to official records and meetings is designed to create the citizen interaction and voter confidence that is essential to free government. And it works.

Individual privacy is also a valued aspect of personal freedom. But government officials, by their need to build citizen confidence in most of the things they do or say as public servants, may have less claim to individual privacy than most of their constituents.

That's why, in this time of pervasive and instant news communication, good conduct, personal candor and responsible disclosure - not stalling - are measures of successful public leadership.

As to Connecticut FOI: happy anniversary!

Art Deco Headquarters of SNET CO, *Church Street at Wall, built for institutional business in 1937, converted to luxury apartments in 2004.*
Dana Collection.

Saturday, April 26, 2003
Editor's note

A Fast Ride On A Spring Evening

It was a Monday not quite like every other Monday for me.

I had finished my next Saturday column - due at the Register each Wednesday afternoon - a day earlier so I could visit an ailing son on Tuesday.

After supper, I took a last look at my comments on ancient Baghdad, checking for typing errors or perhaps a change of phrase. Satisfied, I pressed "p" for print on my keyboard, turned off the lights, and headed for the kitchen.

Once there, I had a heart attack.

It wasn't a crushing attack. But suddenly the fingers of both hands were tingling and there was a definite but bearable pressure across my chest. My first impulse was denial. I took a baby aspirin, already part of my regimen. I lay down on my bed and looked at the clock. When relief didn't come, I recalled that time mattered, by all the testimony about other attacks.

I walked to the foot of the stairs and called my daughter and son-in-law. "I hate to say this," I said, "but I think I'm having a heart attack." Both moved me to a chair, while one dialed 9-1-1 and the other got the car keys.

The private crisis dissolved into public action. In Bethany, handling a heart attack is a volunteer fire department ambulance function. Within seconds, it seemed, there were volunteers in our driveway to support the arrival of the ambulance crew. In the kitchen after the siren's cry, I gave vital statistics and got oxygen. Then I was placed on the rolling stretcher outside and popped into the ambulance. My daughter rode along beside the driver.

Through an oxygen mask, I gave my medical past, my doctors

names, the degree of pain I felt from 1 to 10.

A nitroglycerin tablet was slipped beneath my tongue. And as we swung through the wide, bright Whalley-Amity intersection I thought, for no good reason, of the midnight ambulance runs being made in lightless Baghdad that night.

In the St. Raphael's courtyard I was trundled past my concerned family into the instantaneous, comforting routines of the health givers: blood pressure cuffs, stethoscopes, the open-back gown, a nitroglycerin patch, monitoring points and digital meters, the brightly-lit, throbbing hospital focused on the individual sense of ailment.

As late night drifted into morning, there were chest x-rays, and EKGs, plus the blinks, the protesting squawks, and the whirs of medical machines assessing the 1916-model hominoid hooked into their circuits.

Worn out in the fluorescent dawn of the emergency room, I dangled bare feet at the end of my pallet, reached toward a serving of French toast and coffee, only to hear my cardiologist, the lilt of India in his warning: "No, Robert! No food! No food until the procedure is done."

We talked about the long night's multiple diagnostic readings, about injected dyes that would define the heart's condition, of angioplasty's potential.

Near morning's end, the doctor and I and a small entourage moved toward our basic encounter with the facts.

The prone patient's view of a hospital corridor is of floating faces and remote ceilings. In moving toward the destination called "angioplasty," I was engaged by some design-decorated ceilings. There were arches and curlicued corners above me. Were they, I pondered, images of the chambers of the heart? Something from the Middle East mosques of our current concern in Iraq? Some metaphysical link to the looming "procedure"?

"It's a narrow table," said the nurse, and I found myself like a wounded knight upon his narrow shield, arms and elbows propped outside as the cardiac crew moved in.

Through some gentle anesthesia there was a hum of calm, distantly pleasant voices communicating few understandable words. Then, clear and final, my doctor's voice said, "Robert, we will handle this problem with medicine." Eureka!

There were a few added days under the hands of skilled and attentive nurses, plus the final wheelchair trip to "Patient Pickup" with the Register gang's bouquet in my lap.

It took a total 63 hours to get me out the door and back in during this adventure of the heart.

On the night of the day I came home, I went to bed early. A full moon, moving west above our trees, thrust its long silver rays through the window and onto the pillow where for so many years with my dear wife, Anne, I had slumbered.

I touched the pillow where the moonlight and the memory fused and whispered, "Much ado about nothing, old girl" and went to sleep.

First Prize 2003, best column of its kind, Connecticut Chapter, Society of Professional Journalists, SPX.

Saturday, July 5, 2003
Editor's note

The Day Redcoats Took The Town

This is a day that's remembered locally, but not celebrated. On this date 324 years ago- July 5, 1779 - the sun came up above the Branford ridge to send long shafts of morning light across West Haven beaches near Savin Rock and on the waters reaching back to Morris Cove.

There, at the harbor's entrance, floated 48 vessels, large and small, of the mighty British navy, riding the waves to invoke shock and awe in the name of King George.

New Haven was being invaded by sea. A thousand hidden eyes along the shore, alerted by post-midnight alarm bells and blazing pitch on the east shore's Beacon Hill, watched the enemy.

It was the day after Independence Day, the start of the fourth year of the Revolutionary War. There were about 3,000 troops led by two generals and other regimental officers, plus another 2,000 sailors providing support under an admiral's command.

The outgunned defenders of New Haven, led by Capt. James Hillhouse, commander of the Second Company, Governor's Foot Guard, included a few dozen trained soldiers, an informal militia band or two, and anybody else willing to use a personal musket.

Potential reinforcements existed in the agricultural outback from Derby to Wallingford and Killingworth. It would take fast horses, however, to spread word of the attack.

Defensive action began when Yale's president Ezra Stiles, climbed to the steeple of the college chapel. Across the roofs of a two-story town he saw the British landing barges and brightly uniformed troops mustering at Savin Rock. His warning sent Yale and town families into a frenzy as furniture, silver, and other valuables were moved to inland hiding places. Doors were nailed shut. Women and children fled to the country by wagonloads. (The map accompanying this column was drawn by Stiles after the flight.)

In West Haven, the British moved north with confidence, coming up the beach road to the town Green, pausing for breakfast at the center, dealing roughly with interference.

While safeguarding valuables at the Congregational Church, the Rev. Williston broke a leg in scrambling across a stone wall. As redcoats pounced, British Adjutant William Campbell protected Williston from their bayonets and had him carried to the parsonage.

Later that morning, as the invaders advanced on Allingtown Hill in a push to cross the West River, a neighborhood youth, concealed for sharpshooting, knocked Campbell from his horse with a well-placed shot. He died in a nearby farmhouse. The gallantry of the British officer is remembered still in the name of Campbell Avenue. His burial place is marked by a monument a few yards from Orange Avenue, just across from the main gate of the University of New Haven.

The struggle for a West River crossing is reflected just beyond today's Grasso Boulevard-Columbus Avenue junction. There the city's Defenders' Monument, only two miles from the Green, commemorates the way the British were repulsed.

During the engagement at the river crossing, where a wooden bridge was blasted and burned by New Haveners, the king's men had little patience with the president emeritus of Yale, Naphthali Daggett, who was seized while sniping at them from the woods.

"What are you doing, you damned old rebel?" shouted an enemy. "Exercising the rights of war!" declared Daggett. The British dragged him from his horse, beat him and then forced the old man to walk, at bayonet point, the long ridge (now Forest Road) to the heart of Westville and then along Whalley Avenue to the city's center. Near the Green, local Tories intervened and removed him to a friend's house. He was treated there for several days. Then, wounded and ill, he died at home the next year.

Action on the East Shore was delayed until midmorning. Then the invaders came ashore at Five Mile Point (now Lighthouse

Point). Most of the south end of the original colony was farmed by Amos Morris and his relatives. The extended family moved horses and other livestock inland and tried to secure the spacious house. As a final appeasement, Amos left a keg of hard cider in the kitchen. But the British set the house afire.

Part of it was leveled, but it was rebuilt and enlarged after the Revolution. The old manse stands today as a testament of the invasion and as a museum adjunct of the New Haven Colony Historical Society near the Lighthouse Park gate.

The east defenses were lighter than those on the west, though the British pincer put about 1,500 troops on each arm of the attack. After a small group of defenders at Black Rock fort spiked their cannons and blew up ammunition when surrounded, they were taken prisoner and eventually incarcerated in New York.

A flanking unit penetrated East Haven streets, and farms, as the invasion moved north.

A volunteer from Cheshire, Adam Thorp, faced the onslaught with a declaration: He would not run another step from the British. When he lingered as the redcoats came forward, however, he was caught within their lines and killed by their bayonets.

In the same retreat Chandler Pardee,18, had responded to the local alarms while still wearing Sabbath shoes with silver buckles. In the harbor marsh, one of his shoes was sucked into the mud. As he crouched to fumble for the buckle, a musket ball struck him in the lower back and "traversed his body to the breast." Pained and prone, young Pardee lay there as three passing enemy groups concluded that the wound was fatal.

Then, as the action moved on, friends heard him calling, and got him to shelter and then to surgery. He spent months recovering, but he lived, says the old account, to be the father of several children and to have many grandchildren.

When Beacon Hill was captured, the British eastern contingent marched to the ferry (now the Tomlinson Bridge site) and made its way to a bivouac on the grassy point where the Mill River and the Quinnipiac River meet in the inner harbor.

The British military in the 18th century aspired to a degree of chivalry, as well as civility in its officer corps. But it was also tolerant of excess in its foot soldiers - so that "pillage," "plunder," "drunkenness" and other definitions of abuse appear in documentary reports of the 1779 encounter here.

Unofficial casualty counts estimate British losses at nine dead and 41 wounded; the local losses at 27 killed and 19 wounded.

Edward Atwater's "History of the City of New Haven" (1887) tells of severe outcomes for minor and unproven claims. An elderly citizen, Benjamin English, was found shot dead in his home along the British route through town. The tongue of a mentally disturbed youth was cut out because his mumbling was taken as criticism. He bled to death.

Nathan Beers stayed in his house at Chapel and York; too old, he said, to endanger the monarchy. But a shot, allegedly from his garden, infuriated the troops. When Beers opened his front door and confronted armed soldiers, the gun he grabbed at face level discharged into his hip. He died within the week.

Uncounted numbers of men were rounded up, uncharged, and shipped off to jails or jail ships in New York.

Sarah Lloyd Hillhouse, the young wife of the foot guard commander who led the Elm City's nimble but inadequate defense, wrote a poignant letter to a friend in Danbury:

"I can only tell you that Mr. Hillhouse was the first that attacked them .... Old Aunt Lucas and myself rode off when the enemy was within two miles of us. The excessive heat of the day, the fright, and above all the distress I felt for my best friend's safety had such an effect upon me that we were all fearful of the consequences."

A few months later, Sarah Hillhouse died in childbirth.

On that summer day, many New Haveners suffered.

But what was the British purpose?

Rollin G. Osterweis, the late Yale historian who wrote the definitive "Three Centuries of New Haven," suggests that the invasion was designed to worry George Washington, to take his focus off West Point and Stony Point in the Hudson Valley. American garrisons there throttled traffic between British-held New York City, Canada, and western New England. British successes on Long Island Sound might force Washington to lose his grip.

But the British didn't burn New Haven, as was their original intent. Even town Tories petitioned redcoat generals to treat the college and the community gently. And as their spies told them that large militia forces from central Connecticut were massing outside New Haven, the Brits seem to have swapped a fire-free town for a no-shooting, firing-free troop withdrawal the next day.

And that's what happened. The town went largely undamaged. The redcoats were aboard ships by sundown, their sails set for New York by dawn. They sent fire-setters into Fairfield and Norwalk - perhaps to show they followed orders.

That was a tough July in New Haven. There was much personal loss in a town of only 8,000. But it has never since been invaded - and George Washington was not distracted.

There will be a Foundry Bookstore farewell party on Monday night from 7 to 11 at Toad's, 300 York St.

Never an invader, but always a gentle occupying force, Foundry founder Henry Berliner is heading somewhere over the rainbow soon.

Saturday, October 30, 2004
Editor's note

It's Been A Swift 30 Years In This Corner

October's end on the current calendar means that I've been writing this column for a full 30 years.

The assignment has been a great gift to a hometown boy with much affection for New Haven, for the people and situations of this region, and for the honest, uncomplicated, accurate reporting processes of a community newspaper like the Register.

To be granted a personal word and opinion on local affairs every week for three decades is one way to avoid ulcers.

The length of my run in this corner of the opinion page suggests, however, that I could wear out my welcome - especially in this season when the entire country is split over whether it is, or is not, time for a change. Since procrastination comes easily to me these days, I'll leave decisions in that vein to the politically minded.

To my recollection, I haven't missed a column in 1,560 Saturdays. In that span, there were hard weeks - when I lost my dear wife, Anne, or later when our eldest son slipped away - when the deadline numbed the duty. There was the time I went through St. Raphael's emergency room into the coronary unit while pondering the experience as a subject for the Saturday report. But a modest obsession like that is what keeps curmudgeons mudgeoning.

The column was launched in 1974. It wasn't designed to be a steady-habit for me, or for you. In fact the first example concluded: "Today's Editor's Note is the first in a series of weekly comments on matters that relate to the coverage of news and other questions of editorial interest in the New Haven newspapers." That was not a long view of things.

The Register Publishing Co., then producing the afternoon

Register and the morning Journal-Courier in this city, had recently become the owner of the Hartford Times.

The afternoon paper in Connecticut's capital city had lost much ground to its morning rival, the Hartford Courant. Register publisher Lionel Jackson had the hope that a two-city publishing operation might create what we now call synergy. An editorial comment on the week's journalism in both papers was explored. But the Hartford Times as an institution soon folded. The comment labeled an "Editor's Note" continued in the Register.

Until I took then-compulsory retirement at age 65 in 1981, this essay was generally a comment on the weekly problems and purposes of the Register and its news staff - though the training of 2,500 youthful carriers, new printing technologies, changed advertising concepts, and other unfolding glimpses of today's electronic communications industry were grist for the mill.

After I retired and lost daily touch with the goals and activities of young staffs and new ownership executives at the Register, my range of subjects widened. I linked my old experience with the newspaper as a first draft of local history to an interest in this area as I remembered it in my younger years and as it was in Revolution-era generations.

That brings us back to this morning, when the fact that I've occupied this cozy corner for 30 years is my version of 'October surprise" – with the surprise all mine.

Researching in old editorial pages I came upon one of those do-you-remember? nuggets in a 1974 Saturday Journal by the late Bill Ahern. A reader had inspired in him memories of Congress Square and Carson's long-gone 24-hour restaurant in the 1930s, where Church Street then ended at George Street.

The site today is the project-of-the-moment, where a new Gateway Community College, Knights of Columbus head quarters, the doomed Coliseum, a possible Long Wharf theater, and the Oak Street connector all vie for position. It was a different world for Ahern:

"Carson's was the hub of the city's long-eradicated Congress - Square. Within a block on Church Street were Wood's Drug

Store; Herman Pickus' men's clothing; next door the A.E. Alling Rubber Company (sporting goods); Spencer's; Jacob H. Segaloff and Brothers, woolens; P and Q Clothes; the Fox Poli Palace building; ... Prof. Anthony Pascale, voice teacher; McCusker-Schroeder, coal dealers; Surety Clothes - A.M. Paul jewelers; and above that an oriental restaurant. Thereafter Leslie's Perfumery, Harvey's Shoes, and in its corner basement, the Hof Brau Haus.

"Across the street, and next to Wood's, was Sears-Roebuck, the St. George Hotel, Presto Restaurant, Pages Clothes, Lewis Osterweis & Sons cigars, Postal Telegraph, DeVora Luncheonette, A.A. Perry Jewelers, the Fox-Poli Bijou movie house, American Hat and Shoe Repair; and the First National Bank."

Ahern's litany went on and on. At Church and George, Meadow Street went off on an angle to the railroad station. Congress Avenue took traffic and trolley cars on another angle up into the Hill toward West Haven.

Where there are now only eight or nine buildings, with green space, there were then dozens of side streets with mom-and-pop stores, garages, stables and Civil War remnants huddled close to the center of the city. Ahern said that the sign in Carson's offered "Roast Beef Dinners, 75 cents." There was vitality there, even in the Depression.

Index